EQUIVOCAL DREAMS

STUDIES IN MODERN HEBREW LITERATURE

EQUIVOCAL DREAMS
STUDIES IN MODERN HEBREW LITERATURE

LEV HAKAK

KTAV PUBLISHING HOUSE INC.

Copyright © 1993
Lev Hakak
Library of Congress Cataloging-in-Publication Data

Ḥakak, Lev.
    Equivocal dreams : studies in modern Hebrew literature / Lev
Hakak.
        p.   cm.
    Some of the studies were originally published in Hebrew.
    Includes bibliographical references.
    ISBN 0-88125-466-5 : $25.00
    1. Agnon, Shmuel Yosef, 1888-1970--Criticism and interpretation.
2. Yehoshua, Abraham B.--Criticism and interpretation. 3. Israeli
poetry--History and criticism. I. Title.
PJ5053.A4Z5985   1993
892.4'35--dc20   93-1943
                                                              CIP

Manufactured in the United States of America

CONTENTS

PREFACE

"The Motif of the Cock in *A Simple Story* by S. Y. Agnon" was originally published in *Hassifrut*, Tel-Aviv University, vol. 4, no. 4, 1973, pp. 173-225, and has been translated from the Hebrew. "Sexual Symbols in 'Another Face' by S. Y. Agnon" was published in *Hebrew Annual Review*, The Ohio State University, vol. 10, 1986, pp. 95-108. A Hebrew version of "Society's Judgment and God's Judgment: Agnon's 'In the Forest and In the City' and Dickens' *Great Expectations*" was published in *Moznaim*, The Literary Monthly of the Hebrew Writers Association in Israel, vol. 62, no. 11, 1989, pp. 23-250. Excerpts from "Israeli Society as Depicted in the Novels of A. B. Yehoshua" will be published by Misgav Yerushalyim, The Hebrew University of Jerusalem. Excerpts were published in *Mahut*, Haberman Institute for Literary Research, no. 1, Summer 1989, pp. 254-264, and reprinted in *Hadoar*, Nov. 17, 1989, vol. 69, no. 3, pp. 19-22, and Nov. 24, 1989, vol. 69, no. 4, pp. 20-21. "David Vogel and Natan Alterman: A Comparative Study" was published in *Hebrew Studies*, published at the University of Wisconsin-Madison by the National Association of Professors of Hebrew, 1979-1980, pp. 150-156. "Estranged Nightingales: On Poetry Written by Near Eastern Jews in Israel" was published in *Hebrew Annual Review*, The Ohio State University, vol. 11, 1987, pp. 129-152. The articles have been revised for publication. Some initial remarks related to "A Poem to the Wise Lovers" (chapter 7) were published in Hebrew in *Al hammishmar*, Jan. 30, 1976. Chapter 3 is published here for the first time.

I wish to thank the University of California, Los Angeles, for supporting the preparation of the manuscript; I am especially grateful to Jane Bitar and Betty Baker of the Word Processing Center for their contribution. First proofreading was done by Dr. Arieh Wineman; final proofreading was done by Dr. Carol Dana Lanham.

THE MOTIF OF THE COCK IN
A SIMPLE STORY BY S. Y. AGNON

Several scholars have focused on the cock (*gever* in Hebrew) in the novel *A Simple Story*,[1] by Agnon (1880-1970), striving to point to its meanings beyond the explicit plot. The first to devote a comprehensive discussion to this motif was Kurzweil (1966, pp. 216-223), who emphasized the symbolic identity between the cock-*gever* and the master-of-the-house-cock *gever*[2] (pp. 216, 217)--an identity which, in his opinion, serves a particular goal:

> It is a device to prove the true character of the apparent home. The cock-*gever* which is free in its virility is a contrast to the man who is not free in his manliness, who is coerced and imprisoned by a woman and a society which he hates.... The motif of the cock has a tremendous impact on the development of the motif of the going-out-escaping. The escape, which is an escape from home, from the degenerated relations between him and her, is evidence of the crack in the life of the Jewish family in the small town.

> Boruch Meir[3] already is not a "real" man. His wife, Tsirl, is a person of undisputed authority. (pp. 217-218)

Kurzweil finds both identity and contrast between the cock-gever and Hirshl. He also examines some of the explicit appearances of the cock within a particular group of chapters in the novel, and through them clarifies important aspects of Hirshl's life.

The present essay seeks to clarify the versatile and changing meanings of the cock-*gever* as an intricate repetitive element which develops throughout the novel from beginning to end. I shall examine the implications of various elements in the novel for the understanding of the meanings of the cock-*gever* in its explicit appearances. This task sometimes requires and depends upon references to various Jewish sources which deepen, clarify, and enlarge the meaning of the rooster in the novel.

Specifically, I shall examine the meanings and the effects of the varying semantic uses of "cock" and "gever" in the novel, differentiating between those places where the cock-*gever* appears as an object with realistic substance and those where it has a nonrealistic substance. I shall identify the category of the cock in the realm of poultry and explain the importance of this category in the novel. I shall also describe the place and the roles of the cock in presenting the relations, especially the erotic relations, between Hirshl and Mina. The cock has a role also in formulating our thoughts about Hirshl's murder and suicide, thoughts which are relevant to this study. In addition I shall discuss the roles of the cock as an indicator of the passage of time and of the degree to which Hirshl functions in a society with bourgeois norms. Through an early allusion the cock also reveals the madness which will later seize Hirshl. The latter's attitudes toward the cock, his attempts to evade and avoid being publicly identified with the cock, the degree to which Hirshl himself identifies with the cock and the degree of his alertness to the cock—these accompany the development of Hirshl's character during the course of the novel. The onomatopoetic sounds of Hirshl's froglike croaks sharpen his attempts to communicate through his crowing like a cock. Issues which relate to poultry—its consumption, stories told about it, and poultry trade—will be discussed here because they are elements necessary to the development of the meanings of the cock-*gever* in the novel.

In short: this study intends to clarify the dynamic symbolic motif of the cock-*gever* in the novel (using the term "motif" as an inseparable unit which appears in a specific literary work as a repetitive figure/image or situation through which links of meanings are formed during the sequence of the plot). For the purpose of elucidating the motif of the cock, I sometimes invoke the concept of motif as defined by Thomashevsky (1965, pp. 67-68):

> Thematical unit which occurs in various works.... These works move in their entirety from one plot to another ... within the limits of the given genre these "motifs" are always found in their complete forms. Consequently, in comparative studies one must speak of motifs that have remained intact historically, that have presented their unity in passing from work to work....

I use the concept "dynamic motif" as Thomashevsky (1965, pp. 67-71) defines it. He differentiates between free motifs—"which may be omitted without disturbing the whole casual chronological course of events" and bound motifs—which cannot be omitted "without disturbing the connections among the events."

Thomashevsky also differentiates between dynamic motifs, which are central to the story and change the situation, and static motifs, which do not change the situation. In *A Simple Story*, the motif of the cock is dynamic; it is central and it changes various situations.

The cock appears in the novel as a symbol: it does not represent itself alone and does not demand attention merely to its own merits, but in addition it means something more or something else, an additional or truer meaning rather than just a cock. The cock in the novel unites the actual "concrete" cock with the ideas or conceptions which it suggests and evokes in the text. What is said in the text about the cock becomes clearer, more vivid, effective and intelligible through the use of the symbol.[4]   In determining the additional meaning of the cock and its functions in the novel, we shall refer not only to the text of the novel, but also to human experience, reality, associations and conventions related to the cock,[5] because the symbolic use of the cock in the novel draws also upon its "traditional" or "conventional" symbolic meaning. The latter meaning does not undermine the surprising and innovative effects of the motif but rather enriches them.

The subject of poultry appears frequently in *A Simple Story*. There are eight main categories in which poultry appears:

1.   A rooster-cock drives away Hirshl's sleep (pp. 149–150, 154, 155, 156, 158, 163, 167, 171, 172, 174, 176, 179, 183, 192, 193).

2.   Poultry appears in descriptions of country life (pp. 41, 111, 117).

3.   Raising poultry is a hobby (p. 103).

4.   Poultry appears in figurative language--in similes and periphrasis (pp. 35, 59, 68, 171, 182, 203).[6]

5.   Poultry is the object of imitation (with aesthetic pretensions) in the making of food-serving utensils in the shape of poultry (pp. 78, 115, 227).

6.   The poultry trade flourishes in Szybusz (pp. 100, 111–112, 227).

7.   Poultry evokes religious issues--ritual permits issued by a rabbi confirming that poultry is kosher, and the preparation for slaughtering poultry and the

>   determination of its kosher state (pp.   32, 70,
>   143-144, 170, 183).
>
> 8.   Poultry is served as a standard food in the bourgeois
>   meal (pp. 26, 77-78, 80-81, 106, 115, 118, 186).

We shall focus on the first category, referring to the other categories
only when they supplement and clarify the symbolic motif of the
cock-*gever*.

HIRSHL AS A MAN AND THE COCK- GEVER

The term *gever* (a homonym in Hebrew which stands for both "cock"
and "male," "man") recurs for the cock in a certain period of the
development of Hirshl's character, from his return home after seeing
Blume near the home of Akavia Mazal until the day of his madness.
In this context (reflected in the English translation on pp. 149-150,
154, 155, 156, 158, 163, 171, 172) the original Hebrew speaks of
gever. This period coincides with the climax of Hirshl's crisis. His
madness led to his compromise and submission to trivial life. Once
Hirshl was cured, the term used for the cock is *tarnegol* "cock" and
not *gever* (p. 168, 171, 172, 174, 176, 179, 183, 192, 193).

The cock is referred to as *gever* in the novel during the period
in which Hirshl is sleepless and suffering from nervousness and
hostility toward Mina. He is incapable of choosing to rebel actively
against those who brought on his emotional condition. He is a weak
man, incapable of continuing the way of life of a "son and grandson of
storekeepers" (p. 33), but also incapable of fulfilling himself. His
deviations from his regular course in life are not the result of a
willful decision, but rather of lack of control over his mental and
physical states, something which inflicts upon him suffering beyond
his capacity to deal with it.

The first two instances in which the cock is called *gever* occur
in critical days of Hirshl's life. The first instance follows Hirshl's
return home after seeing Blume near the home of Akavia Mazal:

>   A rooster [original: *gever*--L.H.] crowed and the clock
>   inside chimed twelve as he reached the front door of his
>   home. He paused on the doorstep to consider what to tell
>   Mina should she ask where he had been. I'll tell her I was
>   at Blume's, he decided. (1985, p. 149)

In his imagination Hirshl carries on a dialogue with Mina (Even, 1971, pp. 289-291), and in a dramatic confession which he imagines, he finds the courage to reveal to his wife his love for Blume.

The second time that *gever* relates to the rooster occurs during Hirshl's first sleepless night:

> Several times he had the feeling that something important had happened, yet when he tried to recall what it was it turned out to be nothing at all. Hearing a rooster [original: *gever* - L.H.] crow, he got out of bed to see if it was midnight; before he could look at the clock it crowed again. The whole world is asleep and resting, thought Hirshl, except for me. (1985, p. 154)

In this incident, Hirshl sees himself as different from "the whole world" which, unlike Hirshl himself, is asleep. Hirshl is conscious of the fact that he is different and alone. In both incidents we witness his weakness as a man (*gever*) who did not protest against his parents' taking his beloved woman from him and marrying him to a woman whom he did not love. The cock (*gever*) crows but the man (*gever*), Hirshl, does not protest against the ways of his society.

In those chapters of the novel in which the motif of the cock appears (chapters 23-26), it sometimes appears merely as a rooster, while at other times the cock dominates Hirshl more than a mere cock could. Sometimes the cock's crow is "real" (pp. 149, 154) and coincides with Hirshl's physical and mental revolt as a man (*gever*) against being trodden upon. One may ask--who is the owner of the cock (*gever*) which causes Hirshl's sleeplessness? Where is the cock? Hirshl and Mina discuss the possibility of slaughtering it (p. 167)--what stopped them? Would not the slaughtering of the cock be an expiation for Hirshl which, according to faith, could redeem Hirshl from his illness? Indeed, some of the reader's questions may be answered not in the realistic dimension but rather in the symbolic one.

In the course of the *gever*'s appearances it becomes clear that its effects upon Hirshl are not dependent upon Hirshl's sensory perceptions. The crow of the *gever* affects Hirshl as a kind of internal voice, and therefore all Hirshl's devices to avoid hearing the *gever*'s crow seem naive and simplistic and make us even more aware of the vigor of the *gever*'s crow. In his bed Hirshl hears all kinds of noises, but the one which affects him the most is the crowing of the cock:

> Eventually all of these sounds vanished, leaving only the crowing of the cock. But though Hirshl could crawl into bed feeling more dead than alive, the mere thought of that outrageous squawk was enough to banish all prospect of falling asleep. (p. 155)

"The mere thought" of the crow of the cock is enough to render Hirshl sleepless, and therefore "no matter how much blanket he pulled over his head there was no keeping out the sound of it" (p. 156). This "combined speech" (Golomb, 1968, p. 251) reveals Hirshl's helplessness against the crow of the *gever*, and the reader's anticipation that Hirshl's attempts to escape the *gever*'s crow will fail, is fulfilled:

> There was one other thing that Hirshl tried, which was dipping absorbent cotton in oil and stopping his ears with it. If this made them less sensitive, however, it made the rest of his body more. Whenever a wagon went by, or a rooster crowed, the noise sent shock waves running through his knees, as if that was where his auditory nerves were.

The vigor of the *gever*'s crow becomes a surrealistic issue especially if one recalls what kind of *gever* it is: "But though Hirshl could crawl into bed feeling more dead than alive, the mere thought of that outrageous squawk was enough to banish all prospect of falling asleep" (p. 155). The Hebrew original speaks of "that sound of yellow" (translated here as "outrageous squawk"). This is not a mere synaesthesia. "Yellow" may be understood as "the yellow cock"--the smallest type of European poultry, which is very light. It is just such a cock, the lightest and the smallest cock-*gever*, which suffices to render Hirshl sleepless. The effect of using the term *gever* (man, male) for this cock is ironic--not only regarding the small, light cock but also regarding Hirshl for whom the crow of the cock is an internal voice. The *gever* becomes a literary device to distract the reader's attention from focusing directly on Hirshl; at the same time it is also an indirect means of characterizing him. It becomes a metonymy of Hirshl. This specific *gever* casts light upon Hirshl's weakness: the call of the man in him, which burst forth at a time when he is rebellious, is no more vigorous than the call of the smallest cock.

The author is cautious and meticulous in his selection of words: "When the *gever* crowed Hirshl sought to check if the cock aimed to crow at midnight."[7] The crow of the *gever* is identified with the call which flows from within Hirshl, while the crow of the cock is a "real" one. It is noteworthy that Jewish sources reflect alertness to the possibility of semantic uncertainty: when the addresser is using the term *gever* would the addressee understand *gever* as a man or as a cock?[8]

The use of the term *gever* in the novel stresses Hirshl's weakness. The various meanings of the Hebrew word reveal how weak and helpless Hirshl is as a man. The word *gever* in Hebrew emphasizes masculinity (e.g., Deuteronomy 22:5), heroism (e.g., Job 38:3), and the male organ (e.g., Bekhorot 7:5).

Agnon himself, in another literary work,[9] makes use of biblical verses in which the term *gever* appears meaning "man," as if they refer to a cock. In that same context the reader notes that Agnon is aware of the view that the cock is the strongest fowl.[10] At the peak of his pain, the climax of Hirshl's "revolt" is not that of a strong man but is rather a kind of collapse, which robs him of the possibility of living conflicting internal and external lives. The usages of *gever* emphasize how much Hirshl failed in fulfilling himself as a man.

IN THE BEDROOM OF HIRSHL AND NINA

The crow of the cock recurs in various episodes which take place in the bedroom of Hirshl and Mina and echoes the defects in the erotic relations between them. In the same context in which we find the crows of the cock-*gever*, we find erotic descriptions of Mina in her bed: her deep sleep, the warm somnolent smell emanating from her bed which is supposed to put Hirshl to sleep but does not (pp. 151, 155, 156, 162), her breathing (pp. 154, 155), her nightgown and chest (p. 155), etc. In these situations Hirshl relates to Mina through his senses of sight, smell, and hearing.

The fact that the crow of the *gever* appears in the same context as the above descriptions of Mina is significant. The sexual relations between Mina and Hirshl are psychologically adulterous. While Hirshl sleeps near his wife, his thoughts are occupied by Blume. On his wedding night he already thought about stories of divorce (p. 105) and thus commits a sin because a man shall not marry a woman with the thought of divorcing her (*Yevamot*, 37b). The communication between husband and wife at the beginning of their marriage is replaced by erotic relations: "If not for the hot blood of youth that they shared, there would have been nothing between them. As it is, intellectual compatibility was not everything" (p. 109). At the home of Mina's father, Gedalia Ziemlich, before marrying Mina, Hirshl "looked up to see if anything was left of these abominations, whose smell was making his mouth water, and caught sight of Mina" (p. 80). Of the people gathered around the meal table all except Hirshl crave meat; the attraction to Mina's flesh will not suffice as a substitute for intellectual relations, just as the eating of meat will not substitute for meaning in life.

The crow of the cock also alludes to Hirshl's sexual desire for Mina. The cock's crow is the erotic stimulation of Hirshl when he is awake while Mina is asleep. "One would think that Hirshl had every reason to be content with her. Yet when the feeling was missing, thinking did not help very much" (p. 155). This statement is made by the narrator after describing Hirshl erotically observing his sleeping wife. Hirshl's wakefulness when he studies the depth of Mina's sleep parallels the cock's typical vigilance.[11]

In a grotesque, erotically distorted description, Hirshl is trying to sleep in spite of the crowing of the cock, but his efforts fail:

> At last he would shut his eyes as hard as he could in the hope of dozing off; yet just then the roosters would bristle their combs and break into their horrid screech, while the warm smell from Mina's bed ... reminded him that she had taken all the sleep for herself....
>
> Mina lay on her back in a pink nightgown with satin straps ... her chest rising and falling above her distended stomach. (1985, p. 155)

Mina appears here as a sexual object of many cocks. The bristled combs express sexual desire. In this sense we note in the Talmudic tractate *Shabbat* (110) that one who wants to castrate a cock should remove the cock's comb. The cock's bristling its comb is a male coquetry[12] and coxcombry and also an indication that the cocks are ready to engage in battle (they are like knights prepared to use their shields to defend the beloved woman). Mina deserves at least to be regarded as sexually attractive. The cocks here represent this lust and attraction and remind Hirshl of his lack of manhood since he comes back home when his wife is already asleep and he has no sexual contact with her.[13] The bristled combs of the cocks are an erotic expression of the stimulus which Mina's position should evoke,[14] but Hirshl is not attracted to her. The combs distinguish the cocks from the chickens. In Jewish sources we find that the cock swears by his comb in order to persuade the chicken.[15]

In some Jewish traditions the cock and rooster are seen as a symbol of fertility.[16] The cock appears as an artist of seduction, whose lust is ever present. Viewing the cock as a projection of Hirshl implies that at this stage Hirshl's attitude toward Mina is not that of a refined lover, but is the mere lust of a cock.

THE COCK AND HIRSHL'S THOUGHTS ABOUT MURDER AND SUICIDE

The cock's crow is also connected with suicide and Hirshl's murderous thoughts.   During his sleepless nights[17] the crow of the cock undermines Hirshl's mental balance.   He listens to Mina's breathing and thinks of murder:

> He had already thought of one thing when the sound of her breathing made him think of another, such as a story he once had heard about two business partners who went on a journey in the course of which one was killed.
>
> No one knew who the murderer was. The surviving partner, being both pious and rich, was above suspicion. One day, however, while he was writing to his wife from an inn where he had stopped, a rooster hopped on the table and defecated on the letter. The wrathful man leaped to his feet and tore the bird apart limb by limb. A police inspector who happened to be present seized him and cried, "It's you who murdered your partner!" The case was reopened and the man was found guilty. (1985, p. 156)

The novel has three characters whose roles parallel those of the murder story. Hirshl "might suddenly leap to his feet and kill all the roosters in the world!" (ibid.) and is bitter because his wife is sleeping so soundly while he himself is sleepless.   Mina is the partner to Hirshl's life. If Hirshl acts like the pious and rich partner in the murder story, then he will murder his partner-wife and tear the cock apart--his suicide-killing of the cock will reveal him as the murderer.

In the context of Hirshl's pondering the murder story we find the following:

> When a man lost his temper, he was not in control of himself. Why, he might suddenly leap to his feet and kill all the roosters in the world! It was just as well that Hirshl put away his pocketknife at night. In fact, when sometimes he forgot, he rose from bed especially to do it.

There was no point in looking for trouble. (ibid., pp. 156-157)

Hiding the pocketknife, especially at night, might suggest Hirshl's contemplating murder and suicide. The knife is his knife, a fact which envelops it with mystery. The "trouble" does not relate merely to the possibility of killing a cock. The knife alludes to death and revenge and simultaneously represents—particularly in its short blade—the instincts of the man who draws it: it may represent his male organ.[18] In the same context, Hirshl's putting the knife away may allude to the lack of sexual relations between Mina and Hirshl during that period.

Hirshl's thoughts about murder or suicide are also alluded to in Hirshl's motion and statement when he speaks to Mina about slaughtering the cock: "Don't you think we might take him to the throat-slitter? He just has to go whisk and there's no more cock-a-doodle-doo" (p. 167). In those words Hirshl vividly lives an experience of slaughtering and gives vent to his concealed feeling and thoughts about it.

On the day that Hirshl was seized by madness the *gever* again connects with suicide: "A man can't grow on a tree. He can hang himself from one though. Would he hear the rooster crow if he did?" (p. 172). Hirshl's existence and conflicts created inside him the crow of the *gever*, an involuntary protest against those who stepped all over him. Again, the *gever* is weak and he does not contemplate a willful and conscious protest but instead sees the solution of his problems in suicide, another form of self-effacement.

In this stage of his life Hirshl is not equipped to walk in the path of moderation which excludes total surrender and suicide.

TIME, HIRSHL, AND THE COCK

The cock-*gever* is an indicator of the passage of time. In this context we find the triangle of Hirshl-cock-clock. The cock and the clock remind Hirshl of the time. When the cock and the clock are active, Hirshl is sane; when they cease, then Hirshl ceases to function and is committed to a mental institution which serves as a bridge for his return to ordinary, everyday life.

The *gever* crows at fixed times and distinguishes between day and night. As such, he appears in Jewish tradition as the one who gives the sign to begin a blessing.[19] The cock also calls at midnight, a demonic time of devils and ghosts but also a time of prayers and psalms ("Tikkun hazot"--a midnight prayer in memory of the destruction of the Temple and the Exile of the Shekhinah). The motif of the cock in the novel first appears linked with the midnight chiming of the clock: "A rooster crowed and the clock inside chimed twelve as he reached the front door of his home" (p. 149). The call of the *gever*, the chiming of the clock, and the imaginary dialogue between Hirshl and Mina in which he "discloses" to Mina his love for Blume all occur at the same time. Hirshl suffers from insomnia and since the cock and the clock dynamically express the passage of time, Hirshl feels that both are provocative (p. 162). Hirshl measures the passing of time by the crow of the cock and the ticking and chiming of the clock (p. 154).

During the morning in which Hirshl became insane, he spoke to Mina about both the cock and the watch:

> You know, I'm amazed by people's optimism. If they have to be somewhere on time they trust their watches, though you see for yourself how a watch can take a notion to stop running. You look at it and it doesn't say a word. You turn it every which way--still no answer. Even when you shake it, it doesn't wake up. It couldn't care less how you feel. Why, you come to depend on it as though it were your own father and mother, you carry it around in your pocket, you even make it a gold chain--and it just stands there and laughs at you. Do you suppose being tied to a gold chain all day long isn't good enough for it? Of course, this is all in a manner of speaking, since a watch has no mind of its own. It isn't a rooster that crows whenever it wants to. I suppose you'll tell me that a person should have two watches, one to tell the time by when the other stops, but believe me, two watches are too much for anyone. You'll just forget the second one anyway. It's not as if we had two brains in our heads to keep track of them both. Well, goodbye, Mina. I'll tell the maid you want to get up. If you ask me, though, you're better off sleeping. If I could sleep myself, I'd do it until hell froze over. (p. 168)

Unlike the watch, the cock has a mind of its own, and it can crow whenever it wishes, but Hirshl still contemplates taking it "to the throat-slitter" (p. 167). Hirshl, the watch, and the cock stopped progressing within the motion of time: Hirshl became insane, his watch stopped, and after discussing taking the cock "to the throat-slitter" Hirshl was taken and committed to a distant mental hospital. So long as Hirshl, the cock, and the clock function, time flows mechanically, automatically, ceaselessly and repetitively: Hirshl is under the control of his parents and his environment, the cock crows in a fixed repetitive cycle, and the clock functions in an automatic repetitive cycle limited in time and space. Hirshl's madness is the temporary pause of this mechanical involuntary flow. Parallel to this pause, Hirshl no longer hears the cock's crow and his watch gets out of order, no longer indicating the objective time.

The watch is exposed as unreliable. If one depends on it, he will ultimately be disappointed. It cannot substitute either for a cock or for parents (who, in the specific case of Hirshl, also disappointed him). The watch is controlled, it is carried around in a pocket and tied to a gold chain. Hirshl wonders if the watch rebels against "being tied to a gold chain all day long." As long as Hirshl obeyed his mother, his destiny and conduct were similar to those of the watch. He was married to a woman whom he did not choose; money induced this marriage. Like father like son: "Hayim Nacht, Blume's father, had married Mirl, who was supposed to have married her cousin Boruch Meir, who, blinded by Shimon Hirsh Klinger's fortune, had jilted her and married Tsirl instead" (p. 19). Boruch Meir was "tied to a gold chain" too--money controlled him, blinded him. Boruch Meir "felt a special bond with his patron" (p. 12) who became his father-in-law. "Boruch Meir had worked six and a half years for Shimon Hirsh Klinger" (ibid.)--an allusion to the laws relating to a Hebrew slave[20]--and like father like son, Hirshl followed in his father's footsteps and he too enslaved himself for the money of his in-laws.

Hirshl spoke with Mina about having two watches: "one to tell the time by when the other stops, but believe me, two watches are too much for anyone" (p. 168). Indeed, Hirshl suffers from having to think about a division of two things at a time--such as Blume-Mina, his own home and his parents' home, his internal life and his external life, love and money, etc.

Hirshl expresses his yearning to get out of the claws of flowing time by an escape which resembles suicide: "If I could sleep myself, I'd do it until hell froze over" (ibid.). Such a sleep will not expose the watch again as an unreliable, broken reed.

We know the time that the above monologue took place:

> "Well, I have to go. You don't happen to know what time it is, do you? My watch has stopped. It was tickety-ticking along, and suddenly it just went and stopped."

"It's half past seven," said Mina.

"Half past seven? Then it really is time to go ...." (p. 168)

After Hirshl lost his sanity, he went to the forest, where he asked God: "Father in heaven ... what time can it be?" (p. 172). Once Hirshl's watch stopped, the flow of time froze for Hirshl. And like the watch, which once it stopped could point only to the time when it stopped, Hirshl himself and his responses "froze":

> A doctor was brought to see Hirshl. To test him he asked how old the Kaiser was. "Half past seven," Hirshl replied. "And what is your name?" asked the doctor. "Half past seven," said Hirshl.
>
> The doctor thought that the patient might not know any German and asked him again in Yiddish. "Half past seven," Hirshl said. It was his answer to every single question. (p. 175)

Hirshl's watch shows "how a watch can take a notion to stop running" (p. 168)--and Hirshl himself "stopped running, stopped being interlocked with life." The fact that he repeats in a dramatic way that "it really is time to go" (ibid.), and that he is going to the synagogue (p. 167) as if it were a regular day, is insufficient to interlock him with his environment once he became insane. The "conduct" of the watch when it stopped and its influence resemble the conduct of Hirshl after he became insane: the clock is silent, it is not awake, it is frightened --and so is Hirshl (pp. 174-176). Not only the watch and Hirshl cease functioning, but also the cock--once Hirshl considered taking him to the throat-slitter (p. 167). All three--Hirshl, the watch, and the cock--stopped functioning simultaneously.

The triangle of Hirshl-watch-cock is repeated in the sanatorium:

> Despite there being no Mina to have to listen to ... no ... crowing rooster ... he still lay in bed like a broken watch that could not keep the right time. (pp. 192-193)

Sadan (1967, p. 34) considers Hirshl's staying in the sanatorium an expression of the quarrel between Hirshl's internal persistence and his acts of submission. Hirshl--according to Sadan--seeks an outlet and finds it by being committed to the sanatorium. The watch and the cock, both projections of Hirshl, ceased, like Hirshl, to progress within time.

HIRSHL'S INSANITY AND THE COCK

On the morning that Hirshl became insane, he went to the synagogue. A discussion takes place that morning in the synagogue concerning the law of poultry:

> Midway through service he felt a jolt in his head as if it had been banged against a wall. A moment later he felt another jolt.... He went to look at the floor, then felt his forehead to see if his tefillin had been knocked to the ground.... Two men who had prayed already were discussing a Talmudic text that dealt with the head feathers of slaughtered birds. (p. 170)

The head plays a central role here. The jolt was in Hirshl's head; he "felt his forehead to see if his tefillin had been knocked to the ground"; Hirshl's memory started failing while at home that morning (p. 167), and his loss of memory became more serious in the synagogue (p. 170). The discussion of the two men in the synagogue concerns "head feathers." When birds have erect feathers in the head—should one check, after slaughtering them, to find out if their skull bone was perforated and had a hole? If it did, then there is an issue of a forbidden bird (taref—Mishnah Hullin 3, 1). Hirshl's madness, like the bird's flaw, is related to damage to the head.

On the day of his madness, Hirshl attempts to control himself, to conduct himself like a man and not like a cock, so that he would not be degraded.[21] Hirshl knows that if he crows like a cock he will seem insane (p. 171), therefore he concludes that "it's a good thing I'm screaming like a man then and not going cock-a-doodle-doo" (p. 171).

Hirshl left the study house feeling as light as a feather (p. 171). As a "light" person, Hirshl drifts easily, without deciding upon his own path. From the synagogue—the religious, traditionally established place—he goes to the woods—a place where people usually don't live.[22]

Hirshl makes efforts not to be identified with the cock (pp. 171, 172, 174) as long as his loss of sanity has not become public knowledge. As long as he is sane, he does not crow like a cock, he

subdues and represses this sound, but when his depression dominates
him he becomes possessed by the crow of the cock and at the time of
his insanity he crows like a cock (pp. 172, 174, 179, 183). Hirshl is
afraid of a mistake in identity: "Don't cut my throat! I'm not a
rooster! I'm not!" (p. 174). Shaked correctly states regarding this
statement of Hirshl:

> The motif reaches its grotesque climax when Hirshl
> identifies himself with the cock, when he is seized by fear
> of the society which, so to speak, wants to slaughter
> him.... Hirshl's crow is an indirect divulgence of Hirshl's
> horror of the society which oppressed his manhood. (1967,
> p. 145)

Hirshl crows like a cock--but he states that he is not a cock.
The same thing that caused the cock-*gever* in *The Bridal Canopy* to
feel anxiety causes anxiety to Hirshl: a cock is destined to be
slaughtered.[23] Hirshl is afraid lest he will be the slaughtered one who
will expiate the sins of a violent society, one which imposes its will
on him. Hirshl's panic is evident from his style--"I am not a rooster!
I'm not!" (p. 174).

Hirshl's return to sanity is also connected with the cock. The
effect of the cock's crow on Hirshl ceases: Hirshl's madness was the
bridge to return to sanity and to complete resignation. Already on
his way to the sanatorium Hirshl "neither croaked nor crowed" (p.
176) and the crow became a matter of the past (pp. 176, 183). In the
sanatorium there were no "crowing roosters" (p. 192) and Hirshl "no
longer crowed like a rooster" (p. 193).

The progress of the contact between Hirshl and the cock's crow
parallels some stages in Hirshl's life. In the stage before Hirshl's
madness was known, Hirshl was pleased that he did not crow like a
cock. But once his madness became obvious to other people, he
crows like a cock while strongly denying that he does it. His madness
is a stage in his cure and is connected with his ceasing to crow like a
cock already on his way to the sanatorium, the place where he
stopped hearing the cock's crow.

At the time of Hirshl's madness, in the same context of the
cock's crows, we find Hirshl croaking like a frog (pp. 172, 174, 179).
Hirshl stopped his croaking already the first day of his madness (pp.
176, 193). Frogs became the subject of the singing of romantic blind
beggars (pp. 190, 193, 226), from whom Hirshl disassociated himself
by renouncing his love for Blume and by surrendering to a bourgeois
way of life. The frog reappears, this time to describe Hirshl's joy in

his bourgeois life, when he hops like a frog in front of his baby son (p. 203).

The frog is also connected with Hirshl's yearning for⁄Blume and her touch. At the center of the romantic world represented by Blume stands the scene in which Blume touches Hirshl's head and strokes his hair (p. 34). At the center of the disintegration of the romantic world is the scene of Hirshl's standing near Akavia Mazal's house on a rainy night when Blume recoiled and retreated into Mazal's house (p. 148). Between these two scenes lie various contrasting parallels which point to the vanishing of the romantic "thousand years" and to the loss of the romantic paradise.[24] Instead of Blume's bed which Hirshl desired, the gate-lock separates the two. Instead of Blume's hand[25] stroking his hair, Hirshl "seized his head with his hands" (p. 148) and then "rested his head on the latch of the gate and began to cry" (ibid.).[26] One is not amazed, therefore to note that at the high point of Hirshl's pain, near Mazal's house, he remembers the high point of his happiness with Blume: "Through a curtain of mist so thick that he could not see his own self the image of Blume appeared as brightly before him as it had on the day she had stroked his head in her room after walking out and returning" (p. 148). The image of Blume has a legendary-romantic splendor (pp. 27, 34). The reader remembers the scene of Blume's stroking Hirshl's hair when Hirshl is brought home from the woods on the day he became insane. This time the scene is connected with both a frog and a cock:

> When Mina approached him he smiled at her, yet he burst into tears when she reached out to stroke his hair with her cold hand. At last he pulled his head away and said, "Blume, I didn't go cockle. I just went ga ga ga." (p. 174)

Mina's hand cannot cure Hirshl. At this stage when he remembers Blume, he identifies with the croak of the frog and not with the crow of the cock. "Ga ga ga" is not only the last syllable of the Hebrew word *meshuga* ("crazy"); it also suggests Blume's touch and Hirshl's yearning (*ga'agu'im*) for Blume. Hirshl wishes to return to his romantic paradise. Not only at home but also in the woods Hirshl says "ga ga ga" in relation to Blume, expressing his yearning for her:

> Do you know Blume Nacht? Of an evening in the marsh grass I'll sit like a froggy and go ga ga ga. (p. 174)

HIRSHL, SZYBUSZ, AND POULTRY

Poultry and meat play a role in the life of Szybusz both in meals and in poultry's being an object of imitation (with aesthetic pretensions) in the making of food-serving pieces in the shape of poultry, and also in stories and in the spoken language. Shaked correctly states that "the meal is used as a projection of man's yearning to be exempt from responsibility ... and to return to his earlier state as a nursing foetus" (1967, p. 136). At family meals Tsirl is conspicuous for her lustful gluttony. The rhythm of the novel slows down to describe her meals in detail (p. 26). The centrality of meat in her life[27] is exposed by a detailed description of how she eats, her dishes, and the way they are prepared. When the food came, Tsirl "leaned over it and filled her plate as lovingly as if it were a prize hen being fattened up to be sold" (p. 26), while Hirshl resembled a cock. Thus Tsirl is presented as the big mother who dominates her son and "swallows" him. The rhythm of the plot is slowed down also by the detailed discussion of the law pertaining to "a bird called grechky hiener,[28] that is to say, Greek chicken" (p. 77), a chicken which was served in Boruch Meir's family's first meal at the home of the Ziemlichs, Mina's parents.

In the bourgeois house of Ziemlich we note a china dish shaped like a goose, "its beak angrily open as if the food had been snatched from its mouth" (p. 78). This china dish, signifying the hosts' "good" taste, represents Gedalia Ziemlich in particular. Gedalia is seized by anxiety: "He could not help anxiously wondering with each bite whether there would be any leftovers for tomorrow" (p. 78). The angry beak of the china bird points toward Hirshl, the silent and angry guest whose mother-in-law follows what and how much he eats (p. 115). The angry expression of the goose-shaped serving dish contrasts with Bertha's feelings, something expressed explicitly in the text (p. 227).

Some of the stories told in Szybusz at the time of the meal relate to fowl. During Hirshl's family's first dinner at the Ziemlichs', Toyber tells a strange story about a dinky little town where he once happened to spend a day. "Apart from a flock of geese in the marketplace there wasn't a sign of life" (p. 79). He requested water and was served water in a strange can:

> That water was brought in a black, crumpled can
> that had specks of rust floating in it. While I was trying
> to decide whether to drink it or not I looked up to see who
> it came with. Why, if she isn't a princess, I thought, that's
> only because no princess would ever live in a dump like
> this. (p. 79)

The "flock of geese" are the people who live in that town. The people listening to Toyber's story resemble them[29] none of them understood the story, but they all reacted like stupid geese. The mere telling of the story "made the mood more relaxed," irrespective of the message of the story.

Hirshl's problem is how to join the world of Szybusz, a world inhabited by geese, where people cooked dead flesh (p. 80). The motif of the cock begins here as Hirshl confronts the corpses of fowl and later develops into a living cock. Later, in a flashback, the corpses of the cocks may perhaps be viewed as an allusion to Hirshl's emotional fate.

When Hirshl relates to the cooked fowl, he identifies with vegetarians: "If my mother did not have her heart set on Ziemlich's money, thought Hirshl, I would not have to be sitting here right now with all this cooked dead flesh in front of me" (p. 80). But later, "Indeed, his stomach seemed to have expanded and his interest in vegetarianism and the simple life was a thing of the past" (p. 115). He knows: "The emptier one's stomach, the clearer one's thoughts. Being hungry has made me realize that it's time I made something of myself" (p. 81). However, once Hirshl surrenders to his environment, meat becomes a regular part of his meals (pp. 106, 118, 119).

The change in Hirshl's attitude toward cooked meat indicates a change in personality and in his attitude toward the values of the bourgeois society. In time he ceased being reserved and also ceased criticizing the values of that society. However, the cock-gever, alive, tortures Hirshl by crowing and Hirshl discovers that love is stronger than money. The cock's crow is retaliation for Hirshl's betrayal of himself, his love and emotions, and this crow is internal, it comes from within him. As long as the cock crows Hirshl suffers, while the beginning of his cure connects with the disappearance of this crow. One of the ways in which Hirshl resumes his bourgeois life after he was cured is through meals (pp. 214-216, 223, 225, 227).

THE EGG-TRADE AND THE RELATIONS BETWEEN MINA AND HIRSHL

The poultry trade flourishes in Szybusz (pp. 100, 111-112, 227) and is described in detail in the novel. Arnold Ziemlich and Gedalia Ziemlich are in the forefront of this trade. Though the discussions of the poultry-trade in the novel are realistic, they also expand beyond the needs of the plot and create additional aspects of the cock-motif. "Eggs" in the novel cease to be merely eggs:

> The egg trade made Ziemlich rich: Gedalia Ziemlich had had a bountiful year ... poultry and egg prices were up too.... Hard though it was to believe, the same chickens that cackled in refuse on Gedalia's farm were now ceremoniously received at the railway station by a trainman wearing the peaked cap of the Kaiser who sent them and their eggs off to Germany. Not even in the days of the Mishnah, when a whole tractate called Betsa, which is Hebrew for "egg," was composed, were eggs ever treated with such honors. (p. 111)

Eggs received the care and attention of the trade[30] and were cultivated--and they acquired meaning in addition to simply being eggs. In the same context in which we find a detailed description of the egg-trade (pp. 111-112) we find that sexual relations between Hirshl and Mina flourished in Gedalia's home (p. 112), and "Mina's bed stood freshly made and smelling of cologne" (ibid.). Gedalia provided livelihood "to the carpenters who made the coops and crates" (p. 111), among other workers in the egg-trade. Another carpenter, "Bendit the carpenter," made a fine bed for Hirshl (p. 112). The textual connections between Gedalia's egg-trade and the erotic relations of Mina and Hirshl at Gedalia's home allude to the intensity of sexual relations between Hirshl (the cock) and Mina (the chicken). Hirshl does not conduct himself like a Jewish scholar who even though he is allowed to cohabit with his wife at any time, will nevertheless act with a sacred attitude and not conduct himself like a cock but will cohabit on Friday evenings only, providing he has the strength.[31]

Arnold Ziemlich works in the egg-trade (pp. 100, 111-112, 227). He receives eggs which are then shipped from Szybusz to Germany. While the discussion of his trade is realistic, here too eggs become a means of transferring hereditary features from one generation to another:

> While as for Herr Ziemlich, though his customers were no wiser than the chickens, it being entirely possible to eat an egg without knowing what tree it grew on, he was only too aware of what made them keep coming back for more. Besides, if a German were to eat eggs from China his eyes might grow slantwise, while the eyes of the good folk of Szybusz were big and blue. (p. 227)

Mere eggs are hardly so influential.

We note a Jewish tradition to the effect that eating eggs increases seed (see *Yoma*, 18a). That tradition also emphasizes the large number of the eggs of the chicken: the cock and the chicken were considered symbols of procreation. Szybusz excels in its large number of eggs:[32] Arnold Ziemlich's business in Szybusz "was large and getting larger, which should have come as a surprise to no one who had bothered to count the number of chickens pecking in the town's garbage" (p. 227). Various traditions relate to poultry.[33] In the language of Egyptian hieroglyphics, "the determinative sign of the egg represents potentiality, the seed of generation, the mystery of life" (Cirlot, p. 90, "egg"). Also, "the Chinese believe that the first man had sprung from an egg dropped by Tien from heaven to float upon the primordial waters" (ibid.). Eggs were thought to have magic power. In this novel eggs decide the color of the eyes of the one who eats the eggs. This idea suggests the biological-erotic aspect of the eggs and cocks in the novel.

The cock-motif passes through various stages in the novel, and sometimes understanding the text requires taking into account various Jewish sources to which the text alludes. The motif, its symbols, and the means of its formation all have important functions in the novel.

The motif is ambiguous and is used as an indirect device to characterize life in Szybusz in general and that of Hirshl in particular. It appears in critical stages in Hirshl's life, alluding to his confusion, and it strongly influences him.

Following the motif in the novel the reader will sense the integrity of Agnon's artistic consciousness. The phenomenon of the cock in the novel is objective; its effects are subjective and depend on the interaction between reader and text. Scholars have pointed out various effects of the motif. Band (1960, pp. 250-251) spoke of the complexity of this motif:

> The *gever* is not only a homonym which means both "cock" and "male," an intimation of Hirshl's failure to fulfill his masculinity, to possess his wife as a woman, but is also the sign for rising to pray to the Lord. Hirshl ... a young man of good family, deteriorates to the state of the grotesquely subhuman, part frog, part cock.... The cock ... seems to be a mockery of Hirshl, the man.

Band drew attention to the connection between religion, madness, and the cock in the novel. The cock's crow powerfully affects Hirshl and contributes to his madness. Various traditional Jewish elements are interwoven with the process of Hirshl's madness and cure: Hirshl remembered near Mazal's house "the candle that had gone out at his wedding" (p. 169), Rabbi Joseph de la Reina (p. 150), Jacob and his wives (p. 155) and Elkanda and his wives (p. 156), and Hirshl's madness which becomes obvious in the synagogue (p. 170) where he is afraid lest he will be identified with the cock (p. 171). Also Dr. Langsam, who cured Hirshl, emphasized the positive aspect of traditional values (e.g., pp. 182–183, 189–190, 201).

The motif of the cock requires the active, creative participation of the reader in the text.   Each time the cock reappears, the reader must consider its previous appearances and the mutual influence between the present appearance of the cock and its previous appearances.   Any present appearance also raises anticipations as to future appearances. The active creativity of the reader is stimulated by the text. Through the motif of the cock the reader is bound to the text—to what he has already read (past), to what he is reading (present), and to what he anticipates reading (future).[34]   The fact that the cock constantly changes its implications and meanings makes the reading process particularly intensive and creative. The reader's anticipations are based on the phenomenon of the cock and its effects on the specific reader. Each appearance of the cock has three functions: it connects with the anticipations raised by the previous appearance; it moves the reader to reflect concerning the previous appearance; it raises anticipations as to the next appearance.   The changes in the meaning and implications of the cock do not frustrate the reader but surprise and motivate him to reconstruct the literary elements which caused his surprise.   All this intensifies the reader's creative reading and enjoyment. The motif of the cock is, therefore, one of the devices which unify the novel structurally.

Another function of the cock-motif is its contribution to the closure of the novel.[35] The motif develops throughout the novel, and when it disappears from the novel and from Hirshl's life it does not simply stop arbitrarily but comes to an artistic closure.   Hirshl attained balance by removing from his life the voice of the cock-*gever*. Hirshl's passive, involuntary revolt proves to be ephemeral and he integrates with his environment. He leaves behind him the romantic, enchanting, rural world, the world of snow and melodies:

> Mina ... took a break ... and went for a walk with Hirshl.

The two of them crunched through the snow, which seemed to sing beneath their feet. Or was it really the snow that they heard? Sitting cross-legged in it and strumming as he sung was a blind musician ... his song that was boundlessly sad and sweet seemed to have no beginning and no end. Yet Hirshl and Mina stood perfectly still as if waiting for him to finish it. Suddenly Hirshl seized Mina's arm and said, "Let's go." (p. 226)

NOTES

1.   The references in the Hebrew version of this article refer to the Hebrew version of the novel: *Kol sippurei S. Y. Agnon*, vol. 3, Schocken, 1953, pp.   55–272.   The references here refer to the English translation of the novel, *A Simple Story*, translated by Hillel Halkin, Schocken Books, New York, 1985.   Quotations are from the translation by Hillel Halkin.

2.   The Hebrew text uses the terms *tarnegol* and *gever* for the rooster.   The term *gever* is a homonym which stands for both "cock" and "male," "man."

3.   Names   in   this   essay   appear   according   to   the transliteration of Hillel Halkin (1985).

4.   See "symbol" in Preminger (1965, pp. 833–836).

5.   The cock was used as a symbol in Agnon's *The Bridal Canopy* prior to its use in *A Simple Story*. See: *The Bridal Canopy*, rendered into English by I. M. Lask, The Literary Guild of America, Inc., 1937.   *A Simple Story* was first published in 1935.   *The Bridal Canopy* was first published in 1931.   For some applicable aspects regarding symbol, see Wellek and Warren (1963), chapter 15.

6.   The words "my dove" appear in English as "my darling."

7.   This translation is my own.   Cf. Halkin, 1985, p. 154: "Hearing a rooster crow, he got out of bed to see if it was midnight."

8.   See *Yoma*, 27b.

9,   *The Bridal Canopy*, translated, Lask p. 63.   In the same spirit one finds the coquetry of the cock in his manhood and crest in Chernihovski's idyll, "Brit mila."

10.   "Three are courageous: Israel among the nations, the dog among the animals, and the cock among the fowl" (*Betsa*, 25b).   The rooster is identified with the male: "He who sees a cock in his dream

should expect a male son" (*Berakhot*, 57a). The chicken, however, alludes to a female (*Shabbat*, 151b).

11.   See Cirlot, 1962, p. 69--"as the bird of dawn, the cock is ... an emblem of vigilance and activity.   During the Middle Ages it became a highly important Christian image, nearly always appearing on the highest weathervane, on cathedral towers and domes, and was regarded as an allegory of vigilance and resurrection." The cock believes that he brings the sunrise and is disappointed when it rises without his help. See Aarne, 1961, pp. 46, 114.

12.   The use of a cock in order to demonstrate coquetry and boasting is common, e.g., Genesin in "Ezel" uses the family of the "grown-up" Dutch cocks when he relates to a sentimental-coquettish complaint; one of the characters who feels disgusted by his own coquettish expression sees himself in his dreams as a cock--with tail, feathers, etc. (*Etsel*, Yahdav, 1965, pp. 75-76, 79). See also, for example, pp. 26, 47, 52 in which cock and chicken are used as periphrasis.

13.   David Tsimerman (1962, p. 20) relates to the erotic meaning of the cry of a bird of prey in the story, "Another Face." See also Golomb, 1968, p. 257.

14.   In Agnon's *The Bridal Canopy* Pessele takes the cock to be slaughtered for a meal for her father-in-law-to-be and she "tripped along, cuddling the cock to her bosom and stroking his comb and chanting to him ... sweetheart ..." (p. 353). About the identity of the cock-man-father-lover-groom see Kurzweil, 1966, pp. 204-216.

15.   In *Eruvin* (100b) the cock is described as a seducer of the chicken. When he cannot fulfill his promise to the chicken, he swears that his crest may fall off if he could fulfill his promise but did not.

16.   See *Gitin*, 57a.   There was a custom to put a cock and a chicken in front of the bride and bridegroom to suggest that they should multiply like the cock and the chicken. See also *Shabbat* 30b. See Haefrati (1971, p. 119) discussing the story "Ba'arava" of Chernihovski--parallel to the wedding one finds also the copulation of a bull and a cow, a cock and a chicken. Sometimes it is derogatory to use chicken as periphrasis for a woman, as in the poem of Y. L. Gordon, "Kuzo shel yod." See also in Zalman Shneor's "Anshe shiklov" (Davis, 1960, pp. 73-75), an erotic-humanistic description of the Jewish cock and the non-Jewish cock.

17.   The mouse, quite unlike the cock, has a positively soporific effect on Hirshl (ibid., p. 163).   A friendly relationship is evident between a man and a mouse also in *The Bridal Canopy*. As to the mouse as a friend of the cock see Aarne (1961, pp. 45, 112**) and also Thompson (1966, vol. 1, pp. 414, 2.2, 281B; vol. 4, pp. 201, 132J).

18.   For an interesting example of an erotic literary use of a pocketknife see Gidon Telpaz' story "Shekhunat hap" in his book *Shekhunat hap* (Hakkibbuts hammeuhad, 1966, pp. 37-38).

19.   Blessing of the Lord for giving wisdom to the cock (to differentiate between day and night) based on Job 38:36: "Who hath given wisdom to the rooster?" (Maimonides, *Sheluhin veshutafin*, a prayer, 7, 4).

20.   "If thou buy a Hebrew servant, six years he shall serve; and in the seventh he shall go out free for nothing. If his master give him a wife ... he shall go out by himself. But if the servant shall plainly say: I love my master, my wife, and my children; I will not go out free, then, his master shall bore his ear through with an awl and he shall serve him forever" (*Exodus* 21:1-7).

21.   See Frishman's use of "Because of a chicken and a cock"--meaning something of little value which becomes very consequential (*Kol Kitve, Sippurim*, vol. 2, pp. 171-181; M. Newman, 1964). See *Gitin* 57a.

22.   The madness of Hirshl and Hirshl's uncle is mentioned numerous times in the novel and in that context--the going to the woods, e.g., pp. 15, 18, 64, 80, 127-128, 157, 171-173.

23.   P. 63: "By reason of a certain prayer, in the Order of Prayers ... when he readeth this prayer on the appointed Eve of Atonement he taketh a cock, whirleth it about his head, saith, This cock shall go to death, and handeth it over to the slaughterer."

24.   There are elements common both to the Original Sin (of Adam) and to the meeting between Hirshl and Blume near Mazal's house: God, garden, wind, a questioning voice, walking (Genesis 3:8).

25.   The hand and the gate have romantic applications in Song of Songs (5:1-6): "Open to me, my sister, my love ... for my head is filled with dew. My locks with the drops of the night ... my beloved put in his hand by the hole of the door, and my heart was moved for him. I rose up to open to my beloved and my hands dropped with myrrh, and my fingers with flowing myrrh, upon the handles of the bar. I opened to my beloved." Hirshl hoped that Blume would open the garden gate--but she "stepped out of the house to close it" (p. 148). Blume is "a garden shut up" (Song of Songs, 4:12) to Hirshl and their romantic reunion will never take place.

26.   The following points of comparison between the two scenes (pp. 34, 148-149) are of special interest:

pp. 33-34   *pp. 148-149*

He ... lay his head on her bed. A thousand years might well have to passed....

Hirshl rested his head on the latch of the gate and began to cry.

For the world ceased to exist for him. Never had his body felt so fully alive.

Through a curtain of mist so for thick that he could not

He lay without moving....

see his own self the image of Blume appeared as brightly before him....

He moaned again and again, seizing his head with his hands. Rain began to fall....

He lay ... suffused by a honeyed sweetness.

Hirshl felt utterly crushed, utterly mortified;... He had not yet felt as sad.... Never since his walks to Blume's house began had Hirshl been so downcast....

Never had his body felt so fully alive.

He was sure that he was coming down with something.

He ... lay his head on her bed. A thousand years might well have passed....

The thought of being ill upset him less than the thought of being in a bed next to Mina's.

Blume ... was gone from the room.... Then a woman's hand touched his ... it was Blume's....

Blume recoiled and retreated ... not that he expected head Blume to come out again to comfort him.

Hirshl stood for a while longer in the middle of the room.

Rejected and soaked to the bone, he stood outside Blume's house.

The whole room was filled with her scent, which was like freshly fallen apples.

The air, earth, and grass still good rainy smell.

27.   In some Jewish sources poultry is viewed as a delicacy food of people of means, e.g. *Pesahim*, 114a; Yerushalmi: *Peah*, 71; *Kiddushin*, 31, 32; *Ketubbot*, 67b.

28.   This chicken was brought to Eastern Europe. In the 19th century it became the subject of dispute--some rabbis permitted these chickens while others forbade it, but ultimately it was permitted to eat them. Leviticus 11:13-19 mentions the fowl which should be detested, but not those which may be eaten. The Jewish sages allowed for eating only fowl which were traditionally considered pure, and they provided the signs that characterize pure fowl.

29.   The possibility of degrading the people of Szybusz in certain respects is alluded to later in the novel: "Szybusz ... was, after all, a town like any other, with geese waddling in its streets and poor folk going barefoot beside them" (p. 215). Geese and poor folk have the same status. Toyber, in his story, is also talking about geese (p. 79).   Dr. Langsam sometimes reminisced about his home town, "flanked by tiny houses hardly larger than chicken coops" (p. 182).

30.   See *Horayot*, 12: He who wants to do business and wants to know if he will succeed or not should grow a cock; if the cock grows fat, it is a sign that he will be successful.

31.   Rambam, *Mishne Torah, Sefer hammada*, 5:4.

32.   Compare: *Baba metsia*, 28; *Baba kama*, 79b. Jewish law related to poultry as causing dirt. *Baba Kama*, 92b.

33.   See Aarne, 223 no. 670; Thompson, vol. 4, p. 366, 1065K; vol. 2, p. 23, 166.1.1D; vol. 4, p. 420, 1691.2K; vol. 4, p. 227, 2614.3J; vol. 1, p. 286, 2321.10.1A.

34.   See Iser, 1972.

35.   See Herrnstein-Smith, 1968, pp. 1-4.

BIBLIOGRAPHY

Aarne, Anti. *The Types of the Folktale*. Translated and enlarged by Stith Thompson. Helsinki, 1961.

Agnon, Shemuel Yosef. *The Bridal Canopy*. Rendered into English by I. M. Lask.   The Literary Guild of America, Inc., New York, 1937.

_____. *A Simple Story*. Translated by Hillel Halkin. Schocken, New York, 1985.

Band, Arnold J. *Nostalgia and Nightmare: A Study in the Fiction of S. Y. Agnon*. University of California Press, Berkeley & Los Angeles, 1968.

Cirlot, J. E. *A Dictionary of Symbols*. Philosophical Library, New York, 1962.

Even, Josef. "Haddialog besippure S. Y. Agnon vedarkhe itsuvo: al pi 'sippur pashut', 'shvuat emunim u'fanim aherot'." *Hassifrut*, vol. 3, no. 2 (November 1971), 281-294.

Golomb, Harai.   "Haddibbur hammeshulav--tekhnika merkazit bapproza shel Agnon: Lefy hassippur 'panim aherot'." *Hassifrut*, vol. 1, no. 2 (Summer 1968), 251-262.

Haefrati, Yosef. *Ha'idilia shel Chernihovski*. Sifriyat happoalim, merhavia, 1971.

Herrnstein-Smith, Barbara. *Poetic Closure.* The University of
  Chicago Press, 1968.
Iser, Wolfgang.   "The Reading Process: A Phenomenological
  Approach." *New Literary History*, 3, no. 2 (Winter 1971),
  279-299.
Kurzweil, Barukh.   *Massot al sippure S. Y. Agnon.*   Schocken,
  Yerushalyim vetel-aviv, 1966.
Preminger, Alex, ed. *Princeton Encyclopedia of Poetry and Poetics.*
  Princeton University Press, 1965.
Sadan, Dov. *S. Y. Agnon - massa, iyun veheker.*   Hakkibbuts
  hammeuhad, 1967.
Shaked, Gershon. "Bat hammelekh usudat ha'em." *Gazit*, vol. 24, no.
  5-12, 1967, 135-147. Reprinted in his book: *Omanut hassippur
  shel Agnon.* Sifriyat poalim, 1973, 197-227.
Thomashevsky, Boris. "Thematics." In *Russian Formalist Criticism.*
  Lemon, Lee T., & Reis, Marian J., eds. University of Nebraska
  Press, Lincoln, 1965, pp. 61-95.
Thompson, Stith. *Motif Index of Folk Literature.* Indiana University
  Press, Bloomington, 1966.
Tsimerman, David.   *Al shelosha missupire Agnon.*   Hassuhnut
  hayehudit, Jerusalem, 1962.
Wellek, Rene, and Warren, Austin. *Theory of Literature.* Harcourt
  Brace & Company, New York, 1963.

SEXUAL SYMBOLS IN "ANOTHR FACE"
BY S. Y. AGNON

"Michael was grateful to her for
her not interpreting his dream
according to Freud and his School."
S. Y. Agnon, "Another Face,"
Dec. 12, 1932, edition *Davar*

Sexual symbols play an important role in S. Y. Agnon's short story
"Another Face"[1] (1976, vol. 3, pp. 449-468). These symbols
accompany the progress in communication between Toni and Michael
and thereby enrich the reader's aesthetic experience of the story.
The author dramatizes the couple's emotional world by projecting it
upon concrete objects which function equally as objects and as
symbols.[2]

Sigmund Freud viewed many components of the physical world
as symbols of sexual activity or desire. A brief glance at the things
and settings emphasized in "Another Face" reveals many objects to
which Freud assigned sexual significance: a parasol, hat, flowers, a
garden, to name some of the more prominent. It may be argued that
different readers will relate in different ways to Freudian symbology
in the story. The reader may interpret the attitude of the narrator to
these symbols as complex and ambivalent and as going beyond
Freudian symbology; the reader may even argue that the narrator
employs these symbols as virtual parody; or he may argue that the
narrator employs Freudian symbols as defined by Freud. While the
effect of these symbols may be viewed in different ways by different
readers, ignoring their existence may lead to erroneous interpretation
because it is a means of characterization in the story. The existence
of the phenomena is objective, their effects are subjective. I agree
with Barzel (1975, p. 61), who thinks that "undoubtedly, Agnon was
well-versed in Freudian symbology and knew how key symbols of his
story would be interpreted."

The presence of many sexually charged objects in "Another Face" indicates the presence of symbols. According to the Freudian approach, objects belong to one of two groups, the masculine or the feminine. This strict duality seems to some to have been imposed by a mind psychologically predisposed to find and to unveil universal sexuality. Symbolic interpretation confined to sexuality may, in fact, be a degenerate form of symbolism. Nevertheless, "Another Face" demands that the reader take these symbols into account in interpreting the story and its central relationship. Various elements make it necessary to understand the sexual symbols in the story: the context of marital tension and sexual attraction; the frequent usage of explicitly Freudian objects; the narrator's encouragement of the reader to see these objects as being more than simple objects; and the fact that some ideas in the story which seem at first flat or difficult become emotionally loaded and intelligible only when the objects are read as sexual symbols. These elements and others—such as the associative power and the centrality of these objects in the story and the sexual tension evoked by the interrelations of these symbolic objects—all support my contention as to the necessity of understanding the sexual symbols in this story. Other symbolic meanings for these objects are possible. My focus, however, is to read the text in the heretofore ignored light of Freudian sexual symbolism.

Between 1913 and 1924 Agnon lived in Germany; there he had close access to the ideas of Freud, already well known in intellectual circles. As Barzel (1975, p. 64) points out,

> Certainly one should not relate to Agnon the exclusive following of one psychological approach or another, out of an attempt to imitate it. On the other hand Agnon knew well the spirit of Vienna and was influenced by the modes of thinking, and also by the ways of symbology of Freud and his followers.

Several of his short stories ("The Doctor's Divorce" and "Fernheim," as well as "Another Face") are set in German-speaking countries and concern themselves with crises within marriage. Agnon originally dedicated the story of "Another Tallit" to Max Eitington, who was a loyal disciple of Freud, and who organized in 1933 a Palestinian Psychoanalytic Society.

Freudian interpretation has been successfully applied to Agnon's work by scholars such as Aberbach (1984) and Shryboim (1977). Feldman refers to the "sexual" connotations of the key-motif in Agnon's *A Guest for the Night*, and she thinks that Agnon is quite explicit in his use of dream symbolism, to the point that "he almost challenges the reader to go beyond the obvious in his search for an integrating reading" (1985, pp. 266, 267).

It is noteworthy that when "Another Face" first appeared in *Davar* in 1932, it included the following passage which Agnon later omitted: "after [Michael] finished telling her his dream ... [Toni's] ... eyes became somewhat wet. Michael was grateful to her for not interpreting his dream according to Freud and his School." By telling us why Michael was grateful, the narrator simultaneously reminds us of Freudian symbolism, with which he is obviously acquainted. Toni's eyes becoming wet is a statement to which Freud himself (1953, 5, pp. 358, 359) would give a Freudian significance.

Some critics have hinted in passing at the possibility of giving a sexual interpretation to some objects in Agnon's "Another Face." I intend to demonstrate that this possibility is much more substantial than Agnon criticism has so far considered it to be. Freudian symbols become a device to portray characters and their inner life and relations through an interplay between the conscious reader and the narrator on the one hand and, on the other, the characters, who are (in the final version of the story) unconscious of the implications of some of their actions and objects. This essay does not, however, claim to be conclusive regarding all the objects and situations that may be interpreted sexually in "Another Face." My larger intent is to offer an interpretation of this story which may enrich the reader's experience of Agnon's other short stories and novels as well.

THE CHARACTERS' PERSONAL EFFECTS AND THEIR BODIES

Agnon emphasizes various personal effects that Toni and Hartmann wear or carry with them. Toni's dress, parasol, handbag, and bottle of scent, and Michael's hat, cigarettes, cigars, and cigar-knife, for example, become prominent in the short story. Freud deals in his work with some of these objects. It is noteworthy that, according to Freud himself (1953, 5, p. 685), the symbolic significance of these objects is not confined to dreams; objects such as umbrellas ("the opening of this last being comparable to an erection" [5, p. 354]) and knives may stand for the male organ (5, pp. 358-359; also p. 380 and pp. 683-684).

One object that is mentioned repeatedly in Agnon's "Another Face" is the parasol. The reader first notices the parasol when Dr. Tanzer and Svirsh,[3] the two single bachelors who lust for Toni, welcome her as she leaves the judge's house: "Svirsh took the parasol, hung it from her belt and, taking both her hands in his, swung them affectionately back and forth" (p. 4).   In other of Agnon's love stories, there are substantial obstacles to fulfilling love; but Tanzer and Svirsh do not constitute such an obstacle at all.   Svirsh's lust is explicitly depicted by the narrator through the use of Free Indirect Speech[4] and the symbolic use of Toni's parasol.   Svirsh's swinging back and forth of Toni's hands and his hanging her parasol from her belt denote sexual feelings.

Later (p. 11), in a moment of mutual attraction between Toni and Michael, Michael is busy dealing with his hat while Toni fusses busily with the parasol.   And Michael, desiring his ex-wife, makes gestures in the air as Toni, desiring her ex-husband, pokes the ground with her parasol (p. 17).   Barzel (1975, pp. 63-64) correctly finds the parasol to be a male object while the ground is a female one.   Toni's act with the parasol moves Hartmann because it reflects his own erotic excitement.   Toni and Michael then arrive at an inn where they decide to dine.   Michael is worried that his wife is aware of his sexual thoughts.   He "took her parasol, laid it on a chair, placed his hat on top of it ..." (p. 23).   Hartmann's unconscious wish is that he will be able to accomplish his desires as simply as he was able to put his hat on Toni's parasol.   At dinner, Toni's appetite (p. 24) represents her love for Michael and her frustrated desire for him.   But Hartmann rejects her again: he "got up, took his hat and said: 'Let's go'" (p. 32).   This time Hartmann does not deal with the parasol himself: "The waiter came up and handed Toni her parasol ..." (p. 32).   One concludes that Tanzer, Svirsh, Hartmann, and Toni express hidden desire as they handle the parasol, and it indeed plays the same role as Freud's umbrella.

The appearance of the parasol in the story is often coupled with the appearance of the hat.   Freud states that "a woman's hat can very often be interpreted with certainty as a genital organ, and moreover, as a man's" (1953, 5, pp. 355-356; see also pp. 360-362).   The reader first notices the hat in "Another Face" when Svirsh and Tanzer are defeated by Michael.   "Waving his hat [Tanzer] walked off...."   The word in Hebrew is *henif*, which can be translated as "waving" or "lifting" the hat.   Tanzer doffs his hat and admits the loss of the sexual object.   Now Toni and Michael are left alone.   Michael is attracted to his ex-wife, and he is embarrassed: "He crumpled his hat and waved it about, smoothed its creases, crumpled it again, put it back on his head, and passed his hands over his temples down to his chin" (p. 6).   These helpless gestures with the hat, coupled with his self-conscious avoidance of her eyes, indicate Michael's strong longing and sexual desire for his ex-wife.   In another moment of confusion, when Hartmann is thinking about his separation and divorce, the narrator describes his feelings and his gestures: "he removed his hat, mopped his brow, wiped the leather band inside his hat and put it back on his head" (p. 10). The hat serves as a refuge for Michael, who has a hard time facing his new status as a divorced man, and represents his desire for his ex-wife. Michael now learns that he cannot fulfill this desire as simply as he was able to put his hat on Toni's parasol.

Critics have noticed the parasol and the hat; however, they have ignored their sexual implications. Goldberg (1963, pp. 213, 217, 218), Tokhner (1965, p. 32; 1968, p. 99), and Kena'ani (1977, p. 491) emphasized the awkward, hopeless, repetitive and confused nature of Hartmann's unconscious gestures with his hat. Rivlin (1969, pp. 120-121) thinks that the parasol is Toni's support and protection. Tokhner is aware of the longing and sexual desires between Toni and Hartmann (1968, p. 98), but does not substantiate his claim. Barzel (1982, p. 59) thinks that the parasol is "a combined expression of canopy, defense and erotic symbol." While I do not disagree with these statements, it seems to me that the sexual roles of the hat and the parasol are important to the interpretation and the enjoyment of the text. The characters do not act out of conscious sexual urges; they do not ask themselves why they do what they do with the hat or the parasol. However, the narrator and the reader "must" be aware of those urges.

Additional phallic smbols in the story are cigars, cigarettes, a pipe and a cigar-knife. The story describes Michael's efforts during a frustrating marriage to find a satisfactory substitute for love. Michael tries friendship, reading books, and smoking "cigarettes first, then cigars" (p. 14) as a means of enhancing his unsatisfactory life. On the day of the divorce, Toni and Michael go through the fields from the town to an inn. In a moment of attraction to Toni, Michael thinks about smoking (p. 18), but now he is self-conscious and the cigarette cannot satisfy his desires. After dinner Michael "took out a cigar and trimmed it with his knife then took out a pack of cigarettes and offered one to Toni. They sat opposite one another, the smoke they made rising and mingling.... Toni parted the smoke with her fingers and went on smoking contentedly" (p. 28). Unlike the lonely, isolated smoking at home during their marriage, now Hartmann and Toni, in a moment of good feeling and positive communication, smoke in a way which is satisfying for them both, and their smoke mingles. Michael's knife should not be disregarded (Freud, 1953, 5, pp. 358-360; also pp. 380, 683-684); nor should we ignore the fire in the phallic symbols of the cigar and the cigarettes (5, pp. 384, 395).

It is heavily symbolic and rather humorous that Michael, who was so desirous of his ex-wife, had to leave her room in the inn, in which there was a "broken horn with a bridal wreath on it" (p. 36). Michael's desires for a renewed marriage end at this stage with a "broken horn." When the old man stated that there was only one room free, "Toni blushed, Michael crumpled his hat and said nothing" (p. 36). We have a detailed description of the way the innkeeper deals with his pipe prior to suggesting that Toni will sleep in the only available room and Michael on the billiard table. Toni's blushing, Michael's crumpling of his hat, the innkeeper's knocking the pipe (which "represents the approximate shape of the male organ" [Freud, 1953, 4, p. 86]) against the table, the innkeeper's putting his thumb into the pipe's bowl—all of these are sexually significant acts. There is one attractive woman and two lonely men. I disagree with Barzel (1975, p. 58), who claims that Toni's blushing here is due to her bashfulness and not to her erotic attraction to her husband. Tsimerman (1962, pp. 18, 21-22) recognizes Michael's desire for his ex-wife, arguing, though, that the closer Michael gets to his ex-wife the more distant she becomes. I disagree with Tsimerman's analysis of Toni's feelings, in that it ignores the mutual attraction indicated by Toni's blushing and Michael's playing with his hat.

Michael starts his life as a divorced man by sleeping on a public gaming table (billiard table), made for a game composed of balls, holes, and sticks, rather than in the bed once consecrated to him and his wife by marriage. His grotesque position is indicative of the fact that his sexual desires cannot be resolved without resolution of his relationship. There is another table in the story: When over dinner Michael started telling Toni his dream, sharing his intimate thoughts with his ex-wife, he put the cigar down (p. 38) while communicating with his wife. Now that his wife is asleep and he is alone again, he thinks again about smoking, a thought that is encouraged by the thick cigar under the table, which itself is a symbol of a woman (Freud, 1953, 4, pp. 355, 374, 376, 381).

Freud calls attention to hollow objects such as handbags.[5] In a moment of mutual attraction and self-awareness between Toni and Michael, Toni wets her hands (another act with a Freudian [1953, 5, p. 403] meaning): "Toni opened her handbag, took out a bottle of scent, and sprinkled her hands with it" (p. 18). According to Freud, "Boxes, cases, chests, cupboards and ovens represent the uterus ..." (1953, 5, 354; also p. 373, regarding "purse").

Several times in the story Michael "wanted to take off his jacket and wrap it around Toni" (p. 34). The original Hebrew text speaks of me'il, a "coat" or "overcoat." Michael's awareness of Toni's being cold is coupled with his erotic attraction to her, and the coat becomes a male symbol here (Freud, 1953, 4, pp. 186, 204; 5, p. 365).

In the opening sentence of the story, the narrator mentions Toni's brown dress (p. 4). He later draws attention to it in erotic contexts (pp. 12, 14, 22, 26, 34). Her dress stimulates Michael's thoughts about her nakedness.

The narrator makes frequent reference to parts of the body, such as hands, thumbs, arms, mouths, lips, and tongues. Freud (1953, 5, p. 359) contends that the male's organ may be represented by his hand or foot, the female's by mouth, ear, or even an eye. Undoubtedly, hands and arms are sexually significant in the short story. Indeed, Svirsh's and Tanzer's confident gestures (pp. 4, 6) indicate merely selfish lust, for Toni is to them an object of sexual fantasies; Michael's graceless and uncertain gestures (pp. 4, 16, 17, 19), though, combine sexual desire and love. Portraying Toni as a good listener, the narrator describes her active silence: she listens, she looks, she thinks (p. 8). But her hand and arm motions are activated by men; she is passive.

THE FIELDS AND THE GARDEN

After their divorce Toni and Michael walk through the field from their town to a garden of an inn. The setting is rich with Freudian meaning: they are sitting at a table in a garden near a gate; the garden is full of birds and fruit trees; they discuss rooms, dancing, and an oven. On their way to the inn, Toni thought (p. 20) that the light of the inn was a firefly. The lights of the firefly are the courting strategies of the female and male fireflies. On their way to the inn, Toni is chilled by the wind:

> "Are you cold?" Hartmann asked anxiously.
> "I think I see people coming."
> "There is no one here," said Hartmann, "but perhaps ..."

They should not be touching each other after their divorce, a transgression against Jewish law (see *Mishna Gittin* 8, 9, and also Rivlin, 1969, p. 110). Toni evades Michael's inquiry about her being cold, and then she points out a tall person: "A man with a ladder came towards them." Toni blushes now not because Tanzer is taller than Hartmann, as Kena'ani contends (1977, p. 492), but because of the erotic atmosphere, strengthened by the ladder as a Freudian element (1953, 5, p. 355). At this time, Toni and Hartmann do not communicate verbally. However, this interchange does not seem to be a failure in communication, but rather a display of timidity about their sexual attraction.

Even (1971, pp. 292-293) thinks that here Toni and Michael become distanced. Toni's lowering her eyes and blushing and the abortive conversation are taken by Even as an example of a "dialogue" without any real communication. This opinion seems to stem from ignoring the intense sexual attraction between Hartmann and Toni. Indeed the sexual excitement that marks this part of the story (pp. 20-22) is unmistakable, when one pays attention to the sexual symbols and situations: Hartmann's anxiety regarding Toni's being chilled by the wind, her indirect answer, his incomplete sentence, the tall man with the ladder who lit the lamp, Toni's blushing and lowering her eyes, Hartmann's smiles, the boy and the girl, and Toni looking at her ring and remembering that she is no longer married to Hartmann and that physical contact is now forbidden between them. The narrator here draws our attention to the progress in the attraction between Michael and Toni, not to the alleged regression in their newly developed communication. Because of such moments, the reader understands that Toni and Michael have discovered another face in themselves, in their relations, and in each other as man-husband and woman-wife.

After walking in the field, Toni and Michael see a restaurant (p. 22):

> A little later they came to a garden which was fenced on three sides. The gate was open and to the right of it shone a lamp. Some smaller lanterns in the shape of pears and some apples hung from the trees in the garden.

We are then introduced to a girl who pulls at her skirt when they enter the garden of the inn, and Hartmann thinks that the girl is red-haired and freckled. Talking about the girl (pp. 22, 24) as red-headed with freckles is a way to evade his sexual thoughts about the girl and his wife. The girl appears again when she passes by "carrying a basket of plums with both hands. The juice of the overripe plums exuded an odor of cloying sweetness" (p. 26). Unlike Tsimerman (1962, pp. 17, 19), it is my opinion that Hartmann's desire is for his wife, and not just any woman. When Toni and Michael returned to the garden of the inn, their attraction is mutual as Kena'ani pointed out (1977, p. 492), and it is reflected by the landscape described as they walk in the field after dinner.

Freud discusses gardens (1953, 5, p. 346), fruits (1953, 4, p. 287; 5, pp. 372-373), gates (5, p. 346), trees, wood, etc., as well as keys and locks (5, p. 354) as sexual symbols. When Toni and Michael first enter the garden, "which was fenced on three sides," its "gate was open" (p. 22). After they leave the inn, they come back to it and "Hartmann pushed the gate open and they went up the stone steps" (p. 34). He is full of erotic desires for his wife and her garden, hoping to consummate their relations by sleeping with her. In this context the stone steps and the act of ascending them also have Freudian significance,[6] as do the shape of apples (1953, 4, p. 287) or pears (4, p. 372). As Hartmann anticipates his meal in the inn's garden, it is clear that he is feeling the demands of his sexual appetites as well, he expects "fresh dishes" (p. 24). The sexual connotation is that Toni has now become "fresh" in his eyes.

Leiter (1970, pp. 63-64) refers to various paragraphs in the story (some of which are in this section), such as the boy running with a lighted stick, the gesture of Hartmann with his thumbs, the flowers, the falling from the mount, and he traces them to the Talmud (*Berakhot* 51-53, 53a, 55b; *Gittin* 66a, 81, 90b). This seems to me a significant contribution to understanding the story without lessening the weight of the sexual symbology.

A bird plays an interesting role in this story. While Toni and Michael are eating, they listen to a song of a bird. Toni's face grows prettier, and Hartmann covers his knees with his napkin (p. 24). Now they are content and attracted to each other. The bird's song is indicative of Michael's sexual excitement (Freud, 1953, 5, pp. 583-584). However, when Hartmann later thinks that divorcing his wife was a clever act, he listens neither to his wife's question about the bird nor to the "bird"; nor does he need to cover his knees any more. In Hartmann's dream the "frozen birds" (p. 30) represent a breakdown in warmth and communication in the family.

Toni and Hartmann walk back toward the city. They come close to a river (p. 32), and the river now plays a role in the story: the stream lulling in its bed, the cry of the bird of prey, the echo reverberating through the ear, the waves raising themselves up and falling back exhausted, the stream rocking itself wearily—all this rhythmic motion happens in a moment of mutual desire between Toni and Hartmann. In general, nature in the story is described in a way which reflects the moods and relations of the characters.

We also meet the girl who sold Michael a bunch of asters (p. 10). The reader is told that Toni had always been fond of asters (pp. 24, 26). The flowers are cared for when Toni and Hartmann communicate and are attracted to each other, and they are thrown into the grass (p. 32) when Hartmann starts having negative thoughts about his wife and decides to leave the garden. Freud mentions flowers in various places[7] and points out "that sexual flower symbolism ... symbolizes the human organs of sex by blossoms.... It may perhaps be true in general that gifts of flowers between lovers have this unconscious meaning" (1953, 5, p. 376).

THE DREAM AND THE MOUND

After dinner in the garden of the inn, Hartmann tells Toni about his dream. Various objects play an interesting role in the dream: the apartment, the dance-like walk of the landlady, the oven, the bedrooms, the study, the birds, the windows, and the walls. Amir-Coffin (1982, pp. 187-198) took into account Freudian notions in her important analysis of the dream; she pointed out its erotic aspects, including objects which are associated with feminine sexual attributes and are identified as such by Freud. Band discussed this dream, as well as other aspects of the story (1968, pp. 251-260).

Freud refers to rooms, apartments, and houses in many places.[8] "Rooms in dreams are usually women" (1953, 5, p. 354); "the 'smooth' walls are men" (5, p. 355). It seems reasonable then to interpret the landlady in the dream as representative of Toni. In the bedroom, Hartmann had an oven; an oven represents the uterus (Freud, 1953, 5, pp. 354, 634). Only by completely sharing his life, including his work, with his wife could Hartmann feel the warmth of the "oven" (Toni) outside the bedroom. His ambivalent attitude toward Toni finds expression. Toni's defects may simply be in Hartmann's mind. In his dream, he understands that he has a nice apartment (wife, woman, Toni: "Ishto zo beto. Mah dira? Ish veishto"--"His wife is his home," and "What is home?" "It is a man and his wife") and he does not need to "change it for another" (p. 30), i.e., for divorce and another marriage.

Hartmann's desire to climb the mound may be interpreted by Freud (1953, 5, pp. 406-407, 410) as a sexual desire. Now Hartmann remembers an event from his childhood: he once climbed a mound, then slipped and rolled down to the bottom; "his limbs had felt relaxed" (p. 42). Kena'ani (1977, p. 499) claims that this depicts Hartmann's longing for death. It seems to me that Hartmann simply longed for the womb[9] (see Freud, 1953, 5, pp. 399-400). Now that he remembers his childhood, Hartmann is seized by a fear of falling. His panic is portrayed by content, by repetition of words, and by syntax which affects the fast rhythm (p. 40). But he quickly understands that the fear of falling has had a stronger impact on his life than the actual falling would have had, and he now sees dangers and risk in proportion; he does not have to live as egocentrically as before, and he will no longer be paralyzed by fear.

Freud (1953, 5, p. 56) discusses wooded hills and the symbolic landscape which includes a path into a thick wood leading up to a hill of grass and brashwood (5, p. 366). In discussing dreams of falling, Freud finds a connection to anxiety and to erotic desires (5, pp. 394-395).

Now that Hartmann can relate to his fears in a rational manner, there is a chance for him to communicate better; and, indeed, after understanding his dream of the mound, he starts seeing Toni in his imagination (pp. 42-44). The arm, the red face, the asters, the parasol, the fingers, and the cigarette smoke are all united in a romantic way. The story ends with good memories, compassion, and attraction between them, with the optimistic indication that Toni and Hartmann may again be husband and wife. Peri and Shternberg (1968, pp. 286-287) think that only someone who is "thirsty for sensation" can be interested in the question of what happened to this marriage. Many sensitive readers, however, concern themselves with this question. The ending is undoubtedly a renewal of the family. In Agnon's A Guest for the Night (1967, pp. 391-392; 1968, p. 418), the narrator says: "... one day [Hartmann] gave his wife a divorce, but as they left the rabbi's house he fell in love with her again and took her back." Fictional characters are talked about by the characters in other works of fiction as if they are part of reality, and the author presumes that he is addressing a reader who is intimately familiar with the author's entire work. Hartmann was not a Cohen. I am not in agreement with Leiter, who thinks that "Hartmann's dream of reconciliation is foredoomed" (1970, p. 61) and that "symbolic night" settles over the relations of Toni and Michael (pp. 61, 64). The crisis forced Hartmann to re-evaluate his relations. In the closing paragraph, Hartmann's face gets red as he merely thinks about his pretty wife. All her "shortcomings in no way detracted from her" (p. 42). Several actions and objects (asters, parasol, fingers, cigarette smoke) which we perceived as erotic are now combined in Hartmann's mind as sources for his attraction to and his compassion for Toni.

By paying attention to sexual symbols[10] in "Another Face," we gain a better capacity to enrich ourselves. We, of course, presume that the characters in the last version of the story are unconscious of the symbolism of their actions and their surroundings; however, their repressed wishes allow us a certain satisfaction through these symbolic patterns. Symbols help the reader to understand the characters' unconscious motivations, enrich the reader's aesthetic experience of the work, and fulfill the demands of the text. Some of Agnon's other works will similarly yield rich layers of meaning to the reader who considers their clear sexual symbolism. It is my contention that while Agnon's works are not rich in explicit sexual scenes, they are loaded with sexuality and sensuality which are alluded to in various powerful ways. Sexuality can be understood in Agnon's works only by looking closely at actions, motions, objects, and settings. If this symbolic interpretation is done, the reader will find Agnon a sensuous author, giving to human sexual urges an expression which requires the imagination and the understanding of the reader.

NOTES

1.   Various English translations of this story are available (see Bibliography).   The translation used in this article is from Spicehandler's collection (1967, pp. 2-45).
2.   Concerning various aspects of the symbol, see Cirlot (1962, pp. 11-54) and Preminger (1965, pp. 835-836).
3.   Compare the names *Tanzer* ("dancer") and *Svirsh* ("Cricket") to the name Michael Hartmann, a man of many virtues (an angel) who is a hard man on the outside.
4.   About some fine effects of this device see my article (1976, pp. 249-252). See also Golomb (1968, pp. 251, 262). There are various terms corresponding to the German term *Erlebte Rede* (the concomitant appearance of two voices in one text): "Free Indirect Speech," "Narrated Monologue," "Represented Speech," "Combined Speech." See Golomb (1968, p. 451).
5.   See Freud (1953, 5, pp. 86, 154, 185-186, 188, 216, 225; 1953, 4, pp. 354, 359, 407, 684).
6.   See Freud (1953, 4, pp. 238-240, 247, 355, 364-366, 369-372, 384, 684).
7.   1953, 4, pp. 169-176, 282-284, 319, 325; 5, pp. 347-348, 374-376.
8.   1953, 5, pp. 85, 214, 225-226, 346, 352, 354, 355, 364, 366, 397, 399, 454, 683.

9.   See also Freud on falling into a pit (1953, 5, pp. 399-400)
and existence in the womb.
10.   See also Hakak (1973), pp. 713-725.

BIBLIOGRAPHY

Aberbach, David. *At the Handles of the Lock.* Oxford, 1984.
Agnon, Shemuel Yosef. "Panim aherot." In *Davar*, December 12,
1932.
_____. "Metamorphosis." Translated by I. Schen. In Kahn, S.
J., ed., *A Whole Loaf.* New York, 1957, 139-169.
_____. "Metamorphosis." In *Orot: Journal of Hebrew
Literature*, no. 1, 1966, 11-41.
_____. "Another Face." In Spicehandler, Ezra, ed., *Modern
Hebrew Stories.* Bantam, 1967, pp. 2-45.
_____. *A Guest for the Night.* Schocken, New York, 1968.
_____. "Metamorphosis." In Glatzer, Nahum N., *Twenty One
Stories.* Schocken, New York-London, 1970, 111-134.
_____. "Panim aherot." *Kol Kitve Shemuel Yosef Agnon*, vol.
3. Schocken, Jerusalem and Tel-Aviv, 1976, 449-468.
_____. *Oreyah nata lalun Kol Kitve Shemuel Yosef Agnon*,
vol. 4. Schocken, Jerusalem and Tel-Aviv, 1976.
Amir-Coffin, Edna. "A Dream as a Literary Device in Agnon's
'Metamorphosis.'" *Hebrew Studies*, no. 23, 1982, 187-198.
Band, Arnold J. *Nostalgia and Nightmare: A Study in the Fiction of
S. Y. Agnon.* University of California, Berkeley and Los
Angeles, 1968.
Barzel, Hillel. *Sippure ahava shel S. Y. Agnon.* Bar-Ilan University,
Ramat-Gan, 1975.
_____, ed. *Shemuel Yosef Agnon: mivhar maamarim al
yetsirato.* Am 'Oved. Tel-Aviv, 1982.
Cirlot, J. E. *A Dictionary of Symbols.* Philosophical Library, New
York, 1962.
Eben-Zohar, Itamar. *Iyyunim besifrut.* Ministry of Education and
Culture, Jerusalem, 1966.
Even, Joseph. "Haddialog besippure S. Y. Agnon vedarkhe itssuvo."
Hassifrut, vol. 3, no. 2, 1971, 281-294.
Feldman, Yael S. "How Does a Convention Mean? A Semiotic
Reading of Agnon's Bilingual Key-Irony in 'A Guest for the
Night'." *Hebrew Union College Annual* no. 56, 1985, 251-269.
Freud, Sigmund. *The Standard Edition of the Complete Psychological
Works of Sigmund Freud*, vols. 4 and 5. London, 1953.

Goldberg, Leah.   "Panim   aherot leshay   Agnon."   In *Omanut hassippur*, Sifriyat Poa'alim, Tel-Aviv, 1963, 204-222.

Golomb, Harai.   "Haddibbur   hammehsullav--tekhnika   merkazit bapproza shel Agnon: lefi hassippur' panim aherot."   *Hassifrut*, vol. 1, no. 2, 1968, 251-262.

_____.   "Panim merubbot: al yahase haggomlin ben hassippur 'panim aherot' le-Agnon uven kotarto."   *Hassifrut*, vol. 1, no. 3-4, 1968-69, 717-718.

Hakak, Lev.   "Motiv   hattarnegol   besippur   pashut   le-   agnon." *Hassifrut*, vol. 4, no. 4, 1973, 713-725.

_____.   " Al haddibbur hassamuy be-'mikhael shelli' le'amos oz." *Bitsaron*, no. 324, 1976, 249-252, 263. Reprinted in: *Shedemot*, Winter 1977, 82-85.

Harael-Fish, A.   "Hammesapper keholem bekhitve   Agnon,   iyyun hashva ati."   *Bikkoret ufarshanut*, no. 4-5, 1971, 5-10.

Kena'ani, David.   "Hartmann o haharada."   In Mibbayit, Sifriyat Poa'alim. Tel Aviv, 1977, 69-95.   Reprinted in: Barzel, Hillel, ed., *Shemuel Yosef Agnon- mivhar ma'amarim al yetsirato*, Tel-Aviv, 1982, 481-500.

Leiter, Shemuel.   "The Face Within the Face - A Reading of S. Y. Agnon *Panim Aherot*."   In *Judaism*, no. 19, 1970, 59-65. Reprinted in: Leiter, Shemuel, ed., *Selected Stories of S. Y. Agnon*. Tarbut Foundation, New York, 1970, 162-183.

Peri, Menahem, and Shternberg, Meir.   "Hammelekh bemabbat ironi: al tahbulotav shel hammesapper besippur david uvat-sheva ushte haflagot latteaoria shel happroza."   *Hassifrut*, vol. 1, no. 2, 1968, 263-292.

Preminger, Alex, ed.   *Princeton Encyclopedia of Poetry and Poetics*. Princeton University Press, Princeton, 1965, 833-836.

Rivlin, A.   *Mafteyah didakti lehora'at hassippur hakkatsar*.   Tel-Aviv, 1969.

Shofman, Gershon.   "Freud ubelitristika."   In *Kol Kitve G. Shofman*, vol. 4. Tel Aviv, 1968, 46.

Shryboim, Devora.   *Halomot umabba'aim demuye halomot bayyetsirot hassifrutiyyot shel   Agnon*.   Dissertation, Tel-Aviv University, 1977.

Tokhner, Meshullam.   "Tsurot ve'emtsaim   aestetiyyim besippure Agnon."   *Mea'assef*, vol. 1, Jerusalem, 1965, 31-36.

_____.   *Pesher Agnon*.   Agudat hassofrim beyisrael, leyad Massada, Ramat-Gan, 1968.

Tsimerman, David.   Al shelosha missippure   Agnon.   *Iyyunim*, Jerusalem, 1962.

THE APOLOGETIC NARRATOR AND THE SOPHISTICATED AUTHOR IN "ANOTHER TALLIT" BY S. Y. AGNON

S. Y. Agnon's short story "Another Tallit"[1] is a story of meager plot and little incident. However, the psychological dynamics between the narrator and his grandfather are rich and provocative. The narrator begins his narration: "So now I merely add what happened on Yom Kippur with the tallit which I had left in the synagogue of my grandfather, may he rest in peace" (1960, p. 315). But more than simply telling us about the tallit, the narrator relates what happened to him on Yom Kippur. The story is about the narrator, who failed to observe Yom Kippur. The story has already been analyzed in detail by Abraham Holz (1972). My intent in this article is not to repeat Holz's skillful and illuminating work; I would rather like to point out what seems to me the major device used by the implied author in this story: the unreliable narrator. I find Holz's explication of the text and his seeing the story as an "open parable"[2] a meaningful contribution toward the understanding of the story. I also find his bibliography enlightening and I have drawn from it (Balakian, 1970; Eastman, 1960).

A responsible interpretation of this story must take into account the unreliable nature of the narrator. The implied author is careful to expose the narrator's attempts to gain the reader's sympathy and understanding. Only the naive reader can be misled by the narrator; the more attentive reader will be able to evaluate the narrator in the same way that the implied author does.

Booth differentiated between a reliable and an unreliable or fallible narrator (*Rhetoric*, pp. 158-159). His definitions of these narrators are as follows:

> I have called a narrator *reliable* when he speaks for or acts in accordance with the norms of the work (which is to say, the implied author's norms), *unreliable* when he does not.

Booth further elaborates and deliberates (ibid., p. 159) on what makes a narrator an unreliable one:

... difficult irony is not sufficient to make a narrator unreliable. Nor is unreliability ordinarily a matter of lying, although deliberately deceptive narrators have been a major resource of some modern novelists.... It is most often a matter of what James calls *inconscience*: the narrator is mistaken, or he believes himself to have qualities which the author denies him....

Unreliable narrators thus differ markedly depending on how far and in what direction they depart from their author's norms; the older term 'tone' ... covers many effects that we should distinguish.

Careful "explication"[3] of this non-realistic story reveals significant patterns and themes that have previously been ignored. "Explication" is used here as Beardsley (1958, p. 130) uses it:

... a critic is explicating when he talks about relatively localized parts ... the meaning of a metaphor, the connotations of a word, the implications of a fragment of ambiguous syntax....

"Another Tallit" is an esoteric story in which the implied author addresses the reader.   This author communicates to the reader through a code, whose message the reader can understand only by paying close attention to the author's attitude toward the narrator (Jakobson, 1960).

Band writes of Agnon's technique in "The Book of Deeds" (1968, pp. 187-188):

He developed a highly compressed and suggestive narrative technique ... which was obviously more suited to convey the doubt and confusion of the pious, traditional Jew who is also intellectually a citizen of western Europe with its broad humanistic tradition.... The action always takes place in the mind of a hyper-sensitive, often neurotic, narrator who tells his story in the first person, naturally mixing memory, dream, fantasy, and reality, as the human imagination often does, particularly under psychic stress.

Band's observation emphasizing "psychic stress" seems applicable to our story. In "Another Tallit" the narrator provides the reader with many accurate facts.   However, the narrator's presentation of the causes and connections and causations among the events, and his explanation of motivations, expose his real nature. The narrator of "Another Tallit" is at a carefully preserved distance from the implied author and does not represent that author's moral system or point of view. Through the words of the narrator himself, the author guides the reader toward the proper critical attitude on the narrator's deeds and misdeeds. It is an open question whether the narrator in this story is lying, or whether his perceptions are mistaken. It appears to me that the narrator is manipulative and is consciously attempting to convince the reader to adopt his point of view on himself and on the events he describes. The reader must infer the narrator's feelings and motivation: he feels guilty for breaking the laws of Yom Kippur. The narrator's attempt to convince the reader that he is pious and blameless for his own clear breach of custom and ritual, indicates his strong ties to Judaism and his restlessness when he disregards the laws of Yom Kippur.

The narrator in "Another Tallit" strives to gain the reader's sympathy, as I shall demonstrate later. But the implied author discloses the narrator's real motivations and real nature in spite of that character's attempts to mislead the reader. This interplay between implied author and narrator is central to the story, and analyzing this interplay can inform our comprehension of this story and its main message. The reader must play an active role in the story by identifying this dynamic relationship between implied author and narrator, and discovering its implications. Such an effort provides the key to the story. Without explicitly interfering in the plot, the author develops a subtle communication with the reader which exposes the narrator's real surroundings and intentions: the narrator conceals facts, misleads the reader, and tries to ingratiate himself with the reader, and the author leads the reader to understand the deception. Contrary to Holz who thinks that in "The Book of Deeds" the reader can know only what the writer reveals to him (1973, p. 303), the reader in our story comes to understand more than the narrator tells him. This interpretation will demonstrate how the relationship between author and narrator provides clues to the reader who must discover the story's message. The narrator is in conflict. He is aware of the appropriate observance of Yom Kippur; he chooses, though, to disregard the tradition. Torn by feelings of guilt, the narrator attempts to convince the reader that it is through no fault of his own that he has disobeyed the laws of Yom Kippur. The reader gradually discovers the narrator to be unreliable despite his stubborn attempt to convince the reader that he is a righteous Jew and that he has been prevented from observing Yom Kippur by purely practical impediments. His repeated attempts to present himself as a pious man convince the reader of the narrator's guilt feelings and of his refusal to face the consequences of his actions and his omissions.

THE NARRATOR REVEALS HIS UNRELIABLE CHARACTER

How does the reader conclude that this story's narrator is unreliable? The narrator declares his ability to say things which he does not mean. When he sees that his grandfather is troubled because the boy cannot find a place in the synagogue, he says to his grandfather: "I shall find a place for myself" (p. 315). However, the narrator informs the reader: "I was just talking" (ibid.). Furthermore:

> I deliberated: perhaps I should tell him that I prayed in the morning service at the synagogue in my neighborhood. But it is not nice for one to make his grandfather a cause for telling lies. (ibid.)

But he has already lied to his grandfather. The specific language used in this passage ("It is not nice for one to make his grandfather ...") is impersonal. It does not reflect his real feelings or moral reservations about lying on Yom Kippur. Thus we see that without the implied author's explicit statement, the narrator exposed himself as someone capable of lying. It is also doubtful that the narrator tells the truth about being drawn to Leibel when he says: "I didn't know why he asked me to go with him" (ibid.). The context (the narrator's not finding a seat in the synagogue; his arriving late and being thirsty) suggests the possibility that Leibel knew the narrator was a promising victim for Leibel's temptations.

The narrator also betrays himself as unreliable in the way he justifies his behavior. He was late to the synagogue the morning of Yom Kippur, he tells the reader: "Because I lived far from the synagogue and because I had stayed in bed too long, I arrived after the chanting of *Pesukei Dezimra*" (ibid.). This is only the fourth sentence in the story and it alerts the reader to look for signs of unreliability in the narrator. Had the narrator considered the distance from the synagogue he would have woken up early enough to arrive on time. However, he attempts to insert an "objective" cause, i.e., the distance, for his being late, instead of facing his own lack of religious commitment.

The narrator explains: "Because of the crowding and the heat and the candles and the great number of worshippers, the roof of my mouth was dry" (ibid.). Here are four "reasons" for his thirst that amount to one reason: the heat. By presenting four alleged reasons for his discomfort, the narrator attempts to overwhelm and to convince the reader.

The narrator notices that one of the old people near his grandfather has refused to assist the grandfather in making room for the narrator. The old man speaks in Aramaic to the grandfather; the narrator then paraphrases: "Today I am not obliged to be pushed around to furnish a seat for one who has none" (ibid.). This happened "when I entered the synagogue" (ibid.), which was crowded with worshippers. It is doubtful, therefore, that the narrator could possibly have heard the old man's words to his grandfather; it is even doubtful that this statement, which disregards the Jewish tradition of good deeds, was made. However, the narrator not only quotes the alleged statement of the old man, but he also interprets it for the reader in a way which indicates that the old man has sinned on Yom Kippur.

The narrator subsequently describes the pitcher that Leibel hands him; he describes the fruit juice as supernaturally active, while portraying himself as the passive victim: "Meanwhile, the juice in the pitcher actually began to float up toward my teeth ... it continued bubbling up ... frothing around my nose, gushing up to bring its taste to my mouth" (ibid.). This description is simply unbelievable, nor is it the only instance of improbable scenes described by the narrator.

He sees "a man ... wearing some kind of baker's hat, and chanting hymns which were not from the Yom Kippur service. A small boy--his son or grandson--stood at his side, accompanying the hymns with foolish gesticulations. Half of the congregation was smiling at them" (p. 316). One can hardly accept this description as taking place in a synagogue on Yom Kippur. Only a person who does not connect the gesticulations and their meanings could have such a perception.

Many statements in the story emphasize the skeptical nature of the narrator; it is his inherent character that explains his failure to observe the laws of Yom Kippur, not the fact that he is victimized by others. When the narrator describes his decision to go to his grandfather's synagogue, he states: "That Yom Kippur, I had the notion to pray with my grandfather" (p. 315). This indicates no serious effort to plan his activities on Yom Kippur. As to his being late and missing the chanting of *Pesukei Dezimra*, the narrator states, "This is truly regrettable" (ibid.). He does not, however, state that he truly regretted it.

The narrator also indicates questions about Judaism which have been in his heart since he was a child. Holz, in his perceptive and useful analysis of the story, correctly identifies (1972, pp. 520-521) the word *makom* not merely as a place, as it is translated in the translation we use here, but also as God. When this interpretation is taken into account, we see moments in the story which reveal the narrator's faltering belief in God. This is the case, for example, when the narrator says: "Because I lived far from the synagogue ..." (p. 315), etc. The Hebrew may be translated literally as "because of the distance from God," not only "from the synagogue." One can similarly interpret the following: "This was his synagogue and he could find no place for me. How could I find a seat by myself?" The words "place" and "seat" (in the original Hebrew, 1975, p. 203, both are *makom*) may be interchangeable with the word "God," and thus the sentence means that the narrator doubts if he can find the Lord in the synagogue.

Even if we believe his later excuse that he "often looked" (p. 316) for his tallit "without finding it" (ibid.), we still do not know why he did not replace it after he failed several times to find it. The second sentence of the story already begins the narrator's attempts to excuse himself: "So now I merely add what happened on Yom Kippur with the tallit which I had left in the synagogue of my grandfather, may he rest in peace." This is an attempt to shift the reader's focus from the narrator to the tallit so that the reader will anticipate the story of a tallit and overlook the sins of the narrator. This can be concluded only after the reader has grasped the unreliable nature of the narrator. After leaving the synagogue and coming back, the narrator sees that his grandfather gave him "a troubled glance," and wonders, "Could he have sensed what had happened?" (ibid.). That is, could the grandfather sense that the grandson had sinned by having juice at his mouth on Yom Kippur. The narrator decides to pretend that the issue does not exist at all, and he says: "I acted as if there were some other explanation" for his grandfather's look. He addresses his grandfather on another issue as if his sin did not exist at all. The narrator does not want to admit his lack of commitment to Judaism and Jewish worship. The narrator is not a naive narrator who does not understand his share in the sins which he committed on Yom Kippur. He is capable of lying even on Yom Kippur, and he is consciously attempting to mislead the reader so that, in the eyes of the reader, he will not bear the consequences of his acts.

The unreliable narrator loses the reader's trust by his own words, and in doing so he exposes characteristics which he would not otherwise admit: he is a Jew alienated from religion and capable of lying.

THE UNRELIABLE NARRATOR AS THE MAIN CHARACTER

The narrator is the main character of "Another Tallit." He tells us what happened, and he describes his reactions. The author uses the narrator's point of view to enrich the text by forcing the reader to detect the narrator's partial point of view. The reader has the task of differentiating between the narrator's interpretation and description of the events on one hand, and the objective situation on the other. Therefore, the reader ends up "correcting" the causes and meanings of the events, and the connections between them. The reader finally evaluates the narrator and the other characters in the story independently of the narrator's suggestions. The author bestows on the narrator the author's own sophisticated style in relating the plot; the implied author, however, utilizes the narrator's presentation to uncover the narrator's real world, one very different from that which the narrator attempts to portray for the reader.

It is noteworthy that the story's implied author indicates that, in spite of the time elapsed between the event described and the telling of the story, the narrator is still incapable of making an objective, truthful presentation. When the narrator tells us the story, his grandfather is already dead ("may he rest in peace"). The reader is initially inclined to give the narrator credit; the narrator has had many years to gain his objectivity, to see and present his own past lucidly. But the reader quickly withdraws his trust in the narrator when he reaches the second paragraph, in which the narrator alleges that there were two "reasons" for his being late to the synagogue.

HOW THE NARRATOR ATTEMPTS TO GAIN THE READER'S SYMPATHY

The narrator has several ways of ingratiating himself with the reader. He tells his story in the first person so that he can become close to the reader and invite the reader to identify himself with him; the narrator also addresses the reader directly to achieve intimacy with the reader; he presents various "reasons" for behavior, which portray him as a passive victim of circumstances and people; through ostensibly honest descriptions of his emotions, the narrator attempts to evoke the sympathy of the reader; he also confuses the reader by mixing the imaginary with the realistic and logical, so that the reader's judgment is initially disoriented and he is incapable of understanding the narrator's real role in the events; the narrator also belittles other characters in this attempt to look better than he is.

The first sentence of the story demonstrates the narrator's use of a first-person narration, as he strives for intimacy with the reader: "About my other prayer shawls I have already told" (p. 315). Here the narrator presumes that the reader already knows the narrator's previous stories and that he need only differentiate between this tallit and the other ones about which he has already told the reader. Now he "merely adds" what happened on a specific Yom Kippur. Throughout the entire story the narrator continues to use the first-person narration and give a detailed account of his spiritual and physical sufferings.

The narrator strives to become close to the reader by indicating that the reader is part of the narrator's considerations and thoughts. For example, when the narrator states that he came late to the synagogue, he says that "This is truly regrettable" (ibid.); and when he says "already in my childhood" (ibid.) he apparently shares intimate feelings and thoughts with the reader. Yet in another context he confesses, "I was just talking" (ibid.). Then he states that "It is not nice for one to make his grandfather a cause for telling lies" (ibid.). He talks about "A certain fellow whom we usually ignore though he never ignores us ..." (p. 316); the use of the first person plural hints at identification between the narrator and the reader. In another instance the narrator again uses "we" to link him to the reader: "to paraphrase his statement ... we might say ..." (p. 315). These quotations demonstrate the narrator's attempt to achieve intimacy with the reader not merely by utilizing first-person narration but also by sharing thoughts, childhood memories, and feelings. These remarks are made by a narrator who always has the reader in mind and who strives for intimate relations with that reader.

To justify his behavior, the narrator also attempts to overwhelm the reader by giving several reasons for one consequence. We have already seen the many "reasons" given for his being late, for his thirst, for his not finding a "place" in the synagogue, and for his having the juice in his mouth.... In all these instances the narrator tries to portray his passive role and the objective impossibility of his complying with Jewish ritual. Leibel, for example, "brought" him, "left" him and "offered" him the juice. It was everybody's fault but his. This story is part of "The Book of Deeds." The narrator is passive, though, and according to him other people are the causes, rather than his own deeds. One finds, as in many other stories of

"The Book of Deeds," sadness, thoughts, dreams and imagination, and dilemmas.

The narrator also expresses strong feelings. Thus we find, for example, "I was disturbed that my grandfather should be troubled on my account" (ibid); "I was filled with anger at Leibel" (ibid.); "depression overcame me ... because of this holiday of Yom Kippur which had passed by without a prayer, without anything" (p. 316). By depicting these strong feelings, the narrator attempts to gain the sympathy of the reader, who is likely to identify himself with a person who is full of sorrow, anger, and depression--and according to his presentation, all undeservedly.

Mixing the imaginary with the logical and realistic is another attempt to obliterate the truth and reality as a device to cloud the reader's eyes so that he will not judge the narrator's behavior as severely as it deserves. Such manipulative imagination is found in the description of the old people in the synagogue, who were "different ... from other men in general" (p. 315). In the same way he adds: "a man ... wearing some kind of baker's hat, and chanting hymns which were not from the Yom Kippur service. A small boy--his son or grandson--stood at his side, accompanying the hymns with foolish gesticulations. Half of the congregation was smiling at them" (p. 316). Benches near these two people seem "like the steps of a bath house" (ibid.). Such strange descriptions serve the narrator's effort to confuse the reader's judgment of him. The implied author's use of the non-realistic story corresponds to the narrator's use of such strange description. The term "open parable" suggested as applicable here by Holz (1972) describes some basic characteristics of "Another Tallit"; it is "open" because it does not have an unequivocal interpretation.[4]

Another obscuring device is the various questions which the implied author, the narrator (who is not a privileged narrator), and the reader have no answers to, such as "... how could that man [with the "baker's hat" - L.H.] leave in the middle of their services, and where did he go?" (ibid.). The imaginary and the realistic are mixed in the story: the imaginary is indicated by the many improbable causes, by fantastic shifts and changes, by the unbelievable and perhaps impossible situations. In this context it is interesting to mention Balakian's comments on surrealism (1970, pp. 13-14):

> The surrealists set out to revitalize matter, to re-situate the object in relation to themselves so that they would no longer be absorbed in their own subjectivity.... Seeing

was no longer considered a receiving process but an interchange between subject and object....

The narrator's surrealistic point of view is a device to expose his character, motivations, and dilemmas. The meaning and weight given to these statements should be preceded by our determination of whether the narrator is reliable or not. Holz's explication of the text as an "open parable" (following Eastman's [1960] article) depends on the issue of the unreliable narrator. According to Eastman (ibid., p. 18):

> Like a kind of literary Rorschach blot, the open parable apparently puts it up to the reader to perform the creative act, to take his own direction so that he may find, in the general richness of theme, an ethical pattern which speaks most directly to him....

Some of the narrator's statements have as their major function the task of portraying the narrator as an unreliable one. His peculiar point of view does not warrant the benefit of the reader's efforts to understand the sense behind them. A scene such as the one describing the man with the baker's hat, the small boy, and half of the congregation is simply a fantasy presented by the narrator to support his views.

Another method by which the narrator attempts to get approval from the reader is by accusing the people around him of responsibility for his problems. No generation is clean: Leibel, the grandson of the Tsaddik, is the faulty seducer; the "son or grandson" generation is represented by the small boy making foreign gesticulations and by the absence of the narrator's father; the grandparents are represented by the old people surrounding his grandfather ("... different from other men in general," p. 315). Half the congregation is guilty of simply being physically in the synagogue but not paying any attention to the meaning of the day and the worship, and finally ridiculing the entire worship ceremony and thus emptying it of meaning. Through such accusations, the narrator implies that he has more virtues than most of the people around him, who are guilty, and who are the causes of his troubles and of his failure to adhere to Jewish laws.

THE ROLE OF THE READER

Unfortunately for the narrator and fortunately for the reader, in spite of all the narrator's attempts the implied author is a sophisticated author. Without explicitly stating it, the implied author makes it clear to the reader that the narrator is unreliable.

Reading the story becomes intense and involving because the reader has to watch out for what to believe and what to disbelieve in the narrator's story. Thus the reader has an important role in this story. It seems that the author is striving to describe the modern Jew. The modern Jew has a "grandfather" who adheres to Jewish law. The absence of the father in the story is meaningful. While the generation of the grandfather has no conflicts and worships the Lord and obeys the Jewish law (despite the accusations of the narrator), the generation of the narrator and Leibel has no such easy religious life. Breaching Jewish law does not come easily to this generation; they feel guilt and consequently distort or suppress the truth. By tempting the narrator to join him, Leibel probably wants a companion in breaching the rules of Yom Kippur. The father is not struggling in the synagogue to make room for his son. Nor do we know anything about the father's effort to ascertain that his son is in the synagogue. The "son or grandson" (p. 316) is making "foolish gesticulations" (ibid.) on Yom Kippur in the synagogue. Both generations are remote from the true meaning of Jewish worship.

CLOSURE—THE PAIN OF THE MODERN JEW

By portraying this troubled narrator, Agnon presents the pain and suffering of the modern Jew, who has at the foundation of the family the image of the observing orthodox grandfather, whose "place" is in the synagogue. When a Jew detaches himself from the synagogue, he cannot do it without pain, suffering, and regret, and without the compulsion to make apologies and excuses. The Jew, even when he is secular, is born into a society in which religion has a strong impact and gives meaning to the life of much of the community. He often matures into a world in which faith has broken down, and he is torn between the faithless, disrupted world and the world in which faith provides answers to all questions and gives organization and order to all phenomena. On the one hand, the religious roots of the modern Jew are not strong enough to warrant the continuation of the "grandfather's" generation's way of life. On the other hand, the modern Jew is not indifferent to his roots, and therefore when he ignores the Jewish ceremonies it is accompanied by pain and depression. Indeed, the narrator is overcome by depression at the end of the story.

The generation of the "grandfathers" carries the tradition without questioning. The modern Jew does not carry on the Jewish tradition, and he suffers discomfort and guilt for not doing so. The motif of the "detached" in Hebrew literature is repeated here. The "detached" was a Jew who, on the one hand, had strong roots in Judaism and, on the other hand, could not find full contentment in Judaism. He was exposed to the outside world and could not find his contentment there either, and therefore he became "detached." This motif proves to be not only a nineteenth-century motif. "Another Tallit," which was published for the first time in 1955, presents this dilemma perpetuated in the life of the modern Jew. That the reader does not know when and where the story happened may indicate that the problems raised in the story are faced by Jews of modern times wherever they are. The modern Jew is neither a worshipper nor indifferent to Jewish worship. He simply suffers. Nothing can apply more pressure on him than the "grandfather," whose look is enough to say it all: "my grandfather brought his face out of his tallit ... my grandfather again gave me a troubled glance ... my grandfather looked at me" (pp. 315-316). That look was sufficient for the narrator to encounter his own neglect of Jewish tradition. The pain goes on.

NOTES

1.   The quotations are according to the translation of Jules Harlow in *Commentary*, 1960, vol. 30, pp. 315-316.
2.   Using Eastman's (1960) suggestions, in agreement with Holz (1972).
3.   See Beardsley, 1958, pp. 129-147.
4.   My colleague Herbert Davidson perceives the story as a dream of the narrator in which he visits the world of the dead ones. He supports his view by pointing out the look of the old people near the narrator's grandfather in the synagogue, by the tallit of three fringes, the reaching into a hole in the table and finding there a tallit with three fringes (only dead people wear it). The narrator cannot find a place and the old man did not make a place for him because he is alive and he is not a Tsaddik, a righteous man who deserves a seat near those who led a righteous way of life when they were alive. The father does not appear in the story because he is alive. The "man I do

not wish to mention," a certain fellow whom we usually ignore though
he never ignores us" is the angel of death.

BIBLIOGRAPHY

Aberbach, David. *At the Handles of the Lock.* Oxford University
Press, 1984.
Agnon, S. Y. "Talit Aheret." In *Kol Kitve Shemuel Yosef Agnon*, vol.
6, *Smokh venire.* Schocken, Jerusalem and Tel-Aviv, 1975.
_____. "Another Tallit." Translated by Jules Harlow.
Commentary, vol. 30, no. 4, 1960, 315-316.
Alter, Robert. "S. Y. Agnon: The Alphabet of Holiness." In *After
the Tradition.* Dutton, New York, 1969, 131-150.
Balakian, Anna. *Surrealism: The Road to the Absolute.* Dutton, New
York, 1970.
Band, Arnold J. *Nostalgia and Nightmare: A Study in the Fiction of
S. Y. Agnon.* University of California Press, Berkeley and Los
Angeles, 1968.
_____. "Hammesapper habbilty meheman be-'mikhael shelly'
uve-'bidmi yameha.'" *Hassifrut*, vol. 3, no. 1, 1971, 30-34.
Beardsley, Monroe C. *Aesthetics: Problems in the Philosophy of
Criticism.* Harcourt, Brace & World, Inc., New York, 1958.
Booth, Wayne C. "Distance and Point of View: an Essay in
Classification." *Essays in Criticism.* No. 1, January, 1961, 60-
79.
_____. *The Rhetoric of Fiction.* The University of Chicago
Press, 1961.
Eastman, Richard M. "The Open Parable: Demonstration and
Definition." *College English*, 22, no. 1, 1960, 15-18.
Even, Joseph. "Sofer, mesapper umehabber: nissayon lesinteza
mehkarit shel tehum merkazy bassipporet." *Hassifrut*, nos. 18-
19, 1974, 137-163.
Fish, Harold. "Hammesapper keholem bekhitve Agnon." In *Bikkoret
ufarshanut*, no. 4-5, 1974, 5-10.
Holz, Abraham. "Hahillul hammeshulash, iyunim be-'talit aheret'."
Hassifrut, vol. 3, no. 3-4, 1972, 518-532.
_____. "Hammashal happatuah kemafteyah le'Sefer
hama'asim leshay Agnon." *Hassifrut*, vol. 4, no. 2, 1973, 298-
333.
Jakobson, Roman. "Concluding Statement: Linguistics and Poetics."
In *Style in Language.* Sebeok, T. A., ed., Cambridge, Mass.,
1960, 350-377.

Tamar, David. "Levush vetoh bitsirato shel shay Agnon," in *Bikkoret umassa*. Reuven Mas, 1973, 82-91.

SOCIETY'S JUDGMENT AND GOD'S JUDGMENT

Agnon's "In the Forest and In the City" and Dickens' *Great Expectations*

"In the Forest and In the City"[1] tells of the narrator's childhood encounter in a forest with Franczisk, a murderer who had escaped to the forest from prison. It was near the city in which he lived that the narrator, who was a boy when this occurred, met Franczisk. The boy never told anyone about the encounter and when Franczisk is caught and taken to his death, his eyes express satisfaction upon seeing the boy who never joined those who desired Franczisk's death.

In the novel *Great Expectations* by Charles Dickens, the adult Pip relates his life story beginning with childhood. Pip progresses in the novel from self-deceit to self-fulfillment. At the age of seven, Pip, an orphan child, meets a convict named Magwitch. This meeting has fatal meaning to the lives of both the boy and the convict. Both Pip and Magwitch long for love and thus have great expectations: Pip longs for a parent and wishes to change his social class and become a gentleman. Magwitch longs for fatherhood and wishes to alter his social status by "making" Pip a gentleman. When Pip discovers the identity of his patron, he becomes full of detestation, but over the course of time he becomes less and less snobbish and in his heart he finds compassion and love for Magwitch.

Agnon's "In the Forest and In the City" was published in 1938; Dickens' Great Expectations was published for the first time in 1860-1861 and was well known by the time Agnon wrote his story. Various works of Dickens were known to the Hebrew reader. A Yiddish translation of *Great Expectations* appeared in Russia in 1939.[2] Hebrew translations of some of his other novels had appeared during the 1920s: *David Copperfield* in 1921 and later in 1928; *Oliver Twist* and *The Posthumous Papers of the Pickwick Club* in 1921-1922; *The Old Curiosity Shop* in 1924; and *A Tale of Two Cities*, in 1929.[3] During the years Agnon lived in Germany (between 1913 and 1924) he had close access to European literature. *Great Expectations* had been published in German in several different editions.[4] From this external evidence, it would not be too far-fetched therefore to assume that Agnon was familiar with Dickens' works in general, and--

we might suggest--with *Great Expectations* (in German translation) in particular.[5]

SOME ELEMENTS OF COMPARISON

There are significant similarities between "In the Forest and In the City" and *Great Expectations*, and a comparison of the works will present "In the Forest and In the City" in a new light. It remains the subjective decision of the reader whether Dickens influenced Agnon or whether the similarities between these works are coincidental, a matter of random affinity. If one concludes that Dickens did influence Agnon, comparing the two works may reveal what Agnon retained and what he rejected from *Great Expectations*; and then one arrives at such questions as why, how, and with what success he did that.[6] Parallels between the two works include not only characters, setting, episodes, and plot, but also complex non-conventional elements: emotional coloration, themes, and social ideology.

Focalization ("Point of View")

In both *Great Expectations* and "In the Forest and In the City," the narrative is related after the events occurred; a distance of time separates what happened and the act of telling. The narrators in both literary works are "above" and "superior" to the story in that as adult narrators each relates his story at a time when he knows everything about it. In this respect, both narrators, relating their stories in first-person retrospective narratives, are "extradiegistic" narrators. And in many parts of both works, the character-focalizer is a child. The focalization through children's eyes (those children now grown up) is internal to the stories; the locus of the internal focalization is within the events which take place in the respective stories. In many parts of each story the child is a dominant internal "colored" and "involved" focalizer, a limited observer with restricted knowledge who lacks a panoramic or simultaneous view of the represented world of which he is a part and of the events which take place in various locations and times. The narrator, at the time he tells the story, is situated at a point far "above" the story because he knows everything concerning that represented world. In each story, when the narrator begins the narration he already knows the end of the story. However, the choice of an internal focalizer (the child which he was) explains the narrator's withholding of information in the story.[7]

In each story, in most of the statements which the adult narrator makes about himself as a child, the language is "colored" by the perceptions of his younger self (who is an internal focalizer). In some cases, however, the language is colored by his perceptions at the time of the narration and hence he is an external focalizer. Sometimes ambiguous language creates a situation in which the reader is uncertain as to the nature of the statement in this respect.

The Central Focus of the Stories

The relations between Pip and Magwitch are the center of *Great Expectations*. The encounter between the narrator and Franczisk and what follows between them is the center of "In the Forest and In the City."

The Encounter with the Villains

In both works a child encounters a villain; both the circumstances of the encounters and the villains' characters bear a certain similarity.

Place

Both children meet villains away from the town. In Dickens' story, Pip meets Magwitch in the marshes near a river (1965, p. 39). In Agnon's story the boy meets Franczisk in the forest near a river (p. 95).

Age

In both cases the meeting is between an innocent boy and an adult villain.

Meaningful Meeting

In both works the meeting turns out to be meaningful both to the child and to the villain.

Meeting after Escape from Prison

Pip meets Magwitch after the latter escaped from prison (1965, p. 46); the boy in Agnon's story meets Franczisk after Franczisk (according to hearsay) had escaped from prison (p. 97).

Worried Family

The boy's going to the forest, in Agnon's story, worries his parents (p. 97); Pip's sister, who raised Pip, is also worried when he does not return home on time (1965, pp. 40-41).

Voice

During his first encounter with Pip, Magwitch's voice is described as a "terrible voice" (1965, p. 36); Franczisk shouts when speaking with the boy (pp. 104-105).

Appearance

In both encounters the disheveled appearance of the villain catches the eye of the child who sees him (Dickens, 1965, p. 36; Agnon, p. 104).

Rational Fear

While both villains appear to frighten everyone else, they themselves are fearful (Dickens, 1965, p. 36; Agnon, pp. 104-106)--and with good reason, because the authorities and the society are indeed after them.

Irrational Fear

In both works, mechanical devices fail to put an end to fear. Magwitch warns Pip: "A boy may lock his door, may be warm in bed, may tuck himself up, may draw the clothes over his head, may think himself comfortable and safe" (1965, p. 38) while, supposedly, he is not. In Agnon's story the people of the city are sufficiently frightened by what they have heard about Franczisk: "At about darkness the shutters were closed and the doors locked; and locks were added to locks, and people went to bed in fear" (p. 98). In both cases that kind of fear of the villain lacks a rational foundation: the villains themselves are, in fact, frightened and appear to be good-hearted in their ways.

When fear is irrational, no mechanical device can abate it. But when one is strong, such mechanical devices are not necessary. The conduct of Mr. Jaggers in *Great Expectations* exemplifies this statement: "He never lets a door or window be fastened at night" (1965, p. 228). Time and again Jaggers attempts to tempt a cracksman to rob him, but "not a man of them, sir, would be bold enough to try it on, for love or for money" (ibid).

In Agnon's story, the townspeople believe that Franczisk, following his escape from prison, went first to the judge's home through the chimney. The strength of the villains is assumed by the fear of the people who tell and believe such stories. The townspeople might be projecting their unsocial urges onto the criminals who are actually, in a sense, the victims of society. This projection then culminates in some form of self-imprisonment which is rationalized by an irrational horror.

Superstitions. Bible

Both villains are superstitious. When Magwitch asked Pip where the child's mother was, Pip pointed to the tombstone upon which he was sitting, and Magwitch "stared, made a short run" (1965, p. 37). Franczisk was frightened by the book which the boy held and he continued to be frightened upon learning that the boy was holding the Holy Scriptures (1974, p. 105). While in the forest the boy carried a Bible with him (p. 105), something which made a great impression upon Franczisk; Magwitch apparently carried in his pocket a little black Testament solely to use in cases of emergency when he required someone to take an oath (1965, p. 349). Both Franczisk and Magwitch (1965, pp. 349, 354, 360, 364) apparently believed in the power of the book.

Knowledge that the Villains Were Encountered

One question concerning "In the Forest and In the City" might be crucial to the understanding of the boy's character, to the story's message, and to everything that happens in it following the encounter: when he encountered Franczisk in the forest did the boy know that it was Franczisk whom he met?

It is inconceivable that the child did not recognize that he encountered Franczisk because the child-focalizer lacks the necessary naivete and unawareness.

Critics, however, have assumed that the boy did not then know that it was indeed Franczisk whom he met. According to Dov Sadan[8]

the boy "does not know that he is Franczisk" (1970, p. 98). According
to Sadan (p. 99):

> After the meeting we read that the newspapers deal with
> Franczisk, and the boy who still does not imagine that he
> already met Franczisk reads them, until the day came
> that going to the forest he saw legions of policemen and
> heard that they captured Franczisk and he pushed to see
> him and he looked at him and recognized that he was the
> one who drank with him from Franczisk's canteen, and the
> robber too recognized the boy, and the end of the story is
> the hanging of the robber.

According to Aryeh L. Strauss (1965, p. 151):

> The boy is accustomed to the dark sight of nature, and
> therefore he does not perceive any strange aspect in
> Franczisk, nor does he identify him as the famous
> murderer. This issue, that unlike any reader, the boy does
> not identify Franczisk, is astonishing and is unclear from
> a psychological point of view. But it is correct from the
> structural aspect.   In the eyes of the poet realistic
> psychology is not important here.

Similarly, Arnold J. Band (1968, p. 236) contends that after the boy
met Franczisk in the forest, "several days later, the boy reads many
newspaper accounts of Franczisk's past exploits, but never connects
them with the stranger he met in the forest." Leiter (1970, p. 49)
sees this story as "another story of initiation in which a child grows
from innocence to knowledge."

Contrary to the opinion that the boy did not identify Franczisk
when he met him, we might argue for the view that the boy even then
knew whom he met. This contention, furthermore, might be the key
both to the understanding of the story and to the character of the
boy.

To begin with, the boy was strongly aware of the possibility
that Franczisk might be hiding in the forest. In fact, he had prepared
himself for an encounter with him. The child's parents explicitly
warned their son of the danger of meeting Franczisk in the forest:
both became "alarmed that the murderer might be living there, and
they asked me not to wander about in the forest. It was not good to
meet a bandit in the forest because he made a joke of murder;
especially since his friend had been killed and he had sworn
vengeance" (p. 97). While the words "they asked me not to wander

about in the forest" exemplify indirect speech, the rest of the quotation reflects a combined speech, the concomitant appearance of two voices, that of the parents in the city and also of the child-focalizer. This form of speech vividly reflects and demonstrates the parents' response of horror to Franczisk (pp. 97-98).

Because of his parents' warning, the precautions of the city-dwellers, and also his own apprehension, the boy is alert to the possibility that he might meet Franczisk in the forest and he goes so far as to prepare himself for such an encounter. Seeing footprints in the forest, he concludes that they are Franczisk's, and he ponders what he should say to Franczisk should he meet him (p. 99). Then, upon meeting an old man in the forest, he wonders if that old man has no fear of people, "thieves and robbers, and Franczisk and his companions" (p. 100). The boy understands that, like the old man, he too is unequipped for self-defense against a murderer.

The encounter between the boy and Franczisk is preceded in the story by a description of worms that had run away and hid themselves in the earth, but the boy did not intend to hurt them:

> ... worms spread on the face of the earth, wriggled and fled--wriggled and hid themselves in the ground. The Lord knows I never thought to do them harm!

> While I was walking about, a small man, strong, with long hair, jumped out in front of me and shouted, "What are you doing here?" (p. 104)

Mention of the unfounded fear of worms appears in the particular context of the encounter with the murderer. Franczisk's fearful manner, his jumping, his shouting, his aggressive question, his appearance--these do not escape the boy's eyes, knowing that he might encounter Franczisk. Indeed, the boy suspects that he has met the murderer, and in the course of their encounter he becomes certain of it. The boy's suspicion explains why he follows so closely Franczisk's tone and gestures which are described in detail: Franczisk "jumped and shouted"; "he looked at me in anger"; "He bent his head on his shoulders, glanced and looked"; "He stretched out his hand towards my book and shouted"; "He raised his voice and shouted"; "He gazed at me"; "He stamped and shouted" (pp. 104-105).

Thus, contrary to other scholars' opinions, there is reason to read the dialogue between the boy and Franczisk in the light of the boy's awareness that he is, in fact, encountering the murderer. Such a reading suggests that the boy is alert and sophisticated, that he has a sense of a philosophy of life, and that based on his philosophy and faith he proceeds to enter into a covenant with Franczisk. The boy agrees to be silent and to refrain from telling anyone that he had met Franczisk on the basis of his belief that everything happens according to God's will. And so the boy, who is not enamored with the people of the city, does not inform anyone of his meeting with Franczisk.

In the dialogue that takes place during their encounter, the verbs describing the verbal acts are "said" for the boy and "shouted" for Franczisk. Whenever the boy succeeds in calming Franczisk down and diffusing his fears, however, instead of the verb "shouted" relating to Franczisk's manner of speech, we note that he "said" or "asked." Franczisk shouts when asking the boy what he is doing in the forest, and the boy responds that he is wandering in the forest; in Hebrew, "mehalekh any baya'ar": the use of *mehalekh* ("stroll") and not *holekh* ("walk") serves the boy's need to appear innocent, aimless, harmless. The simplicity of the boy's answer embarrassed and confused Franczisk, who repeats the answer. "Walking in the forest? Indeed, indeed, walking in the forest!" (p. 104).

The sensitive boy senses Franczisk's confusion, suspicion, and compassion and even though no question was posed, he nods his head to reconfirm and stresses the innocent circumstances, saying: "I am just taking a walk here" (ibid). Instead of "mehalekh ani" ("I am walking") he now says: "metayel ani li kan"--he is hiking here for his pleasure. This answer defuses Franczisk's fear of danger, and the nodding of the head and the use of the singular ("I") reassure Franczisk that he is not in danger. Indeed, the boy achieved his goal; Franczisk calmed down, he bent his head towards his shoulder, glanced and asked: "Are you not afraid?"

This time Franczisk did not shout; he is suspicious, anxious, and interested in the conversation. The question: "Are you not afraid?" is the very same question that the boy had asked the old man whom he met previously in the forest, and the boy now responds to it with the same answer given by the old man: "Whom have I to fear? There are no lions and leopards here: there are no bears or other wild beasts here, so why should we be afraid?" (p. 104). The boy suspected that there might be a connection between the old man and Franczisk, especially in light of a hot dish which the old man had carried in the forest (possibly for Franczisk). The boy is using the same words which the old man had used. These might possibly be the words that the old man agreed with Franczisk to use in the event that someone would ask the old man if he were not afraid.

Possibly the old man had an agreement with Franczisk. The boy feels that he is offering the safest possible answer to the question. If Franczisk and the old man agreed that it is the most natural and acceptable answer, then repeating it should satisfy Franczisk. Furthermore, the answer differentiates between Franczisk and beasts. Both the boy and Franczisk belong to the human category and it is only beasts that they both need fear. In this way, Franczisk becomes part of human society, sharing a fear of the same natural elements, and he is neither excluded from nor confronted by human society: "There are no lions and leopards here ... so why should we be afraid?"

In his meeting with the old man, the boy goes on to ask him if he is not afraid of "thieves and robbers, and Franczisk and his companions" (p. 100)--so aware is the boy of the possibility of an encounter with Franczisk. Now, the encounter is a fact.

In response to a question, the boy mentions to Franczisk that he had met an old man in the forest. The boy is possibly aware that because he is using the same exact words and answers of the old man, Franczisk may have concluded from the boy's answers that the boy met the old man. The boy, therefore, goes on to tell Franczisk about his meeting the old man. The fact that the boy's meeting with the old man did not result in any danger to Franczisk indicates that the boy is not damaging to Franczisk. The boy wants to join in the secret of Franczisk and the old man.

Once Franczisk loses his fear of the boy, his interest turns to something which poses no immediate danger: the book which the boy is holding in his hands. But when he learns that it is the Holy Scriptures, he becomes fearful. Franczisk is a simple man, afraid of the Bible, and it is conceivable that he is jealous of the boy who is capable of understanding the Bible while he himself is unable to do so.

The boy acquires Franczisk's trust and perhaps the latter acquires a liking and yearning for human society. And so as the boy leaves, Franczisk calls him back to ask whether he might want a drop of brandy. The boy, relating tactically to the question, responds in gratitude and pretends to be accustomed to such drinking: "I think that a drop of spirits on a day like this is nice for the throat" (p. 105). Their drinking together represents the making of a covenant between the boy and Franczisk.

The boy then recites the Hebrew blessing, "Blessed are Thou, O Lord our God, King of the Universe, by whose word all things exist"--

the words suggesting, in the story, that everything happens according to the will of God. When the boy explains the blessing to Franczisk, the latter remarks: "Perhaps, perhaps it is so; it is so perhaps" (ibid). In the light of the words of this blessing, God will decide the destiny of Franczisk and the boy will not interfere with that destiny. After all, it is the boy's philosophy not to interfere in the affairs of others:

> "I am a modest man, and I do not push myself into the affairs of others, especially the affairs of the universe, because one can't interfere with the business of the universe, or disturb its work, and tell it to do what it does so well itself and does it much better than either you or I could do it." (pp. 95-96)

All these considerations unite to suggest that the boy in "In the Forest and In the City" identified Franczisk when he met him in the forest. Similarly, a short time after meeting Magwitch, Pip understood that he had met a prisoner who escaped from jail.

Trust. Oaths

In both plots the villains trust the boys not to tell anyone about their encounters with the villains ("Well, I believe you," in Dickens' story, 1965, p. 50; Agnon, p. 106). Indeed they are trusting the children with their very lives.

And in both works, the villain is concerned with the possibility that the child will disclose the fact that he saw him. Magwitch warns Pip: "You do it and you never dare to say a word or dare to make a sign concerning your having seen such a person as me, or any person sumever ..." (1965, p. 38; see also p. 50). Franczisk is also disturbed by the fear that the boy might inform someone that he saw him: "He said to me, 'Don't tell anyone that you met me.' I said to him, 'I shall not tell'" (p. 106). Magwitch made Pip swear fidelity in the churchyard (1965, p. 271); Franczisk also wanted the boy to swear that he would not tell anyone that he met him (p. 106).

"'Did you not say that there is no-one here?' and I said, 'No-one is here,'" (p. 106). The boy has understood Franczisk's fear. There is a contradiction between the boy's talking to Franczisk and his telling him that "there is nobody here," the boy's words implying that from that moment on he will maintain that all he "knows" is that there is no one in the forest. Franczisk requests assurance and, confirming the understanding between the two, he asks the boy to swear that he will not tell anyone that he has met him. This request can leave no doubt in the boy's mind that he is indeed speaking with Franczisk. The boy, however, rejects Franczisk's request to take an oath: "He said to me, 'Swear,' and I said to him, 'Why should I swear? I don't know who you are'" (ibid.). The boy is not objecting to Franczisk's request; he implies, rather, that he already erased the encounter from his consciousness and so there is no need to swear not to relate what he does not know.

Franczisk fully grasps that the boy knows with whom he is speaking, but he knows also that the two have now made a covenant of silence. Franczisk examines the boy's face to determine whether or not the boy is trustworthy: "He looked straight at me" (ibid). When he leaves Franczisk, the boy begins walking and reading so that Franczisk will not think that the boy has ambushed him. Both the boy's manner of speech and the content of his statements, together with his anticipations of Franczisk's responses and feelings, all reveal that he is quite aware that he has met up with Franczisk. Due to his covenant, the narrator "does not tell" the reader that he knew when he met Franczisk, that it was indeed Franczisk that he met--a device which makes the story especially intriguing.

Following that encounter, the boy leaves everything in God's hands; as he compares the various statements in the newspapers concerning Franczisk, the comparison occupies his thoughts more than does Franczisk himself.

Food

In both works the escaping villain requires someone to bring him food from outside--Pip in *Great Expectations* brought food to Magwitch, and apparently the old man in Agnon's story brought food to Franczisk.

Brandy

In *Great Expectations* Pip goes so far as to bring brandy to Magwitch, giving him more than Magwitch expected. In Agnon's story the boy and Franczisk drink brandy together. Both Pip's bringing brandy and the drinking of brandy by the boy and Franczisk signify compassion and covenant.

Blessing and Compassion

In Agnon's story, the boy wanted to bless Franczisk *lehayyim*, "to life" (p. 105), but he did not know how to express that in Franczisk's language and so he said instead, "to health." Both blessings--to life or health--signify that the boy was not influenced by the townspeople who wished Franczisk neither life nor health, as according to their unfounded anticipation either would place them in danger. Franczisk noted the boy's lips moving. "He asked me, 'What did you whisper?'" (p. 105)--and the boy proceeded to teach him the blessing which ultimately changed Franczisk's life.

Pip observed how Magwitch ate the pie which Pip had brought him, and said: "I am glad you enjoy it." Magwitch asked: "Did you speak?" When Pip repeated his words, Magwitch expressed gratitude: "Thankee, my boy. I do" (1965, p. 50). This is a critical moment in the relationship between the two. The lonely and ostracized Magwitch, in quest of love, is touched by the boy's compassion and care. It could be that human compassion surprised him so much that he was skeptical and so wished to make certain of the boy's words and to hear once more the boy's expression of compassion, sympathy, and care.

In both works, then, a portion of the conversation requires repetition which turns out to be critical.

Gratitude

The ending of "In the Forest and In the City" can be understood only on the basis of the above interpretation of the encounter between Franczisk and the boy. Franczisk was apprehended; on his way to be executed, surrounded by policemen, he noticed and recognized the boy. Franczisk was not angry at him; on the contrary, "He looked at me and recognized me, and it was apparent that he had nothing against me; although I had not sworn to him he did not suspect me of revealing his hiding place to others" (p. 108). The boy understands Franczisk's look as conveying: "Although I leave the world and all the world means nothing to me, I am grateful to you that you did not join those who sought my life" (ibid.).

Only if we believe that the boy knows that he encountered Franczisk and kept it a secret can we understand why Franczisk is satisfied. He is content because the boy did not betray him but treated him as an equal fellow human being; the boy acted upon Franczisk's own belief that everything happens according to God's will, and the boy's word proved trustworthy even without an oath. In all respects the boy conducted himself according to their covenant. A moment before he was hanged, Franczisk uttered the word "tcsakel"—meaning *shehakkol*—alluding to the blessing that he had learned from the boy ("everything exists by His Word"), and so Franczisk died content, with trust in at least one member of society, namely, the boy. He also expressed in *tcsakel* his faith that the world is conducted according to God's will and so he justified the judgment against him. The story reminds us that a frog may surpass King David in singing and praising God; similarly, Franczisk in his *tcsakel* might be praising God even more than others are able. In Leiter's words (1970, p. 52): "God wants man's deepest feeling, not the prescribed formulae of tradition." The grace of Franczisk, the victim-villain, expresses his deepest feeling.

Our reading of the story provides a different meaning to the encounter between the boy and the criminal and to their dialogue and relationship. It also portrays the boy himself in a different light and clarifies his pronounced impact upon the criminal. Faithful to his belief that everything occurs according to divine will, the boy refrains from telling anyone about his encounter with the criminal. The boy's conduct pleases Franczisk, and the very fact that the boy accepts him as his fellow human being redeems Franczisk from being a total outcast from human society.

While looking for the convict, Pip was concerned: "I considered ... with great dread, if we should come upon them, would my particular convict suppose that it was I who had brought the soldiers there?" (1965, p. 65). The looks exchanged between Pip and the convict are critical:

> I looked at him eagerly when he looked at me, and slightly moved my hands and shook my head. I had been waiting for him to see me, that I might try to assure him of my innocence. It was not at all expressed to me that he even comprehended my intention for he gave me a look that I did not understand, and it all passed in a moment. But if he had looked at me for an hour or a day, I could not have remembered his face even afterwards, as having been more attentive. (p. 69)

Magwitch recognized Pip, was attentive to him and agreed that Pip did not cause him to be recaptured; Magwitch furthermore recognized that Pip cared enough for him to want him to know that he, Pip, did not cause Magwitch to be recaptured. This, to

Magwitch's eyes, was a mark of compassion, friendship, and respect for Magwitch as a human being.

And this gesture redeems Magwitch from his lonely and isolated existence as an outlaw. From that point on Magwitch makes the effort to protect Pip and for the rest of his life he is indebted to Pip's human gesture of compassion and giving. The convict becomes a good-hearted victim of society who acquires respectful concepts of human give-and-take. Similarly, in Agnon's story, the trust which the convict displays in the boy justifies itself in that the boy accepts Franczisk as a human being made in the image of God, and this for Franczisk is a source of satisfaction, faith, and reconciliation with God and with God's world. The ostracized and persecuted Franczisk and Magwitch need love and warmth. They recognize the gestures of the narrator-boys and are affected by them. In both stories the innocent children are the ones who bring the convicts back to society. The adults are too prejudiced, indifferent, preoccupied, and frightened to do such acts.

Concealing the Encounter

Pip continues to conceal his encounter with Magwitch after he well understands that the latter is a fleeing prisoner. In Agnon's story, too, the boy conceals the fact of encounter.

Thinking about the Encounter

In both cases the boy, after his encounter with the villain, reflects upon that encounter (Dickens, 1965, p. 53; Agnon, p. 106).

The Capture

And in both stories the villain is captured while the number of officers involved in apprehending him is excessive to a ridiculous degree (Agnon, p. 107; Dickens, 1965, pp. 61-71).

Cain and Abel

Magwitch's given name was Abel (1965, p. 345). Abel, in Genesis, was killed by Cain, and while Abel in *Great Expectations* is partially a victim, he is treated like Cain (1965, p. 360). In Agnon's story, the old man indeed tells the boy that Abel killed Cain. This reversal of roles causes us to ponder whether society is a victim of villains or whether convicts are victims of society. In this context, Magwitch's reflections at the time of the trial are meaningful: "I sometimes derived an impression ... that he pondered over the question whether he might have been a better man under better circumstances" (1965, p. 465). The answer is obvious.

The old man whom the boy meets in the forest tells the boy how Abel killed Cain. This is, of course, a distorted version of the story from Genesis. The fact of the distortion, however, does not alter the validity of the old man's perception that human history is a history of wars. The old man is aware that "he who is destined to die dies, and he who does not have to die lives" (p. 101). Therefore, the mere error regarding Abel and Cain does not alter the facts, because again, everything happens according to the divine will. Even a sword placed on his neck will not kill the person who is destined to live (ibid.); Franczisk, however, was destined to die, and so a rope around his neck sufficed to hang him.

Furthermore, the murderer is himself a victim of social injustice to the same degree that those he allegedly hurts are his victims. The hangman placed the rope around Franczisk's neck and pulled the rope until "Franczisk's soul took flight from his body" (1974, p. 278). This passage reminds us of the description of the death of Abel as found in the midrashic sources: Cain did not know from what part of the body the soul departs. So he took a stone and he injured Abel in various parts of his body until he reached Abel's neck; only then did Abel die. In the light of this association, the death of Franczisk reminds us of the death not of Cain but of Abel. This same association may also recall Cain's argument to God: Cain agreed that he was jealous and wroth because God had shown respect only for Abel and his offering and not for Cain and his offering (Genesis 4:4-5). God is the keeper of all human beings and yet He allowed Cain to kill Abel--therefore Cain, according to his own argument, is not guilty.[9] Furthermore, we read an interesting interpretation of "instead of Abel; for Cain slew him" (Genesis 4:25). We are told that Cain died as a result of Abel's sin, because what occurred between the two is analogous to two trees which were close to each other: when the wind broke one of them, it fell and broke the other tree.[10]

When Franczisk whispered "tcsakel" just before he died, the boy was the only one who understood what he was saying. Franczisk rejected the conventional prayer pronounced at such an occasion and in his last moments he invoked his faith in the divine will. The boy's wisdom, sophistication, and faith played a critical role in bringing

Franczisk to his faith in God and to his acceptance of his death sentence.

The Convict's Good Character

Franczisk and Magwitch were caught and destined to be hanged. Just prior to Magwitch's death, Pip states: "I only saw in him a better man than I had been to Joe" (1965, p. 457). Both convicts appear to have good sides to them that society as a whole failed to see. Both convicts are human and have need for love and acceptance. Each died grateful to the one person who did accept him.

Society's Judgment

The boy in "In the Forest and In the City" identifies with the forest, not with the city. In the forest he is free of society, parents, work, formal studies and synagogue ritual. Both the old man, an emancipated serf who serves others even after he has been legally freed, and Franczisk, who violated the law, are found in the forest. We also find there the boy who dislikes the city for its faults: hypocrisy, cowardice, insensitivity, cruelty, injustice. Horror alone unites the city's population, a horror which fuses truth and fantasy: exaggeration is common in the city where the attitude to a villain is sometimes mitigated as long as he is successful. The city people are merciful toward someone who is dangerous, while they can be creatively cruel after the danger has passed; they are biased and utilitarian. The city's being what it is drives the boy away to the forest. The only other city inhabitants who visit the forest are wood-cutters and lumber merchants. Mazor stated (1987, p. 95) that "the sober, balanced standards of the city are boldly confronted in this story with the forest's uncurbed impulses and murderous features." But in light of this story, the standards of the city are not "sober, balanced" and the "impulses" of the forest are not "uncurbed."

The narrator, at the time he relates the story, understands that sometimes "the heart acquires a grudge against the universe in which there are so many evil things; and a man takes the law upon himself to be judge and find some excuse" (p. 98). The boy's sympathies are with the people he finds in the forest; he does not believe in human justice and discretion. Only in the forest, where nature takes its course, can he find refuge from a society which applies laws but is not concerned with justice.

Also in *Great Expectations* the reader is not meant to be pleased with the ethics of the city. Shrewdness, financial ability to retain legal criminal defense, and apparent strength determine much of one's destiny in the city. Emotions are often abused. The apparent social order does not necessarily imply the existence of happiness or justice in the city. In both works society's judgment appears to be dry and mechanical. The court of law is not the court of justice. The social structure is sometimes insensitive enough to put Cain's sign on people of fine characteristics.

The Acceptance of the Sentence

Magwitch accepted his end. "I'm quite ready to take my chance," he remarked to Pip (1965, p. 457), and showed submission and resignation (1965, p. 465). We are reminded in *Great Expectations* about the judge and the people who were given into his hands for questioning, "how both were passing on, with absolute equality, to the greater judgment that knoweth all things and cannot err" (1965, p. 467). Agnon's story concludes with Franczisk's expressing faith and hence accepting his death.

We do not know the nature of that "greater judgment." But like Franczisk in Agnon's story, Magwitch too accepts the judgment: "My Lord, I have received my sentence of death from the Almighty, but I bow to yours" (ibid.). Both Magwitch and Franczisk die with that submission or resignation which is the consequence both of love of a human being and of a philosophical acceptance of the divine decree. The last sound which the hangman heard from Franczisk was "tcsakel." The narrator well understood it:

> The murderer justified his own sentence, for all exists by the Word of the Holy One, blessed be He! When he heard these words first he doubted and said, "It may be, it may be"; and at the hour of death he found in them complete agreement. (p. 109)

CONCLUDING REMARKS

It is not enough to observe the similarities between the two texts. One has also to observe and evaluate the differences between them and to ask why they exist.

In both stories we find the following four elements: narrator, convict, society, God. Agnon had the Jewish reader in mind when he wrote his story. The story is structured to remind us that "everything exists by His Word." This prominent belief appears in the critical stages of the story--i.e. at the time of the encounter with the convict and at the closure of the story, which is its climax and catharsis. The application of the Jewish prayer ("everything exists by His Word") to the non-Jewish convict strengthens the universality of the idea of the prayer. The faith that "everything exists by His Word" may explain one of the differences between Pip and the boy in Agnon's story. Pip strives to be a gentleman in order to change his course of life; the boy in Agnon's story is easygoing, free of any yoke: "I had thrown off the yoke of Torah and had not bent my shoulders to the yoke of earning a living, and all 'my burden' fell on my father" (see Psalms 55:23: "Cast thy burden upon the Lord"). The world according to the narrator in Agnon's story is explained by the will of God. The narrator tries to understand it by reading the Bible and understanding nature. The boy's character is different from the character of Pip as depicted by Moynahan (1960). Moynahan points to the "great expectations fantasy, that dream of huge and easy success which has always haunted the imagination of children and also haunted the imaginations of adults in the increasingly commercial and industrial society of nineteenth-century England." According to Moynahan, "In *Great Expectations* ... the theme of ambition is treated under the two aspects of desire and will, the search for a superbalance of love and the drive for power" (ibid., p. 158). The boy in Agnon's story is not searching for power but for God's love. On the other hand, "Pip's ambition is definable under the aspect of aggression as well as in terms of the regressive desire for passive enjoyment of life's bounty" (ibid., p. 160). Faith plays a much larger role in Agnon's story than in Dickens'. According to Moynahan, "Pip cannot redeem his world ... he can only lead himself into a sort of exile from his society's power centres. Living abroad as the partner of a small, unambitious firm, he is to devote his remaining life to doing the least possible harm to the smallest number of people, so earning a visitor's privileges in the lost paradise where Biddy and Joe, the genuine innocents of the world, flourish in thoughtless content" (ibid., p. 168). Agnon's hero did not harm people and did not lose his paradise. He is motivated by faith and not by earthly ambitions.

Miss Havisham and Estella are too remote for Agnon's reader, i.e. Havisham's wealth, isolation, fatal love, detachment from the community, may be remote for the reader of Agnon. If Miss Havisham and Estella believed that "everything exists by His Word" they would not be what they were.

Jewish elements are present throughout Agnon's story. Among them we note the Torah, the Zion Club, the Holy Scriptures, Psalms, King David, the synagogue, the blessing, and the story of Cain and Abel—even though Franczisk himself is not Jewish. This structure serves to present Agnon's thoughts and gestures concerning social injustice, the lack of clarity concerning who really is victim and who is villain, the dichotomy of city and forest, human compassion, and the basic faith in the One "by whose word all things exist" as points that go beyond religion, time, and place. In this way the Judaization of the story goes hand-in-hand with the universality of the message and the issues. Agnon could eliminate various characters which are structurally essential to Dickens' *Great Expectations.* Agnon's plot and characters are tied to his message. Usually, Agnon emphasizes the Jewish world in his literary work, and the narrators in his works are involved witnesses in the given place and time of the plot. In "In the Forest and In the City," Agnon avoids providing a specific time and place so as to emphasize the universal aspects of the plot. The tensions between society and the individual, society's judgment and God's judgment, the apparent and the real, cast doubts on the social structure of any society, Jewish or non-Jewish. Justice and injustice are not absolute concepts. Even Jewish tradition, to which Agnon alludes in his story, struggles with them. The court of law is not always the court of justice. Reading "In the Forest and In the City" in light of its universal implications, it now becomes obvious that in the opening of the story when the narrator says "and all my trust was directed toward my father" (1974, p. 267)--father, *abba* in Hebrew, is not only the narrator's father but also God. The boy has no doubt: "The Lord is good," he repeats again and again (p. 269), feeling what he had learnt from the Bible: "The Lord is good to all; and His tender mercies are over His Works" (Psalm 145:9). The Lord created everything according to His will and by His word "all things exist"-- all times, places, and creatures. Again we note that the narrator's approach to crime and punishment in Agnon's story is founded on Jewish tradition at the same time that it has universal implications.

Both Pip and the boy in Agnon's story experience social aloneness and solitariness. Dickens' novel opens with Pip's conscious experience of his aloneness (1965, p. 36) when Magwitch comes from behind a gravestone and suspends him upside down (see Van Ghent, 1960, p. 59). The boy in Agnon's story wonders about being alone in the forest; he speaks to himself and to ants; he stays alone at home and he reads books, and in the Society of Zion Club he does not socialize but reads newspapers. Aloneness and solitariness in both cases support human sensitivity and perception. The boy's feeling of separateness in Agnon's story is strong in the city, but it does not exist in the forest, where there are no other people but him, because he feels at one with God's nature. Again, the strong role of faith in the day-by-day life of Agnon's character differentiates Agnon's character from Pip. The social aloneness and solitariness of the boy in Agnon's story is outweighed by his constant thinking about God and the understanding that "everything exists by His Word."

Dickens emphasized the demolition of traditional values, the dehumanization of man by industrialization, imperialism, and exploitation of the human being for profit (Van Ghent, 1960, pp. 128-132). In Agnon's story the people of the city "did not know that there was a world outside of markets and shops" (p. 99). The city itself "was built to enslave the body and afflict the heart" (ibid.). This explains why the boy never found anyone in the forest "except the foresters who cut down trees and come there on business" (ibid.). Nature is used by them for profit only. However, it seems to me that Agnon emphasizes the human nature in general, and his message is not bound by certain social-political factors.

The sheer number of similar components suggests that the similarities are not a matter of random affinity. The number of parallels, and the accumulation of structural similarities, are striking. In determining whether we have a case of influence or of random affinity, we must take into account the uniqueness of these elements and the fact that they are not conventional either in theme or form. For example, in both stories we find meaningful encounters in the childhood of the narrators with adult fearful and superstitious villains after the villains had escaped beyond town, while the families of the children are worried about them. The similarities are in plot, characters, and ideology.

Using the indicator of integrity in order to ask whether we have here a case of coincidental resemblance or influence, we should note that the parallel materials are complex and that there are sufficient patterns common to both texts to assume not only random affinity but also literary influence.

Using the indicator of coherence, we again find sufficient parallel components and patterns in these works to consider literary influence. These components are in atmosphere, ideology, themes, and emotional aura.

Thus in my opinion the quantitative indicator, and the indicators of uniqueness, integrity, and coherence, make it likely that Agnon's story was influenced by Dickens'.[11]

Many critics of modern Hebrew literature have dealt with the influence upon modern Hebrew literature of European culture in general and its literature in particular. Mark (1980) referred to various critics who have discussed the influence of European literature on Agnon; Barzel (1972) published a comparative study of Agnon and Kafka, while Mazor (1987) focused on Agnon, Hamsun, and Strindberg. Agnon himself spoke of reading Homer, Cervantes, Tolstoi, Gogol, Hamsun, Balzac, and Flaubert (Yardeni, 1961). Agnon was influenced not only by Jewish sources--such as the Bible, Mishna (collection of oral laws which forms the basis of the Talmud), Talmud (the commentaries on the Mishna), Midrash (homiletic interpretation of the Scriptures), Aggada (non-legal passages in rabbinic literature), and rabbinical *responsa*, but also by world literature as well. The reader may conclude that the resemblance between the two literary works discussed here is a matter of coincidence. Or, he may conclude that it is a concomitant influence. If so, the fact that *Great Expectations* influenced Agnon's "In the Forest and In the City" in no way detracts from the literary achievement of Agnon's story, for the literary world of "In the Forest and In the City" is Agnon's own artistic complex.

Considerations of this nature point to a new direction in the study of Agnon.

NOTES

1.   Hebrew: "Baya'ar uva'ir," *Ha'arets*, April 15, 1938. Reprinted in *Kol Kitve Shemuel Yosef Agnon*, vol. 2, *Elu ve'elu*, 1974, pp. 267-278. Quotations and references are from the translation of Weinberg and Russell, 1983. (In the translation, the name of the villain was transcribed as "Francisco").
2.   See Bibliography, under Dickens, Charles. The work was translated into Yiddish by B. Marshak.
3.   See Bibliography, under Dickens, Charles. The Hebrew translations by M. Ben. Eliazer, A. Ovasi, Hillel Bali, J. H. Taio, and B. Krupnik appeared in Tel-Aviv, Jerusalem and Warszawa. I thank Professor William Cutter, Hebrew Union College, for providing me with this information.
4.   See under Dickens, Charles, the various German editions.

5.   Various   Hebrew   translations   of   *Great   Expectations*
appeared after the publication of "In the Forest and In the City"
(1950, 1955, 1956, 1983).   See the various Hebrew editions under
Dickens, Charles.
    6.   Regarding the meaning of literary influence see Mazor,
1987, pp. 33-57.   Mazor's book focuses on "Where Hebrew and
Scandinavian Literature Meet"--particularly: Agnon, Hamsun, and
Strindberg.   I have employed here the four indicators of literary
influence suggested in Mazor's work, pp. 48-49.
    7.   See   Shlomith   Rimmon-Kenan,   *Narrative   Fiction.*
Methuen, London and New York, 1983, pp. 71-85.
    8.   The quotations from Sadan and Strauss were translated by
L. H.
    9.   *Tanhuma Bereshit; Bereshit Rabba,* 22; *Shemot Rabba,* 31.
    10.   *Bereshit Rabba,* 83.
    11.   I have employed here the four indicators of literary
influence suggested in Mazor's work (1987, pp. 48-49).

BIBLIOGRAPHY

Agnon, Shemuel Yosef. "Baya'ar uva'ir." In *Kol Kitve Shemuel Yosef
    Agnon,* vol.   2, *Elu ve'elu,* Schocken, Jerusalem and Tel-Aviv,
    1974, 267-278.
_____. "In the Forest and in the City." *In A Dwelling Place of
    My People.*   Translated by Weinberg, J., and Russell, H.
    Scottish Academic Press, 1983, 94-109.
Band, Arnold J. *Nostalgia and Nightmare: A Study in the Fiction of
    S. Y. Agnon.* University of California Press, Berkeley and Los
    Angeles, 1968.
Barzel, Hillel. *Ben Agnon Lekafka.* Bar Uryan, Bar Ilan University,
    Ramat-Gan, 1972.
Dickens, Charles. *Great Expectations.* The Penguin English Library,
    New York, 1965.
_____. *(Great Expectations). Groyse 'oysezikten.* Translated by
    B.   Marshak.   Melukhe farlag far de-nazyonale minderlayten,
    Kiev, 1939.
_____. *(A Tale of Two Cities). Shete 'arim.* Translated by M.
    Ben -Eliezer. Tel-Aviv, 1929.
_____. *David Copperfield.*   Translated by M. Ben-Eliezer.
    Jerusalem, 1921; Tel-Aviv, 1928.

_____. *(The Old Curiosity Shop)*. *Bet mimkar 'atikot*. Translated by A. 'Ovasi. Warszawa, 1924.

_____. *Oliver Twist*. Translated by Hillel Bavli. Warszawa, 1924.

_____. *(The Pickwick Papers)*. *Ketavim meizvon bet hava'ad hapikwiki*. Vol. 1, translated by I. H. Taviov; Vol. 2 by B. Krupnik. Warszawa, 1921-1922.

_____. *(Great Expectations)*. *Grosse Erwartungen*, roman. Ubersetzt von Paul Heichen.

_____. *(Great Expectations)*. *Grosze Erwartungen*. Ubersetzt von Dubois, L. aus d. Engl. Stuttgart, Hoffman, 1964.

_____. *(Great Expectations)*. *Grosse Erwartungen*. Ubersetzt und hrsg. von Richard Zoozman. Leipzig, M. Hesse, 189[?].

_____. *(Great Expectations)*. *Grosse Erwartungen*, roman: Aus dem Englischen übersetzt von Siegfried Long. Zurich, Manesse-Verlag, 1947.

_____. *(Great Expectations)*. *Pip pa'ut*. Adapted by Z. Son, 1950.

_____. *(Great Expectations)*. *Tikvot gedolot*. Translated by K. Katsenelson, 1955.

_____. *(Great Expectations)*. *Tohelet gedola*. Translated by Y. Levanon, 1956.

_____. *(Great Expectations)*. *Tikvot gedolot*. Translated by Ester Caspi. Sifriyat Poa'alim, Tel-Aviv, 1983.

Leiter, Samuel. Introduction to "In the Forest and in the City." In *Selected Stories of S. Y. Agnon*, Tarbuth Foundation, Inc., New York, 1970, 49-55.

Mark, Y. "Ben Agnon le-Hamsun." In *Bikkoret ufarshanut*, vol. 15, 1980, 153-182.

Mazor, Yair. *The Triple Cord: Agnon, Hamsun, Strindberg*. Papyrus, Tel-Aviv, 1987.

Moynahan, Julian. "The Hero's Guilt: The Case of *Great Expectations*." In *Assessing "Great Expectations"*, Lettis, Richard, and Morris, E. William, eds. Chandler Publishing Company, San Francisco, 1960, 149-169.

Rimmon-Kenan, Shlomith. *Narrative Fiction*. Methuen, London and New York, 1983.

Sadan, Dov. *'Avne bedek*. Hakkibbuts hammeuhad, Tel-Aviv, 1970, 97-100.

Strauss, Aryeh L. *Bedarkhe hassifrut*. Mosad Bialik, 1965, 148-153.

Van Ghent, Dorothy. "On *Great Expectations*." In *Assessing "Great Expectations"*, Lettis, Richard, and Morris, E. William, eds. Chandler Publishing Company, San Francisco, 1960, 57-73.

Yardeni, Galya. *16 sihot 'im sofrim*. Hakkibbuts hammeuhad, 1961, p. 162.

ISRAELI SOCIETY AS DEPICTED IN THE
NOVELS OF A. B. YEHOSHUA

> "If you believed half you heard, the
> whole country had been falling
> apart for years, and yet everything
> was still there. In fact, wherever
> you went there was a tractor
> clearing new ground."
> (A. B. Yehoshua, *Five Seasons*,
> 1989, p. 170)

THE AUTHOR, THE STORIES, AND THEIR IMPLICATIONS

A. B. Yehoshua, born in Jerusalem in 1936, is one of the most
important Israeli authors of the generation that began writing after
the State of Israel came into being. The characters in the fiction of
that generation of writers relate in an individualistic and ambivalent
way to the constantly changing reality described in their works. In
the prose of that generation the boundary between the fantastic and
realistic is sometimes unclear; their works differ from the realistic-
naturalistic prose of the preceding generation whose writing centered
around the Israeli War of Independence. The prose written in the
years of the struggle for the establishment of the State of Israel and
during the early years of the State (Shaked, 1971, pp. 11-70; Gerts,
1983; Sadan-Lovenshtein, 1981, pp. 9-12) focused on the collective
problems and experience of that tempestuous generation, on problems
of the "here" and "now," and presented characters with a clearly
defined system of values, characters who identified with the basic
values of the State of Israel and of Israeli society. The shift from
this stage of Israeli literature to the later stage which concentrated
on the individual conveyed a sense of rupture concerning the
individual's identification with his society; the writers depicted the
individual as lacking values and faith and portrayed his life as restless
and undermined. The individual was described as wandering
aimlessly, as lonely and desperate, and also as rebelling futilely
against his feeling of estrangement and detachment. The firm
ideological orientation which was common to the characters and
authors of the period of the War of Independence and the years

immediately following does not exist for writers like A. B. Yehoshua or Amos Oz.

The work of A. B. Yehoshua broke with the themes of the earlier literary generation whose writing was naturalistic and realistic in nature.   In the writings of that earlier generation, characters were judged by their social conduct and by their attitude toward Zionism, toward pioneering and humanism, socialism, the land, struggle, and the building of the land. Literature had a definite social role for that literary generation as it strove to promote Zionism, pioneering, and socialism.   It sought to express and emphasize an optimistic attitude (Gerts, 1983, pp. 16-17), to portray a typical and positive character who proudly represented the Jewish nation; it created a thrilling, realistic plot in which struggle leads to a positive outcome. The style was rich and drew upon various layers of the Hebrew heritage. "We" was stressed more than "I," and the characters were described in terms of the pattern and framework of their society.   Smilanski, Bartov, Meged, Shamir, and Shaham all presented such issues as the acceptance of social rule, the preservation of friendship, the readiness to obey the commands of the State and to struggle against the enemy, the significance of the group and the justification for toeing the social line; they presented the values of pioneering, of the building of the State, the war, and identification with the active life of the Jewish community in Israel before and after the War of Independence. The characters in their works were stereotypical--they were born in Israel, went through the youth movements and then to the wars and were concerned with the problems of their time, their place and their generation (Shaked, 1971, pp. 11-70).

Following the establishment of the State, the writers who comprised the literary generation of the War of Independence yearned for the pre-State days in which the values of the labor movement prevailed. The contrast between past and present, the disappointment with what followed the breakdown of their social dreams, produced a satiric-ironic attitude toward Israeli reality. These writers focused instead on the individual and on his desire for independence; they portrayed new character-types and distanced themselves from what they perceived as naive beliefs and values and no longer portrayed monotonous situations and characters. Yehoshua himself was not influenced by this literature (ibid.); his early works, writings of a symbolic-allegorical nature, were influenced by the non-realistic writing of Agnon ("The Book of Deeds"), which ignored and negated the limits of time and place to allow for the creation of meaningful metaphorical situations.   The works of Yehoshua discussed in this study, however, display a stronger contact with specific reality.

Yehoshua is an author who is rooted in Israeli reality, to which he responds both through his political activity and through his literary work. His understanding of the virtues of Brenner (1881-1921) might contribute a great deal to explain his novels: according to Yehoshua (1971), Brenner is a relevant author who wrote about his surroundings and thus abandoned perspective and who judged the reality around him according to his personal, reliable approach. Yehoshua's statement that people and their freedom are more important to him than literature (Yehoshua, 1977) may explain the focus on ideological issues in his novels.

The literary works discussed here do not deal with the Israeli reality alone. In addition to issues typical of Israeli existence--such as the relations between secular and religious Jews or between Sephardic and Ashkenazic Jews--the reader also encounters issues which relate to Jewish existence in a larger sense, such as the relationship between Israel and the Diaspora. Yehoshua, in addition, confronts in these novels such universal conditions and problems as the loneliness and alienation in modern life. Our focus, however, will be on those issues which specifically relate to the Israeli situation.

In 1975 Yehoshua discussed some of the newer issues which he was dealing with in his writing at that time (Peri-Kalderon, 1976). He realized that he expanded the contact of his stories with specific details of reality (also Sadan-Lovenshtein, 1977); he expanded his gallery of literary characters. He consciously contrasted the literary work of his generation, the "State of Israel generation," with that of the Palmach or the "War of Independence generation." The latter focused upon the individual in his relationships within a small society; the values of the characters of that earlier generation remained limited. Yehoshua's literary generation, in contrast, reacted against the suffocation it found in the social context of the works of the "War of Independence generation" and did not have a great deal of interest in the values central to that former literary generation. These differences resulted in what Yehoshua describes as a style which is infinitely more intellectual and abstract. The former generation, attached to and submissive to reality, did not have the ability of abstraction. As for the present, Yehoshua maintained that authors should take more initiative in various areas--sociological, economic, historical, and ideological. The feeling that life has become complicated and that everything requires an expert should not discourage authors from expressing their opinions, especially since the experts have not proven themselves as experts and since things are actually less complicated than they appear. Yehoshua's attraction to Brenner (ibid., p. 287 and Yehoshua, 1971) is due to the latter's ability to find the point at which the psychological and the actual come together. The wars of 1967, 1973, and 1984 and the political situation in Israel caused various Israeli authors to become involved through their literary work with the Israeli reality and its ideological crisis.

Yehoshua's tendency in his novels both to relate to reality and to search for the general, the symbolic, and the intellectual is hence a result of well-formulated concepts. Searching for the components that shape Israeli society in his novels, one has to remember that the implied author neither detests nor judges his characters but simply attempts to understand them.

We will examine some major aspects of Israeli life as described in Yehoshua's novella, *Early in the Summer of 1970* (1972), and in his novels, *The Lover* (1977), *A Late Divorce* (1982), and *Five Seasons* (1987). *Early in the Summer of 1970* is a novella and not a novel; however, its time of publication and its themes allows its inclusion in our study of his novels. These works, like Yehoshua's earlier works, his short stories and plays, contain harsh messages directed to Israeli society, with little consolation. The author portrays the social, political, and economic reality of Israel through astonishing situations which express disastrous and destructive elements in the souls of his characters. The reader witnesses the disintegration of stable middle-class families. Many of the characters appear as frustrated and deprived people, distressed, restless, lonely, and yearning for love. In a condition of perpetual conflict both with themselves and with their environment, they are neurotic people attracted to sickness and living a disturbed way of life in the shadow of wars, an absurd existence marked by death, fatigue, and aimlessness. Yehoshua's characters in these novels compose a problematic and complicated nation rather than a "chosen people" with an exemplary, model society, a light to the world.

The pre-existing perversions of these characters are exposed through the distressful and complicated events described in the novels. The characters formulate their various opinions concerning the distressful events, opinions which in themselves are neither right nor wrong. An ambivalent attitude toward their reality lacks any unequivocal criteria to judge reality.

In his earlier works, Yehoshua had to struggle with a norm, common to some Israeli authors and critics, according to which the writer avoids social and political materials in his work. Consequently

Yehoshua utilized symbols in order to comment on Israeli social-political reality. The works discussed here display a more realistic trend in his writing. The shift from his earlier symbolic-allegorical writing to writing realistically about specific and well-defined reality was a difficult one. Meron (1979, p. 96) sees *Early in the Summer of 1970* (and "Missile Base 612") as the beginning of the shift; these two stories, however, according to Meron, remained "cardboard" in nature. The time and place of Yehoshua's novels are familiar to us. The characters are occupied not only with general intellectual issues but also with daily problems such as food, sex, medicine, etc. The style is accordingly suited to the individual character.

Yehoshua's pessimistic view of the Zionist dream is not new in Hebrew literature. However, while in the 1960s this view was voiced more through symbols, in the 1970s the author expressed this view much more directly. Perhaps both readers and critics were better prepared for direct social and political criticism, especially after the 1973 war.

Yitshak Barzilai (1984), describing the bitter social criticism in the books of some major contemporary Israeli authors, concludes (p. 537),

> ... the fact that prophets of wrath ... appeared, among us, is not all negative. On the contrary, it is in the spirit of our old prophetic tradition ... it is good, hence, and encouraging that now, too, we have among us people who are zealots for the truth, and even if the truth is bitter and depressing, it may be assumed that the bearers of this truth will not allow us to rest while they see us failing and falling, but that they will elicit in us positive and creative powers.

In both *The Lover* and *A Late Divorce*, Yehoshua was influenced by the technique associated with Faulkner: the author allowed the characters to speak in monologues without interference from the narrator or other characters. Yehoshua explained his choosing this technique (Carmel-Flumin, 1986):

> ... when I started writing *The Lover* I felt that the center [of Israeli society - L.H.] is disintegrating, that there is a definite gap between people, and were I to write a novel in third person or in first person as an authoritative narrator, I would then be judging that reality and speaking in its name, speaking in the name of a non-existent center.... The feeling of the disintegration of the center

showed that the most correct way to write is to allow
every character to talk with the total point-of-view
accumulating from all the points-of-view together. This
was both an aesthetic consideration and my own outlook
as to the correct way to respond to the Israeli situation.

In the frame of this presentation, our focus will be on certain facets
of Israeli life as they are described in the works of A. B. Yehoshua:
family life, and conflicts between Arabs and Jews, between Sephardic
and Ashkenazic Jews, between secular and religious Jews, and
between Israel and the Diaspora.

Early in the Summer of 1970 is a story about a father who was
suddenly notified that his only son, thirty-two years old, a lecturer at
the Hebrew University, was killed while serving in the Israeli Defense
Army Reserve. The father, a secondary-school Bible teacher, later
discovered that there had been a mistake in identification and that
his son was alive. The story is written as a retrospective monologue
of the father, who reconstructs the events of his crisis in order to
understand them and also to understand himself. The use of nature in
the story, along with the plot, objects, and minor characters, are all
directed toward the real focus of the story which is the father.
Through the father, the reader is introduced to problems of Israeli
society. The father interprets events according to his own fancies;
yet the fantastic elements in the story are limited, unlike in
Yehoshua's early stories; and landscape, place, and plot are all
realistic.

The story does not provide us with the names of the father and
his son, and the very lack of proper names might imply their being
representative of their respective generations. This novella deals
with the period following the Six-Day War and the War of Attrition
which followed in Israel.

The Lover focuses on the period of a few months before and
after the Yom Kippur War of October, 1973. It is the story of an
"average" Israeli family, a couple who knew one another from before
the War of Independence. Adam, who in 1973 turned forty-six years
old, and his wife Asya attended the same schools, the same youth-
movements and youth-camps during the period before the War of
Independence. When married, they met at first with economic
difficulties but later attained substantial economic success. Their
family and social life, however, met with failure. Through the events
in the life of this one family, the reader views the story of Zionism
and of the population in the land of Israel over the period beginning in
1881 (when the first Bilu settlers arrived in the land of Israel). The

six characters in the story are developed simultaneously both as individuals and as representatives of social groups. They are both speakers themselves and objects in the reflections of other characters and witnesses in the novel.

Each of the interrelated characters, three men and three women, views the identical events in monologues representative of that character's one way and style, so that the reader comes to know each character both as it perceives itself and as it is perceived by the others. The best parts of each character are disclosed when that character reveals its own wounds. Adam, his daughter Dafna (or Dafi), his employee Na'im, and his wife's lover, Gabriel Arditi, discuss their experiences; Asya, Adam's wife, reports her dreams when they occur; a stream of consciousness marks the monologues of Veducha when she loses consciousness. In this novel, Yehoshua, who was influenced by the symbolic surrealistic fiction of Agnon, also distanced his approach from that of Agnon in various ways including his use of spoken Israeli Hebrew.

The novel *A Late Divorce* is set during the period of Kissinger's trips to the Middle East, the end of the Labor government, and the rise of the Likhud. *A Late Divorce* tells about Yehuda Kaminka and his family, an educated middle-class Israeli family going through the crisis of divorce. Yehuda and his wife, Naomi, were married more than thirty years, a marriage full of quarrels, hostility, and frustration. Three years before the divorce, Naomi attempted to murder her husband and was consequently committed to a mental institution. Yehuda left for the United States and, at the time of the story, has returned to Israel for a week's visit in order to divorce his wife before returning to America to marry Connie, an American Jewish woman about twenty years younger than Yehuda, who has become pregnant through him. The crisis of divorce generates the reactions of Naomi and Yehuda's two sons, Zvi and Asa, and of their daughter, Ya'el, who reside respectively in Israel's three largest cities: Jerusalem, Tel-Aviv, and Haifa. The divorce crisis generates reactions also among those people who are connected in various ways with Yehuda and Naomi's children. Following the divorce and prior to his return to the United States, Yehuda goes to his wife's mental hospital in order to steal the divorce agreement in which he had agreed to release to his wife his share in the community-property apartment. Acting insanely, he is murdered by one of the inmates of the hospital.

There are nine chapters in the novel: eight chapters consist together of eight monologues of the Kaminka family and of those connected with them, and the last is a dialogue between Zvi and his psychologist. Each character presents its own perspective of the events, and the narrator strives to adopt for that character a typical style, vocabulary, syntax, and rhythm which represent its psychological, educational, and sociological setting, e.g., childish (Gadi), literary (Dina), intellectual (Asa), neurotic-dramatic and somewhat clumsy (Kedmi). After these variations the author turns to technical devices; there is a shift to dialogue in the case of Zvi and his psychologist; and the reader does not directly hear the other characters' speaking to Calderon who also has an emotional and clever style.

In 1987, Yehoshua published his novel *Five Seasons*, which describes one year in the life of its leading character (the Hebrew title of the novel is *Molkho*). The novel begins with the death of Molkho's wife when her husband is fifty-one years old. Her death followed seven years during which she fought cancer. The number seven reflects a prolonged period of commitment on her husband's part. The death has a practical and emotional impact on Molkho and on his two sons, the one a secondary-school pupil and the second a technical student, and on their daughter, a soldier, as well as on Molkho's mother, his mother-in-law, and his friends. During the lonely year (fall, winter, spring, summer, and again fall) following the death of his wife, Molkho travels from his city, Haifa, to Jerusalem, to the Galilee, to Paris and Berlin. He meets various women who trigger his memories of his late wife, but he concludes that he is still attached to her after a marriage of thirty years and that it is meaningless to enter into any new relationship without falling in love. The novel deals with the death of Molkho's wife in the first chapter and with the death of his mother-in-law in the last chapter; both deaths occur in the autumn, a year apart.

The story is placed in the early 1980s. The exit of Israeli forces from Lebanon is mentioned (pp. 158, 189), but the war is not central to the story. Some critics, though, have read the novel as a work which relates to the Israeli reality in a general way. Bartana (1987) comments, for example, that the description of the middle-aged Israeli in the novel is destructive: Molkho, who is passive, lacking sexual urges and the ability to love, represents an entire generation of middle-aged Sephardic Jews as impotents, people who have reached a dead-end, bankrupt spiritually and wretched. Paz (1987) suggests that if this novel depicts the national situation of Israel, then the illustration is saddening because Molkho is physically and mentally poor, weak, gloomy, helpless; he is hesitant, greedy, and also petty. This opinion, however, overlooks the cautious, wise, and sensitive sides of Molkho, who in many ways represents the Israeli middle class.

The principal events of the novel connect with the seasons of the year. The novel is divided into five chapters, each relating to another season and another time, a structure which conveys a sense of the flow of time. In the fall Molkho's wife dies. In the winter Molkho is sad: he travels to Berlin in search of a woman, the legal counsel of his office, who resembles his wife in some aspects; their cold relationship is mirrored in the Berlin snow. In the spring Molkho makes a trip to the Galilee where new flowers sprout and where he is attracted to a little girl, eleven years old, who awakens him sexually. In the summer he meets Ya'ara, whom he had loved in his youth. And in the fall he travels to Europe with Nina Zand, whom he helps in her desire to return to Russia; and also his mother-in-law dies in the fall.

The Lover and *A Late Divorce* present events from the points-of-view of various characters, while in *Five Seasons* there is but one main character and his point-of-view dominates.

STORIES OF INDIVIDUALS OR STORIES OF ISRAELI SOCIETY?

Do these stories portray Israeli society or are they simply stories of the individual characters? It would seem that the author's ambition went beyond describing the lives of various individual members of Israeli society and that he strove in these works to depict Israeli society as such.

Feldman, discussing the new literary trends in Israel, concludes that "Zionism--once the 'cure for Jewish Diaspora neurosis'--is now perceived as a pathology in its own rights, a new Israeli neurosis." She contends that "the madness he [Yehoshua - L.H.] pictures is made tangible by his characterization, but its meaning grows out of the interpersonal relationships among them.... Yehoshua is immersed, then, in the collective Israeli neurosis. This may explain why *A Late Divorce*, although presented almost as a collection of family case history, is liable to be read as a political allegory" (1987, pp. 34, 91).

Early in the Summer of 1970 compels the reader to reflect upon issues that relate to the Israeli reality, issues such as the gap between generations, the rights of the individual versus his obligations to the State, the attitude toward war, old versus new, words contrasted with action. National events play a central role in the story and find expression in the lives of the individuals portrayed.

Yehoshua has himself related to the question whether he intended to portray a whole society or just individuals. While an author's statement of intent is not necessarily the basis for judging his actual intent in writing, some of his statements concerning this question are certainly worthy of consideration.

In an interview with Michael Ohad (1977) regarding *The Lover*, Yehoshua told Ohad: "Amos Oz read the manuscript and said: 'You wrote a book which is a eulogy for the State of Israel.'" Indeed, the message of the novel compels Israeli society to recognize its dark and self-destructive aspects (Shaked, 1977). This is a story not about individuals but about the Israeli psyche. The very names Adam and Asya might even allude to this. Asya bears the name of a continent, while Adam can mean "everyman." The author addressed himself to the novel's pessimistic point-of-view in his interview with Aharoni (1978):

> It was said that *The Lover* is a harsh book about the State of Israel. I do not wholly agree with this opinion. Literature, usually, is not optimistic; it is interested in the dark, problematic sides of life and also exaggerates them. And one must remember that *The Lover* is about Israel in the period after the Yom Kippur War, not the Israel of today when we saw the light again. There is also an optimistic thread in *The Lover*: Here we have a group of people which had lost its identity, especially Na'im. At the end there is some degree of order and everyone resumes his place.

Feldman (1987, p. 92) offers a psychoanalytical interpretation of this novel: the return of Arditi to Israel brings back to life two mother figures in the novel—Veducha and Asya, who are presented initially through their dreams. Veducha represents Zionism and Asya represents the State of Israel. The dreams of Veducha and Asya represent the loss of the reality principle. Arditi, unlike the classical model of Oedipus, does not have to fight his way to his "mother"—Adam brings him to Asya. All this distorts the Zionist metaphor of the sons coming to redeem their motherland.

In still another interview (Beser, 1982), the author defined this novel as "partially political." In his interview with Carmel-Flumin (1986), Yehoshua stated: "Undoubtedly, there are in my texts some kinds of allusions to the larger structure. The question is the measure of its significance in the work.... a good critic is one who stands before the living text and finds in it what there is in it, unlike those who approach a literary work and use it as way of organizing their own ideas."

Early in the Summer of 1970 marks Yehoshua's attempt to depart from the allegorical-symbolic style of his earlier works and to employ a well-defined and specific historical reality. This tendency is even more pronounced in *The Lover*, in which Yehoshua uses spoken Hebrew in order to evoke specific aspects of Israeli social reality. In his earlier works he suggested this reality by depicting one aspect or another in a symbolic-allegorical illustrative manner; in this realistic-psychological novel, the author directly portrays various aspects of Israeli society. True, symbolic-allegorical aspects are present in *The Lover*, but the principal achievement lies in the openness to the diverse nature of Israeli reality. One may find a similar struggle to shift to the clear, specific, and concrete also in the works of such writers as Appelfeld, Oz, and Orpaz (see Meron, 1979, p. 103).

The reader wonders if *A Late Divorce* is an allegory about Israeli society and its deterioration. In this family, the unsuccessful marriage of Yehuda and Naomi affects the lives of three generations (Yehuda and Naomi, their children, and their grandchildren) and leads to a mental institution, divorce, family quarrels, homosexuality, a heart attack, emigration, and even murder. Is this an account of the Israeli family in general or is this novel about a peculiar Israeli family which is not representative of the complexities of Israeli society with its failings or problematic aspects?

Yehoshua was asked in an interview (Beser, 1982):

> Almost all the characters in the book ... are psychologically undermined in one way or another.... I have heard a hint that this book relates not to a family but to our society and to our national and social situation in Israel. You, too, a few moments ago, hinted in that direction. Are you saying, in other words, that we live in a mental institution and that our destiny has already been determined like that of the Kaminka family?

In his response, Yehoshua said:

> ... one has to differentiate completely between literature and life in the sense that literature speaks out in ... higher tones ... undoubtedly there is great danger in drawing unequivocal conclusions from literature about life. It is true that writers try to test the center by testing the margins and they turn the margins into the center, they place the margins in the center of their works, and in doing so they indeed want to understand

better what is defective or sick in the center. But in the end, in this respect, works of prophecy and wrath and whatever is connected with them have been disproved many times. In spite of the fact that sometimes there is in literature a piercing vision that can all of a sudden--by magnifying the illness--really aim and strike some specific illness, the corpus is big and very complicated and it has some sick spots and some very healthy spots, but this does not mean that the entire system is sick. Therefore by all means I don't want to push the novel into some kind of diagnosis of Israeli society. I don't think this way and I also think it is dangerous. I truly and seriously intended to write a book about a family.

But literature also experiments and tests situations. It tries to take a certain situation and to go with it to the end. It tries to show in some place what will happen if.... This means that it would be wrong to read it as mere reflection of a situation, but also as a wish or a nightmare.... The nightmare ... will not materialize because you know that nightmare and you can take precautions so that it does not occur. So what I am saying is that one has to be careful in all this symbolizing ... [one has] to preserve the people in ... uniqueness and in the fact that this person is a particular person. Aside from this he also bears, partially, some more general substance, he belongs to a certain class, he represents certain aspects, but that is all. One has to maintain the proportions between these two components.... I would not see them [the characters - L.H.] as mentally damaged....

Yehoshua's refusal to give "approval" to any single interpretation is persistent (Pomerantz, 1983).

While we do not intend to read the novel as an allegory of Israeli life in a particular time and place, we will seek to point out the realistic, psychological and social elements in it. The work presents a complex of relationships which are open to various interpretations; the concrete struggles with the abstract; the materialistic, with the spiritual. It is interesting to note the complex nature of the characters about whom the author writes in this novel, characters many of whom write or think about writing (Dina, Asa, Kedmi, Kaminka, and Ehud Levin).

Employing the techniques of realism and stream-of-consciousness and distancing himself from the style of Kafka and

Agnon, Yehoshua deals in *A Late Divorce* with the deterioration and the distortion of the Zionist dream and of its ideology. In the novel we see the Israel of the 1970s and the early 1980s; we catch a glimpse of its university- and school-life, its literary scene, along with banking, the stock-exchange, mental institutions, religion, emigration, and family life in the country during that period. We encounter both Ashkenazic and Sephardic Jews, secular and religious Jews; we read about Jerusalem, Tel-Aviv, and Haifa. We view three generations: grandparents, children, and grandchildren. Everywhere we find loneliness, a desire for divorce and emigration, misery and a lack of communication. Behind the facade of organized life, madness, destruction, and schizophrenia are hidden; the Sephardic Calderon is a husband and father who at a late stage in life has discovered his latent homosexuality; Asa is successful in the academic world but is deprived of spiritual and physical contact with his wife, Dina, who is nourished more by her fantasies and literary ambitions than by her human relationships and contacts. And, on the night of the Passover Seder, a rabbi speaks to the patients in the mental institution, addressing them as "chosen," as people with a "spark of holiness," while the patients "blink and gape with drooling mouths staring back at him in alarm as though he were about to attack them" (p. 293).

Pain characterizes all forms of human relationships in the novel: love, parenthood, marriage, and divorce. It is true both that this painful condition typifies modern man in general and that the author chose to write about it in an Israeli setting.

The years of the Kaminkas' marriage are the years of Israeli statehood. Leaving Russia, Yehuda Kaminka came to Israel with a sense of purpose; later, however, he decided to leave, and he blames Israel for his decision. As in *The Lover*, the emigrant is insane. Israeli life is illustrated in the novel by a family plot portraying a neurotic or insane way of life in which the family framework has disintegrated, marriage lacks meaning, and emptiness leads to divorce and suffering on the part of children and grandchildren. Israeli existence is represented by the Kaminkas and their environment, and it is filled with contradictions, madness, and violence; it is a reality of sick and mad people--Yehuda, Naomi, Asa, Zvi, Calderon, Dina. Through this dark family scene we witness the collapse of national, spiritual, and family frameworks in the social and cultural life of the country. As a historian, Asa perceives this as a time of confusion (the old age has died, the new one has yet to be born, p. 157); and Yehuda wants mercy from history ("Asa, do you hear, historical mercy--there's a concept for you to work on," pp. 319-320).

In the novel *Five Seasons,* Yehoshua returns to focus upon the individual; ideological aspects are not prominent. The ideological message in *Five Seasons* was best defined by Yehoshua himself (Huppart, 1987):

> The ideological message of the story is that we must be more patient and more tolerant, that we have to abandon the kind of nervousness which seeks immediate and unequivocal solutions to our conflicts.... Now I feel that greater patience is needed, that processes require time, that we need to fight, but not to expect immediate results.

> From this point of view, Molkho's hesitancy symbolizes this quiet element. Here there is an issue of identity that did not protrude until now in my literary work. Molkho has his family roots in the old Sephardic community in the Land of Israel, the "old settlement," those who do not belong to what is called "the Near Eastern Communities," in the classical meaning of the term. The persona in the novel came from an assimilated class, but he has his own voice, a patient voice, irritating in his inability to act, but a voice of wisdom and of moderation.

> It becomes clear that in the year in which Molkho did nothing, he actually did a great deal. This is the way in which things have to be done in order to achieve improved results.

Gerts (1983, pp. 87-95) investigated the relationships between literature and politics in Yehoshua's work up through 1978 and the literary devices used in order to accomplish the connections between the two. We will draw upon some of her ideas in addressing our question whether these are stories of individuals or stories of a society.

The fact that national events are so strongly connected with the lives of the characters in these novels leads us to think that these are not only stories of individuals but stories which also depict Israeli life as such. For example, the War of Attrition provides the father in *Early in the Summer of 1970* with an excuse to continue teaching after his retirement and regenerates his life. In *The Lover*, the Yom Kippur War exposes more sharply the selfish individualistic deserter-nature of Arditi. The years of Kaminka's marriage in *A Late Divorce* are the years of Israeli statehood. And while *Five Seasons* focuses on individuals, issues such as Arabs and Jews, monetary retributions from Germany, and the political situation in Israel are interwoven with the presentation of the lives of the individual characters.

The characters themselves connect and combine the individual and the national-political-historical dimensions. For example, in *Early in the Summer of 1970* the father tries to use his experience as a "bereaved" parent so that out of the "private sorrow a common truth would illumine us all" (p. 38). Asa in *A Late Divorce* (p. 335) talks about the possibility that we might draw conclusions from history so that people might innoculate themselves against catastrophe, "to isolate the meaning, the secret code of the past, and distill from it a serum that can be injected into human beings to prepare them for the coming catastrophe: that's the story of history in a nutshell." This catastrophe is "the one that can't be helped" (ibid.). Asa thinks here of preparing for his own catastrophe as well, and indeed it was a short while after this very conversation that his father who came to Israel to divorce his wife, Asa's mother, was murdered.

The relationships between the characters in these novels are sometimes representative of some aspects of Israeli society-at-large. In *Early in the Summer of 1970* the father is detached from his son and students, something which represents the gap separating the father's generation from young Israelis. In *The Lover*, the relationship between Veducha and Arditi represents the differences between the generation of the founders and many of the younger Israelis. In *A Late Divorce*, the attitude of Kedmi toward Levana represents certain issues in the Ashkenazic-Sephardic conflict. In *Five Seasons*, when the leading figure rejects his wife's bitter criticism of Israel, the Sephardic Molkho is rejecting criticism voiced by German Jews.

Sometimes a character's personal situation or attitude is clad in a national or political argument. In *Early in the Summer of 1970*, the father refuses to retire because of the war, while the principal of the school "did not see any connection between the war and myself" (p. 11). The father does not say that he is lonely and that his life would be empty without his teaching but rather chooses an explanation related to the political and national situation in order to explain his own personal desire. Similarly in *Five Seasons*, the chief character's wife attributes her bitterness not to her own tendency to be unhappy (p. 138) but rather to the political situation in Israel. The seriocomic officer in *The Lover* thinks that he seeks Arditi because of issues of national character, but in truth he does so because he is personally a troubled, honor-seeking man who uses war and national-historical terminology for purposes of self-glorification. The officer has a kind of will, "written in elevated tones and a poetic style, something about himself and the people of Israel. It was a strong mixture--destiny, mission, history, fate, endurance. A bloated anthology of righteousness and self-pity." The officer connects the national and the individual, and the reader, like Arditi himself, looks at his attempt with irony, because, after all, "he hadn't seemed really involved in this war" (p. 309).

The recurring appearance of a national situation in the work conveys the feeling that this situation is static and dominates the novel. *Early in the Summer of 1970* both opens and ends with the "death" of the son in the War of Attrition, a war which is constantly present in this novella. In *The Lover*, the Yom Kippur War both opens and closes the novel and is mentioned repeatedly in the monologues of the various characters.

THE ISRAELI FAMILY

In the novels *The Lover* and *A Late Divorce*, Yehoshua characterizes the life of the Israeli family as one of routine and boredom. Destructive elements dominate the disintegrating families: death, anomaly, madness, deviations, fights, and severance of husband and wife. Also, the novella *Early in the Summer of 1970* makes us aware of problems in the Israeli family. The Israeli family which the author portrayed in *The Lover* was expanded in A *Late Divorce*, which depicts three generations of an Israeli family. In *Five Seasons* the devotion of the husband to his family is admirable: we observe Molkho himself, his mother and mother-in-law, and his three children; his wife dies at the beginning of the novel but remains powerful in affecting Molkho's life through memories.

A complexity of issues marks the relationship of father and son in *Early in the Summer of 1970*.   When the father finally meets his living son in the military camp after he had previously been informed of the son's death, the son looks at his father just as "he would look" at him "when he was small," when the father "would beat him" (p. 63). Silence and lack of communication characterize the meetings between father and son (pp. 19, 24)--the son neither shows interest in his father's life nor thinks that his father can understand his work, while the father admires his son and thinks about him in terms of a prophet with a message (pp. 19, 23, 32, 63).

The father is aggressive toward his son because he thinks his son is remote from Israeli reality (p. 19):

> "And you're still teaching Bible there ..." (already he has nothing to say to me).
>
> "Yes, of course. Only Bible."
>
> "In that case"--still smiling--"everything's as usual."
>
> "Yes, as normal"--and another long silence--"except, of course, for my pupils getting killed."   I spit it out in a whisper straight into his face!

The motives of the father in this conversation are mixed: he wants to make a point to his son that a lot has been going on in Israel (death of pupils) while the son was away, studying in America; but the father also senses that the son is distant from him. It is also possible that the father feels contempt for the son whose life is dynamic in some sense as compared with his own more static life. He, who never served in the army (pp. 50, 55), tries unsuccessfully to convey to his son "some point, some meaning" in military service, while the son feels that this same service is "such a loss of time ... so pointless ..." (p. 64).   Besides ideological and mental differences between the narrator-father and his son, language creates an additional barrier between them.   The son writes in English (p. 24) and his American wife speaks English (pp. 16, 17, 24, 25), while the father's is "an impossible English" (p. 17).   The absence of the mother from the story, even as a memory, might imply a faulty family life.

The major failure of Israeli society is that of family life as depicted in *The Lover* through the family of Adam and Asya. They represent the generation of the War of Independence along with a society which has lost the clues to the goals of its existence. Loneliness, rapid aging, and disloyalty typify their family life. Adam, Asya, and their daughter, Dafi, live next to each other but not with one another.   They are loveless, sensitive, and lonely, lacking affection and drifting apart.   Adam, a wealthy garage owner, is a tired father and husband surrounded by Arab employees; he is bored and lacks social and spiritual outlets.   Asya is a secondary-school history teacher, intelligent and responsible as a working person, but frustrated, a woman with neither warmth nor a sense of beauty. Adam is not attracted to his wife.   He gave the key to his house to Na'im who became his daughter's lover, and he brought to his home Gabriel who became his wife's lover, acts of self-destruction on the part of a man who is tired of his role as a father and as a husband.

His search for Gabriel is indicative of some sort of mental collapse. It is hardly normal for a husband to seek to bring back his wife's lover. In Adam's quest for Gabriel, Asya's lover, furthermore, he is seeking the death-blow, the *coup de grace* of his disintegrating family life which has reached a dead end. On the surface, Adam appears an influential character both at home (bringing the lovers together) and at his garage (he is the owner); however, he has no control over his life. Indeed, he depends upon other people to do his work: he neither manages his garage nor works in it. Nor does he act as a husband but rather brings another to substitute for him; he is, in addition, a passive father and does not participate in the war. Money is his substitute for love, while for Asya (who likes old women), books substitute for love. Dafi's awareness of the lack of love in her family brings on her insomnia. Adam loses his authority as a father vis-a-vis his daughter Dafi.

Eros leads nowhere in the novel. It is distorted, as in the examples of Adam-Asya, Asya-Gabriel, and Adam-Tali, or obstructed, as in the case of Na'im and Dafi. And while Na'im and Dafi are able and willing to overcome the tension between Arabs and Jews, it would probably be significantly more difficult for them to do so if they were older (Shaked, 1977).

In the framework of these relationships, Adam's belief that he and Asya spared their daughter the impact of destroyed family life--"broken homes, families splitting up" (p. 251)--sounds naive or self-deceptive and evokes irony.

The monologues of the lonely, unhappy, and lost characters in *The Lover* reveal the misunderstandings of the characters on both an individual and a national level and their flight to money (Adam, Dafi, and Gabriel), to sex (Dafi, Asya, Gabriel, Adam, and Tali, his fifteen-year-old daughter's friend), and to learning (Asya). The monologues interrelate and make for continuity in the plot and stress certain meanings and characteristics of the characters. Gerts (1979, p. 426) is correct in stating that the fact that we do not have one subjective opinion about the events results in a multiplicity of points-of-view which brings the reader closer to reality. The confines of social and sexual tabus are destructively threatened in the novel in the arenas of family (Gabriel-Asya, Adam-Tali), of nation (Dafi-Na'im, Adam's daughter and his young Arab employee), of state (Gabriel is an emigrant, *yored*), and of age (Adam-Tali). The disruption of family tabus (Asya-Arditi, Adam-Tali, Dafi-Na'im) and the national tabus (Arditi's deserting the army) neither brings vitality to the lives of the characters nor resolves problems (Barzel, 1977). Adam and Asya do not become young; Dafna and Arditi remain restless. War produces only death and wounds. Yitzhak ("will laugh" in Hebrew), the orphan-immigrant from Teheran who joined Asya's class, was killed in a war; Yigal, the first-born of Asya and Adam, was deaf and, not sensing danger, was killed in an accident.   Yitzhak did not laugh; he sacrificed his life as a victim of war; Yigal ("will redeem" in Hebrew, Shamir, 1977) did not redeem. Tali ("my dew") did not refresh Adam's life. Dafna ("laurel") does not possess the qualities required in order to triumph over life. These issues represent the national condition and not only that of the particular individuals portrayed in the novel.

Some of the motifs of the novel had already appeared in the author's short stories (Shaked, 1977).   The energetic Na'im who conquers the daughter of Adam, the tired Jewish father, recalls the active Arab and the passive Jew in "Facing the Forests"; Adam may remind us of another tired and helpless Israeli ("Continuing Silence of a Poet") and of impotence as an expression of the helpless Israeli ("A Long Hot Day"). The garage of Adam and his attitude toward the contact between Dafi and Na'im in this novel recall another lad who courts a daughter and another father who attempts to obstruct him ("A Long Hot Day").

In *The Lover*, the generation of the strong laboring settlers whose ideology matched their life-style is no more; the present is in the hands of a tired generation, that of Adam who has lost his values and much of his feelings and that of Asya who invests very little in her family. The future is in the hands of a declining generation, as represented by Dafi. The affluence of the generation of the settlers' children (Adam and Asya) does not bring happiness.   The novel presents the generations in a condition of entropy: Veducha, Gabriel's grandmother, is a survivor; Gabriel's mother died; Gabriel, Adam, and Asya lead restless and aimless lives; Dafi has neither the working energy of her parents nor the intellectual drive of her mother; the Jewish characters are all troubled, while at the end of the novel, it is Na'im, the Arab boy, who is full of hope. Terrorism, troubled relations between Arabs and Jews, war and tension--these will persist.

The Israeli families in *A Late Divorce* are in a state of collapse. The parents' home and their family-lives are no longer a uniting factor. After a prolonged bad marriage, Yehuda and Naomi divorce, but the effects of their bad relations continue to impair the lives of their children. Their son, Asa, does not engage in sexual relations with his wife, Dina, who is distant from her husband. Asa is "weak" in bed, and he ends up licking the feet of a prostitute (pp. 163-164). As substitutes for family life Asa escapes to books and knowledge of terror while Dina, who remained a virgin after her marriage, escapes to neurotic literary fantasies. The patronizing and overprotective attitude of Dina's parents caused her to distance herself from them; conversely, the lack of protectiveness of the parents in the Kaminka family produces a distance between them and their children. Asa is full of self-pity and under stress he hits himself in hysteria (p. 169). Zvi, Asa's brother, who physically resembles their father Yehuda, is a homosexual. Ya'el, the daughter of Naomi and Yehuda, is married to Kedmi, a vulgar, domineering, and demanding husband rich in paranoid fantasies. His character explains away his many mistakes regarding other characters, including their morals and honesty (his client is not a murderer, his secretary and her family are not criminals), or their health (his son is fat and sick, not strong and healthy as he thinks), etc. He is the victim of his own megalomania. Kedmi's status and livelihood depend upon people's troubles; if crimes are not committed and if people don't seek divorces, then he stands to lose both livelihood and status. The name Yisrael Kedmi (Eastern) possibly alludes to some collective characteristics given expression in him. He is a prattler, rough, arrogant, and pretentious. Only Ya'el's passive attitude allows her marriage with Kedmi to continue. Her father wonders (p. 259), "You just agree with everyone.... How can you be so passive?" and she responds: "You're right. I really have no opinion. I never had one" (pp. 259-260). In this sense, she reminds the reader of the narrator who simply observes. She is in charge of remembering: "I'll remember ... you leave the remembering to me, because there is no one else to do it" (p. 235). Ya'el is a passive observer who reconstructs events rather than a character that molds them.

Kaminka's sons cannot have offspring; of his daughter Ya'el's two small children, Gadi and Rakefet, the former suffered a heart attack due to overweight, while his grandfather, Yehuda, is thin and physically healthy. Emotionally, Zvi and Asa feel hostility toward their parents.

Troubled relationships are typical not only of the Kaminkas and their children. Dina, Asa's wife, is remote from her parents; she left their traditional way of life but she is nonetheless detached from her adopted secular environment. Calderon's latent homosexuality destroys his family life along with religious values and family honor. Zvi, a homosexual, lives as a leech; he is willing to give his body to Calderon in order to receive "tips" about the market, to speculate and to enjoy a "good" earthy life. Ya'el, the most "normal" of the lot, is a passive introvert who may end up suffering even more than the others. The child that Yehuda will have from Connie is evidence of the destruction of his family rather than fertility and the continuation of Israeli family life.

Names are significant in the novel. The names Zvi, Ya'el, and Gadi (deer, mountain-goat, kid) may remind us of sacrificial animals. Calderon's surname, Rafael, shows how remote he is from being an angel. The name Rakefet (cyclamen) may indicate ironically the difficulties of growth in such a family. The insanity of Yehuda and Naomi was transmitted to their children and to their grandchild, Gadi, who overeats, wets his bed, fights with his schoolmates, and ends up with a heart attack.

Family life in the novel is deeply affected by the mentally troubled characters. Technically only one principal character in the novel—Naomi—is insane. However, it would seem that insanity marks the Kaminkas and also their in-laws, Dina and Kedmi. The father, Yehuda, who seems to be the most stable and economically well-off in the Kaminka family, is exposed in his insanity at the end of the novel as he goes to his wife's mental hospital to steal their divorce agreement. He puts on her dress, apparently a symbolic act of identification with her madness and an unconscious attempt to reveal his own insanity. Yehuda's latent illness succeeded in influencing the entire family. He was one of the sources of Naomi's illness, as Yehoshua stated in an interview (Beser, 1982): "the other characters, indeed every one of them, pulled another string from the father's pathology." Yehoshua thinks (ibid.) that there is a wide dynamic range of mental health and illness: one person can be ill and recover, while another can be sane and commit suicide after a short time. Indeed, we are made aware of Yehuda's madness in various parts of the novel (pp. 75, 90, 353). In exemplifying a "sickness of Diaspora," Yehuda, who strives for a new emotional, economic, and professional life in America while his children continue to struggle in Israel, is "factually" crazy and the metaphor of "sickness of Diaspora" becomes real in the novel.

Kedmi thinks that he "caught" some of his mother-in-law's madness (p. 63), and Dina's life is heavily influenced by fantasies. Their family lives are affected accordingly. All these characters, together with those such as the strange father in *Early in the Summer of 1970* and Arditi in *The Lover*, who was once in a mental institution, are not without impact upon their environment.

The characters in *A Late Divorce* compose a microcosmic description of a "mad country." Yehuda's insanity, Naomi's attempt to murder, her schizophrenia and kleptomania, all affected her children. Naomi, admitting that she wanted to murder her husband, explains her reason: "Because you disappointed me" (p. 282). Yehuda attempts to "confront" this argument within himself (pp. 312, 320, 335, 348): "Disappointed you that I didn't go crazy too. Forgive me but that far I wouldn't go. And did I ever really promise?" (p. 312). And then again: "Disappointed her how?" (p. 335). While we do not know what the promise was, Yehuda admits that he made some kind of promise: "promiscuously doubling herself demanding the impossible from me to keep a promise meant only as a metaphor as a landmark for longing. But is it thinkable?" (p. 320).

Feldman states that Yehoshua dramatizes in this novel the mental consequences of the political issue: "The mother (Naomi, Israel) is torn to a point of no return, each of her children has his/her own pathology, and her husband attempts to avoid the conflicts by the typical 'neurotic solution,' escape into Diaspora existence" (1987, p. 92).

The name Yehuda (the tribe of Judah; Jew) is not incidental; Yehuda represents certain Jewish characteristics. The best description of his overall personality is offered by his former student: "He was a sharp fellow. An odd person, though. And one who got on your nerves. Still, he did make me think.... An odd fellow. Complicated. He made life tough for us.... A strange man. Talented but wasted..." (p. 75).

And Yehuda exemplifies a "sickness of Diaspora"--he moved to America. Mental illness as an important theme in the characters' lives appears not only in A Late Divorce. Arditi in The Lover was committed to a mental institution for years, and in Early in the Summer of 1970 there are marks of mental instability in the father (pp. 12, 13, 30, 34, 35, 39, 64, 67). He suspects that other characters in the story perceive him as insane: "he thought I had gone out of my mind" (p. 12); "and I realized suddenly: they take me for mad" (p. 34); "the driver ... thinks I have gone out of my mind" (p. 39). The father is obsessed with madness: "it's been a mad day" (p. 64); "and I, crazed and exhausted with hunger" (p. 67). His acts at times are peculiar: "for the first few weeks I scarcely left the school grounds, would haunt them even at night" (p. 13); "start winding among them, over them, step on their flabby, Diaspora limbs, strike them lightly with the branch that has reappeared in my hand" (p. 36). Undoubtedly these aspects of the character influenced his relationship with his son. (Gerts analyzed the father's personality in order to support her contention that the father is an unreliable narrator [1985, pp. 197-204].)

Fuchs thinks that "gender-conscious analysis of Yehoshua's model of characterization reveals some important differences between male and female characters, most of which reflect traditional preoccupations of roles." According to Fuchs, the "blankness" and the "referentiality" of the women in Yehoshua's work "are necessary results of an inherently androcentric perspective that identifies humanity with masculinity, and that essentially views women as supporting characters in the drama of life" (1984, p. 80). The arguments of Fuchs are sharp; however, due to the fact that nearly all of Yehoshua's characters are troubled, one could build a similar "case" as to Yehoshua's male characters.

In *Five Seasons*, the major struggle of the chief character after his wife's death was to free himself from his attachment to her so that he might go on to develop a new relationship. He discovered, however, that his attachment to his late wife, his love and devotion to her, was too strong. At the end of the first year following her death it became clear to him that only new love and depth of feelings could take him out of his loneliness and that his emotional recovery would therefore necessarily be slow: "Lovingly, he tried thinking of his wife, but for the first time he felt that his thoughts grasped at nothing, that each time he cast their hook into the water it bobbed up light as a feather. Am I really free, then? he wondered. And if I am, what good is it? Somewhere there must be other, realer women, but for that a man has to be in love. Otherwise it's pointless, he fretted, a man has to be in love" (pp. 358-359).

Molkho's devotion to his wife, his care and tenderness during the years of her illness, are described in detail. His wife's nature did not become dominant during the years of their marriage. His devotion to her and his complete identification with her suffering resulted in his becoming a kind of androgynous being, an impotent, lacking sexual life, and he even developed small breasts on his chest at the end of the story, a sign of his giving of himself wholly to his wife which projected itself in his disregard for his sex and sexuality.

Molkho's love for his wife explains why he cannot relate to the women who show interest in him after her death. Indeed, he remained in Berlin with two different women on two different occasions; he discovered, however, that his wife, who was born in Berlin and who had refused to return there to visit, was so intensely "present" in his consciousness that she did not leave space for a new woman and a new relationship. Bartana (1987) may have gone too far in concluding that Molkho's lack of sexual relations during the years of his wife's illness and the year afterward indicates his inability to love and that he is a kind of middle-aged Sephardic impotent. Certainly Molkho felt toward his wife--the first and only woman he "knew" (p. 145)--"compassionate love, fine endearment, complex of human relations" (p. 33). The legal counsel who tried to seduce Molkho and failed accused him of wanting to cause his wife's death and of actually killing her (p. 126).   Urian (1987) thinks that he killed his wife through his devotion lasting to her death and through his anxiety, a view that is not supported either by Molkho's conduct nor by the implied author.

The insertion of Molkho's reading of *Anna Karenina* during the first year after his wife's death has various implications.   In this context let us refer to just one.   The ties and the emotional impact of a marriage do not cease with death but continue their weighty effect on the surviving spouse.   If the hope that a new tie will cure the wounds turns out to be false, then the feeling of a lack of outlet and resolution in a second marriage will bring inevitable destruction. Molkho, realizing this, is cautious about reestablishing married life. Uri, Ya'ara's husband, also knows this, and in his own way he is protective of Ya'ara (lest she commit suicide) even though he offered her for marriage to Molkho.

Ramras-Rauch (1987) asks if Molkho's care for his wife is a "self-sacrifice or a self-deceit?"   She concludes that Molkho is only pretending piety.   During her illness his wife ceases to be the dominating one, and he becomes in a sickly and obsessive way the master of his home.   Ironically, while he is defined in the novel as a "loyal staff officer" (p. 5), he is merely a merciful nurse.   Molkho's desire to please his wife, his passive nature, his central role in the drama of his wife's illness (pp. 47-48) indicate, according to Ramras-Rauch, that he is not sacrificing himself but rather deceiving himself. Even though he is pleased (to a degree) to have the roles shift in a way which places him in a stronger position vis-a-vis his wife, Ramras-Rauch's view overlooks some prominent aspects of self-sacrifice in Molkho's conduct.

Viewing the families in these stories as microcosms of the Zionist society, the reader senses that this society is declining.   *Five Seasons* may be viewed as a pause in this decline, thanks to the healthy and moderate nature of the Sephardic Molkho.   Many of the characters in these stories are troubled to the point that they cannot function properly, and they also affect other characters connected with them.   The father in *Early in the Summer of 1970* and Asya and Adam in *The Lover* function in spite of being troubled.   Even Arditi finds some direction in life after leaving the mental institution.   But in *A Late Divorce* three family generations are troubled to the extent that one is committed to a mental hospital (Naomi) where another is murdered (Yehuda) while behaving insanely.   The mental state of some of the characters finds expression also in their state of physical health--the grandson Gadi in *A Late Divorce* suffered a heart attack and Molkho's wife in *Five Seasons* died of cancer.   In addition, the mental state of one generation is perpetuated into the next: Dafna in *The Lover* struggles with her insomnia and Gadi in *A Late Divorce* struggles with his heart condition--both conditions resulting from a family situation. While in *Early in the Summer of 1970* we find no disruptions of the family tabus, such a disruption does occur in *The Lover*, while in *A Late Divorce* we find such disruptions (Asa and the prostitute; Yehuda and Connie) coupled with deviation (Calderon-Zvi).

With the exception of Molkho, the relations between parents and their offspring deteriorate in these stories. While the son in *Early in the Summer of 1970* is an adult with his own family life and does not focus on his relationship with his parents, the lack of resolution of those relationships in his life is apparent. In *The Lover* Dafna, though still dependent upon her parents, is aware of the distanced and cold relationships in her family. Zvi in *A Late Divorce* values the money he may acquire through his parents more than his relationship with them, and like his brother Asa he is also hostile toward them. Only in *Five Seasons* do we witness a more normal type of relationship.

Similarly, decline marks another aspect of the Israeli family: the relationship of husband and wife. The absence of the wife-mother in *Early in the Summer of 1970* is significant; *The Lover* also deals with the husband-wife relationship and depicts it as empty of emotional, intellectual, and physical bonds. In *A Late Divorce* the husband-wife relationship declines to such an extent that the wife attempts to murder her husband, and the husband is eventually murdered under circumstances relating to their divorce and the division of their community property. Molkho's resentment of his wife's bitterness, his fear of her, and his awareness of her intellectual superiority partly explain his devotion to her--with her sickness she becomes the weak and needy one. In *Early in the Summer of 1970, A Late Divorce,* and *Five Seasons* only one of the spouses survives. In *The Lover,* while both spouses are alive, both are depicted as emotionally dead. The deaths both of Yehuda in *A Late Divorce* and of the wife in *Five Seasons* are related to their emotional states. The events leading to Yehuda's murder are dictated by his insanity, while the cancer which consumes the body of Molkho's wife symbolizes her inability to accept Israeli life and to be content.

In *Early in the Summer of 1970* no woman shares the life of the father. For years Adam in *The Lover,* Kaminka in *A Late Divorce,* and Molkho in *Five Seasons* have no physical contact with their respective wives. When Molkho's wife died he wondered: "was he about to become a sexual object ... even though sex itself was but a

dim and distant memory of a bondage cast aside for a more
compassionate love, for the greater subtleties of affection, for the
finer complexities of human relationships?" (p. 30). The husband-wife
relationships are not fulfilled either physically or emotionally.
(In the novel by Binyamin Tammuz, *Besof ma'arav*, published in 1966, it
does not take much to convince the narrator, an Israeli man, that he
should not suffer just because his beloved woman has been ill for
several months, that he should physically enjoy another woman.
Molkho and Eliakum respond to their situations differently.) In both
The Lover and *Five Seasons* the wives have social and intellectual
advantages over their husbands: Asya is better educated than Adam,
whose father was a public figure; Molkho's Ashkenazic wife is more
intellectual than is her Sephardic husband. It is possible that Molkho
exaggerates when he describes his wife's intellect to the legal counsel
(who is three ranks above him in the office): by describing his wife as
intellectual he is flattering himself because she chose him over
others.

Taking into account the above relationships, the reader is not
surprised to discover that the father in *Early in the Summer of 1970*
is attracted to his daughter-in-law; that Adam in *The Lover* sleeps
with Tali, his daughter's friend; that Kaminka in *A Late Divorce*
wants to marry a substantially younger woman; that Molkho is
attracted to a little girl. Molkho also decides to purchase a certain
car because of its "womanly" appearance. He found the French
Citroen to be "feminine": "just look at those curves, how she bellies
down below, the flare of that rear of hers" (1989, p. 154; see also
p. 215). It's convexes, belly, and buttocks--a sublimation of his
sexual desires. His wife's breast was removed (ibid., pp. 23, 45),
while he "had even sprouted little breasts" (p. 301; see also p. 303).
The attraction of these men to girls may be explained by their desire
to recapture both their own strong traditional role and their lost
youth. In this context it is noteworthy that Yehuda in *A Late
Divorce* was murdered after he dressed himself in his wife's dress;
and the husband of the legal counsel collapsed while cleaning dishes
in the kitchen, a woman's role according to some social norms in the
background of the story. Kaminka died while he feigned to be a
woman, and the legal counsel's husband died while fulfilling a
traditional female role. Molkho himself put on an apron and served
meals (1987, p. 50). Ramras-Rauch (1987, p. 42) has pointed out that
in Yehoshua's novels the woman becomes more "manly" while the man
in turn becomes more womanly. The many beds in *Five Seasons* are
connected more with death and illness than with sexual activity
(Molkho's wife's medical bed; his bed near or under hers; the bed in
which Molkho's mother-in-law dies, etc.).

"All the world is a stage--and all the men and women merely players"--and the stage reflects the world: in a world in which a man takes a woman's role and vice versa we find that in *Five Seasons* a fat woman acts as Orpheus in an opera in Berlin.

THE ISRAELI-ARAB CONFLICT—LIFE IN THE SHADOW OF WAR

As depicted in *Early in the Summer of 1970*, life in Israel at that time is one of nightmares, with funerals, tension, and horror, all resulting from the Israeli-Arab War of Attrition. The victims of the war include both son and father and their respective generations. The war-generation (as in Yehoshua's "The Last Commander") is not interested in the war. The war-situation goes far to explain the erosion in understanding between the generations. Both older and younger generations confront confusion, guilt, pain, loneliness, and a search for meaning. The father employs terminology from the Binding of Isaac (Genesis 22); sometimes he feels that he is the sacrifice in the war (p. 53); he is "pinioned" (Hebrew: *akud*); then he is inside the "thicket" (Hebrew: *sevakh*--this is omitted in the translation, p. 62). But at other times either he feels that he is sacrificing his son or he is accused of doing that (pp. 12, 17, 21, 68). Ironically, the "death" of the son has in some ways a positive impact upon the father; he becomes energetic and feels that he and his wisdom are needed; he becomes the center of attention and receives compassion from others. Following the notice about his son's death, the father is surrounded by concern and love and a sense of solidarity which typify the Israeli experience in such circumstances (pp. 14, 15, 20, 23, 34, 35, 40, 45, 48, 49, 50, 54). The status of the father who is bereaved of offspring is thus connected not only with pain and sorrow but also with attention and compassion which he sorely needs. When his son was believed dead, the father was revived socially and psychologically, becoming active and developing plans for the future; however, he weakened and became passive upon learning that his son was still alive. The father's attempts to flee his loneliness by continuing his teaching, by communicating with his son, and by "discussing" his son's death, all ended with the father's confronting once again his basic loneliness. Both the beginning and the end of the novel deal with the memory of the notice the father was given of his son's death; this conveys that the passing of time does not necessarily indicate progress but rather that situations may indeed remain static. Light and darkness, dryness and water, horizon and landscape, past and future are employed in the story to allude to the connections between the father and his environment and the father's enduring loneliness (Gerts, 1983, pp. 197-204).

The war situation has a strong impact upon the teacher's relationship with his students. He feels that he is not "important to them any more" (p. 69) and has lost his control and influence over them. In the latter years, when his students are discharged following their military service and begin a family life, the teacher perceives barriers between them and him:

> This pain of theirs is the result of an experience in which I have not shared.   And even those who do come back--there is something veiled in their eyes; they stare at me blankly, almost ignore me, as though I had deceived them somewhere ... I mean as though with the material itself I had deceived them, as though everything we taught them--the laws, the proverbs, the prophecies--as though it had all collapsed for them out there, in the dust, the scorching fire, the lonely nights, had all failed the test of some other reality. (p. 70)

The teacher is representative of his generation and its values, values which collapsed in the reality faced by the younger generation who could not apply them but who are nonetheless sacrificed in their name.   Experiencing the barrier between teacher and students, the father still seeks contact with the younger generation. He uses words such as "gospel," "as though," "resurrection," "ancient," "prophet," due to his feeling that he lives in a twilight time, in a transition period because of the possible "revolution" and "gospel" of the young generation.

We learn about the relationship between the students in the graduating class and their teacher from the three occurrences in the story in which the narrator-teacher recalls and reconstructs (with fine, meaningful variations) that moment in which he was told of his son's "death." From the description of the tense relations between teachers and students in the first recollection (pp. 9-10) the story shifts in the second recollection to war-terminology (pp. 45-47) and, in the third, to estrangement (pp. 69-72). The second recollection employs war-terminology to depict a kind of state of conflict between them. Some students "spy me from afar and curse, hurry inside to warn the others." The students are tense, their papers spread "like flags of surrender." The teacher is aware of "the tyranny," the "hard" situation (Hebrew, "cruel") he enforces during his test in Bible. The students "exchange despairing glances" and some of them raise their fingers at the teacher, but he "mows them down" (p. 46). All these result in their "revolt" (p. 47). The language tells a story of conquest;   its components are spies, warnings, surrender, tyranny, cruelty, despair, mowing down, and revolt. The teacher employs war-terminology out of a desire for closeness to his students and their world: he prefers "war" with his students to a remoteness from them because the war is evidence of his impact.

The teacher imagines his speech before his students, their parents, and the secondary-school faculty during the graduation ceremony which will take place at the conclusion of the academic year (pp. 36-38, 60-61). In his fantasized speech the father intends to deal with the issue of the younger generation's death in the war, from psychological, historical, and philosophical points of view. The result is a meaningless, pretentious, confused, and vague "speech," lacking any message (pp. 60-61):

> "On the face of it, your disappearance is nothing, is meaningless, futile.... Your death will again be but a weary repetition in a slightly different setting.... Yet ... your disappearance fills with meaning, becomes a fiery brand, a source of wonderful, lasting inspiration.

> "For to say it plainly and clearly--there is not history. Only a few scraps of text, some potsherds...."

The future is a repetitious death; the past, scraps of text and potsherds. History is not a gradual process of any kind, rather everything is repetitious. Destruction, death, and the death of the younger generation as a source of inspiration to the older one--these cannot provide "meaning." This is an implied statement that nothing meaningful can be said concerning those deaths. Gants (1976) emphasized the fact that Yehoshua, like other contemporary authors, did not protest against war, death, and bereavement but rather abandoned all hope of bettering the reality which his characters inhabit.

When the father found his son, the son--"heavy, long-haired, sleep-walking, lonely"--was urinating on the chain of the tank, "the rifle clanging from his shoulder like a broom-stick" (p. 62). We do not wonder, therefore, when the son says to his father, "such a loss of time ... so pointless" (p. 64), and the father wonders "how to give him some point, some meaning" (p. 65). Ramras-Rauch (1978) stresses that the father indeed lost his son even though he found him because the son, like the father's students, does not uphold the values of the father and his ideological heritage. The secular generation of the founders of the State of Israel witnesses the ideological collapse of its values because the younger generation has lost interest in the values of the founders.

Feldman (1986), relating to the ideological world of Oz, Shabtai, Tammuz, and Yehoshua, concludes that the works of these authors reflect a guilt-feeling and self-criticism regarding Zionism and rejection of the petrifaction of principles, ideas, and ideologies which further the use of power without questioning. The potential result of those ideas could be either a new generation that blindly follows the slogans of the fathers or a generation that rebelliously surrenders that heritage. The attempt to build upon pain, experience, and goodwill so that out of the "private sorrow a common truth would illumine us all" (p. 38) is not successful.

In the speech which the father fantasizes, he "settles his accounts" with the principal of the secondary school who prefers administrative to educational work and yet seeks to "hold forth as a guiding spirit to these youngsters." "And who is not eager to address the young these days?" asks the father, rhetorically, fantasizing his speech.   The students are "inarticulate, slightly obtuse ... vague graduates without ideals ... with the strength and readiness to die" (p. 37).

Here are some of the basic implied differences between the generations as they are expressed in the context of the Israeli-Arab war: the older generation talks while the younger listens and acts ("the class is listening absorbed," p. 13); the older generation is privileged with the honor of guiding and commenting on the acts of the young—the young suffers from the doing of the acts; the old expects while the young is expected and obeys; the old pretends to know, to be a "guiding spirit" while the young does not conceal the fact that they are "slightly obtuse"; the old pretends to have a clearly defined ideology and ideals while the young does not; the old pretends to be articulate but remains vague, the young is "vague" and "inarticulate" (p. 37) but sincere in its acts. The educators fail, one might suggest, "to give some point, some meaning" (p. 65) to war and death, and their describing death as "a source of wonderful ... inspiration" (p. 60) does not lend "meaning" to it. This death provides the father with an excuse not to retire (pp. 11, 12), and it offers the principal of the school an opportunity to pretend to be a spiritual leader. Furthermore, the story of the son's "death" verifies how this death inspires the father who loves and admires his son and gives the father vitality and strength, taking him out of his condition of loneliness.

It is ironic that the Arab cleaning-woman of the son's house is the first person to whom the father attempts to communicate—in Arabic—the news of his son's "death" (pp. 27-29); he speaks to her over the loud heroic Arabic singing on the radio.   The language barrier is difficult; the Arab woman, however, is emotional; she tries to help, to understand. She feels, she awaits orders, she speaks and sobs or screams, and when she finally understands the father's message she is stricken, stunned and unbelieving; she takes a step backward. The differences and conflicts between the two nations are not so strong as the personal contact between individuals which makes for care and sympathy.

In *The Lover*, A. B. Yehoshua presents meaningful differences between Na'im, the Arab boy, and some of the Israeli characters. The reader cannot but compare Na'im with Adam, Dafi, and Gabriel. Unlike Adam, Na'im, who is Adam's employee, is full of life and vigor. He is an ambitious survivor, desirous of education and progress, emotional, bright, productive, and diligent in a country in which physical labor has ceased being a value. Economically he is dependent upon the Jewish economy. Na'im breaks into Veducha's apartment (which belonged to Arabs) through the windows, but he becomes a legitimate tenant, essential to her life emotionally and physically. Na'im desires Dafi and sleeps with her; he reminds Adam and Dafi of Yigal, Asya and Adam's son who was killed; he reminds Veducha of her grandson, Gabriel. He thus has many aspects and might parallel different characters. He lives in Peki'in, the one place in the land of Israel continuously inhabited by Jews. On the one hand he has no particular hostility to Jews (pp. 185-186); he absorbs Israeli culture. He can recite Bialik's poem (p. 166) and he uses the melody of "Jerusalem of Gold" as a whistling signal. At the same time one should not disregard the fact that of all Bialik's poems, he recites "Dead of the Desert" (p. 166), a poem in which the dead of the wilderness have risen "in spite of heaven and its wrath" to be "the last generation of bondage and the first of deliverance." The Arab Na'im identifies with heroes and heroism no less than the Jew and is capable of applying the expression of the Jews' rebellion against oppression to his own situation. Na'im captured Dafi's heart and body; he became indispensable for Veducha. Adam gave Na'im the key to his home, the "home" which is run by a tired and lonely family. This makes Na'im's work simple. Dafi has what Na'im wants: the opportunity to study, to progress, to live in comfort; however, she does not use her opportunities well, but rather she is negligent, unambitious and materialistic. She considers using her parents' occupations as a means to survive at her secondary school. She is direct. In the future, the diligent, hardworking, life-thirsty, hopeful Na'im will prevail and consequently the Jewish future in Israel will be in danger.

Adam's garage is a scene of power, energy, mobility, repair. It depends upon Arab labor. While the cars and the firm are owned by

Jews, the Arabs provide the labor. The car repairs as well as the garage's income depend upon the labor of the Arabs and their Arab garage leaders. Adam does not even know his employees; he is tired as an employer and as a businessman, while the Arabs provide the energy required to maintain his garage as a going enterprise.

Arab-Jewish relations bear promise of healing only when both peoples know one another up close on an individual basis. Adam knows the Arabs better than do many other Jews who speculate concerning them. Veducha is suspicious and unappreciative of Arabs; Dafi simply does not know them. But they all like Na'im once they know him and stop thinking about him as a stereotype. Adnan, Na'im's brother, ends his life as a terrorist, but Na'im learns that "it's possible to love them and to hurt them too" (p. 352).

Economically, Israel depends upon Arab labor. Morally, Jews claim a right to their land because they need a home, but this home, in which Arabs once lived, is enriching those who had left it and who returned only in order to claim that home as an inheritance and to leave once more (Gabriel).

The war-syndrome in Israel, with its victims, corpses, people missing in action, is described in a low key. The working and personal relationships which develop are sometimes in conflict with the prevalent estrangement on a national level.

In a history lesson taught by her mother, Dafna asks (p. 250) whether war was the only way to establish the state. "All this suffering around us ... wars ... people getting killed ... generally ... why was that the only choice?" This question, which was posed at the end of a class session and which generated laughter in the classroom, is indeed the basic question of Zionism and it remains unanswered in the novel. Oren (1977) thinks that in this question Dafna provides the author with the clearest evidence for the end of Zionism.

Adam raises still another issue in the area of Israeli-Arab relations (p. 124). The Israelis speak about Arabs but they do not know them. The pressure, tension, and suspicion between Arab and Jew explain why Adam sees the Israeli Arabs as leading a "double life" (p. 150, in the original Hebrew version: "a double bottom").

In *A Late Divorce*, the Arab-Israeli conflict is marginal. While an Arab headwaiter in a restaurant, "a heavy-set, immaculate" waiter, thinks that the Kaminkas came to the restaurant to celebrate Yehuda's birthday, presuming togetherness and love in this Israeli family, Kedmi told him that "it's actually a divorce party." "The headwaiter laughed incredulously," probably because from his cultural perspective this seems a joke, not a possibility. Yehuda is leaving for America. The Arab asks, "Why leave Israel? What's so bad about it?" Kedmi, rough and insensitive, responded, "Maybe it's not so bad for you ... after all, you people think you own it" (p. 333). Arab boys are employed to push the shopping-carts in the supermarket (pp. 93-94), and the headwaiter briefly presents the problem of the Arabs' status in Israel.

In *Five Seasons*, it is ironic that Arab janitors prepare the convalescent home for the religious needs of the Jewish Sabbath (p. 69) and Arab nurses care for the health of the old Jews who live in it. An Arab driver takes Molkho on a trip to Zeru'a, a new Israeli settlement (p. 179). The road, as in *Early in the Summer of 1970*, goes through Arab villages. Molkho cannot reach the new Israeli settlement without going through those villages, which are old and vital, while the head of Zeru'a asks concerning his settlement, "But how can you develop a village that's starving to death?" (p. 194). Molkho was surprised (p. 180) that the Arab restrooms were clean; again, only personal contact can alter prejudice. In one of Molkho's trips to Vienna, he met an Arab and felt close to him (pp. 302-303).

The Israeli-Arab conflict becomes less and less a central issue in these works of Yehoshua. Israeli society is deeply troubled from within as many internal issues threaten its destruction. It must confront the possibility that "Thy destroyers and they that made thee waste shall go forth from thee" (Isaiah 59:17). The period following the Six-Day War and the War of Attrition clearly affects the lives of the characters in *Early in the Summer of 1970*; similarly, the Yom Kippur War of October 1973 clearly affects the lives of the characters in *The Lover*. But the problems of the Kaminka family in *A Late Divorce* and of the Molkho family in *Five Seasons* are not related to the Israel-Arab conflict. The impact of the conflict depends to a large extent upon the Israelis themselves.

How long will the youngsters described in *Early in the Summer of 1970* agree to continue sacrificing themselves in a war which does not interest them? Adam's family in *The Lover* and the Kaminka family in *A Late Divorce* lack the vitality needed for a secure survival. Characters such as Nina and Molkho's wife in *Five Seasons* are self-defeating; their criticism fails to improve Israeli life and they end up with death (the wife) or emigration (Nina). Under the circumstances, the Israeli-Arab conflict becomes less prominent: murder, ailments, madness, deviation, immigration, fatigue, ennui, loneliness, social tension, disregard of tradition--all these suffice to threaten the destruction of Israeli society even without the existence of an external enemy and a war situation.

THE ASHKENAZIC-SEPHARDIC CONFLICT

For a long time A. B. Yehoshua avoided the Sephardic[1]-Ashkenazic conflict in his literary works.[1] In an interview with Yitshak Betsalel (1969, p. 154) he stated: "I underwent a process similar to that which Jews experienced in non-Jewish society. I assimilated amongst the Ashkenazic Jews...." However, in *The Lover*, Yehoshua described two Sephardic characters, Arditi and his grandmother, Veducha; later he described Calderon in *A Late Divorce* (note also his play, *Hafatsim*). Yehoshua commented about this (Carmel-Flumin, 1986):

> I also write about what is called the "old *Sephardim*" because they are part of me. Most of my identity as Sephardic consisted of an interaction with the Ashkenazic society, and this issue of uncovering one's identity more clearly was concealed with me in some drawer. This drawer was opened. This is not the Sephardic-Ashkenazic problem in general but the family myth ... your blood and flesh, to seek roots in order to search for yourself. This is not particularly a response to a political or social problem. In general, everything is of one texture: politics, power struggles, family myth, psychological theology. People approach my work and isolate the elements which appear to them political or social, for example, the Sephardic-Ashkenazic issue, but it does not occur to me to neutralize this element just because of this. I ask them: Gentlemen, please read my text carefully.

Yehoshua, like Calderon in *A Late Divorce* and Molkho in *Five Seasons*, differentiates between the Sephardic Jews of the old settlement in the Land of Israel and Near Eastern Jews such as Levana in *A Late Divorce*. In an interview following the publication of *Five Seasons* (Levi, 1987), Yehoshua expressed his recognition that the Likhud party was successful in reducing the feeling of alienation of a large part of the population of Israel who now felt that they became hosts rather than guests; they participated in the government and were accepted on the inside. The social restlessness was somewhat cured. According to Yehoshua, the struggle between Ashkenazic and Near Eastern Jews started with the mass-immigration following the establishment of the State of Israel, while he himself belongs to the old Sephardic settlement in the Land of Israel who cannot speak about deprivation in the same sense as can Near Eastern Jews and who attempted to assimilate into the Zionist mentality of Ashkenazic Jewry of Eastern European origins or roots. His own emphasis is on his being an Israeli. It was probably following his relating to the Sephardic-Ashkenazic issue in his novels that he felt personally less hard pressed and threatened by those of the Near Eastern Jews, the later immigrants, who accused him of deserting and betraying them.

In 1981, Yehoshua reached the height of his hatred toward the "second Israel" which was largely responsible for bringing the Likhud to power. This feeling passed, however, and he began to display more positive feelings about them.   Molkho's visit to Zeru'a, a new immigrant settlement, mirrors Yehoshua's own reconciliation with the "second Israel" (ibid., p. 22). Indeed, Molkho feels very good in Zeru'a among the Sephardic Jews there. His attachment is described as something biological in nature. When he was served food in a restaurant in Zeru'a, "he decided first of all to eat before the food got cold, trembling with desire, immediately smelling from the food which was in front of him a succinct deep smell, like the smell of his father" (p. 154). This smell is so strong that he needs an assurance that indeed he is eating beef and not some other kind of meat. Such a smell is stronger in its impact than any concepts which are intellectually acquired. Molkho's attachment to his Sephardic origin is undeniable.

Calderon in *A Late Divorce* (p. 193) is worried lest others might not differentiate between the Sephardic Jews rooted in the older settlement and the other Near Eastern Jews (the "trouble-makers from North Africa"). Yehoshua, whose father, like Molkho, was a fifth-generation Jerusalemite, and whose mother came to Israel from Morocco in 1930, gives his own perception of some of the issues informing the relationship between the older Sephardic settlement in Israel and the more recent Near Eastern immigrants (Fuks, 1987, p. 20):

> After the establishment of Israel these Jews [the old Sephardic settlement - L.H.] suffered shock and turbulence in confronting the immigration from Arab countries and North Africa. They had been a protected minority in Ashkenazic society and now they became exposed as they were identified with the Near Eastern Jews.

> Some of them were not prepared to say that these are their authentic brothers ... they were not able to establish contacts of solidarity and trust [with the newer immigrant-population - L.H.].   So they hurried to assimilate ... [this was - L.H.] a kind of castration, a surrender of values....

Gabriel Arditi, whose name is ironic (Gabriel--an angel; Arditi--vigor), is of a Sephardic family of the "Old Settlement." Gabriel had left Israel twelve years before he later returned to visit; he lives in Paris where he spent a few years in a mental institution. He feels neither guilt nor shame for having left the country. He abandoned his land, his army, his grandmother, and his family together with his benefactors (Adam's family). He is ruthless and spineless, committed only to what serves him best. He came to Israel to claim the legacy which will be left by his grandmother, her car and her apartment (which belongs to Arabs). In this way the value of a home which had belonged to Arabs will end up enhancing the life of an Israeli who has left Israel and does not make Israel his home. The basis of the argument that Arabs left Israel as a result of the justified Jewish need for a home does not apply in his case.

Throughout most of the novel, our impression of Gabriel is based mainly on the way other characters view him. In his long monologue toward the end of the novel, however, we find him resourceful and perceptive, a person of style (Shenhar, 1977). Both Gabriel, the military deserter, and the seriocomic military officer who wants to acquire heroic rank and status are tainted. In order to desert the Israeli army Gabriel changed both his appearance and his life-style, joining the ultra-traditional Ashkenazic fringe-society which never accepted the values or the concept of the Zionist state.

The Sephardic ninety-three-year-old Veducha, Gabriel's grandmother, belongs to the generation of the founders and pioneers. Her story is really the story of Zionism, for she was born in 1881 when the very first Bilu settlers arrived in the Land of Israel (p. 139). When she is conscious she is vital, wise, and clear and exhibits a sense of humor; when she is unconscious she resembles a stone or a plant. During the war she was unconscious, a state which represents the sleep or the death of the old settlers in the 1973 war. Like Veducha, that generation too will at times be conscious and at times unconscious.   Gabriel's mother's death, which coincided with the founding of the State of Israel, may allude to the demise of the values of the older generation. Considering Arditi's human qualities and Veducha's present physical condition, the reader infers that the novel does not depict the Sephardic Jews as a redeeming element in Israel.

Generally speaking, contact between Sephardic and Ashkenazic Jews in *A Late Divorce* ends badly. Naomi's grandmother came from the Sephardic Abrabanel family (p. 272), a fact that fascinates and attracts Calderon to the family because of the bloodline (p. 273). Yehuda came from Russia and married Naomi; this marriage culminated in the murder of Yehuda and in Naomi's entering a mental hospital. The curse follows the generations and we note its marks on the two sons and the daughter of Yehuda and Naomi and also on Gadi. Zvi and the Sephardic Calderon have a destructive relationship. Asa is married to the Ashkenazic Dina but receives his sexual satisfaction from "Natalie" (p. 163). (Is this a trade-name of a Sephardic prostitute?) Each woman, Dina and Natalie, satisfies different parts and needs of Asa. The name of Ya'el's husband is Yisrael Kedmi ("Eastern"), alluding to his connection with the East; their marriage, too, is substantially troubled. It appears that there is an attraction between Sephardic and Ashkenazic Jews but that this attraction does not make for constructive relationships. The novel describes also how the Sephardic rabbi in the novel manages to dominate the Russian rabbi and to process the divorce between Naomi and Yehuda.

In this context one has to remember two characters, patients at the mental institution, both close to Naomi: Musa and Yehezkel. In the initial meeting between Kedmi and Musa, the latter is described as "a crazy giant even taller than I am, a colossus with the straw broom on one shoulder," while Yehezkel, in turn, is described as "a pale old man" (p. 49). These two residents of the mental hospital are described once again: "that skinny, rotten-tooth old fellow ... pulling behind him a moronic-looking giant who carried a rake on one shoulder" (p. 139). Yehezkel, possibly Ashkenazic, is the intelligent one but he needs Musa, bearing a Sephardic name, the physical force, for his own safety and possibly also in order to carry out his intentions. However, when at the end of the novel Yehezkel is not present, Musa then must act independently; he becomes a "fateful man" (p. 354) and kills Yehuda with a pitchfork when the latter put on Naomi's dress, stole the divorce agreement, and attempted to leave. The broom which was carried on Musa's shoulder (p. 49) was later exchanged for a rake (p. 139) and at the end for a pitchfork (p. 354), a powerful tool with which he killed Yehuda. The meeting between Sephardic and Ashkenazic Jews is fatal once more: the Russian Yehuda comes to his death near the fence of the mental hospital, and Musa is doomed to remain in the mental hospital forever. Yehoshua, of course, avoids dealing with the lack of any rational, legal significance in Yehuda's act, as the mere theft of the copy of the divorce agreement from Naomi would not constitute its cancellation.

A unique version of the Ashkenazic-Sephardic conflict is voiced in Yisrael Kedmi's attitude toward Near Eastern Jews. Kedmi is a professional person, educated in his field; however, his education does not enrich him culturally and he is prejudiced against Near Eastern Jews. Through Kedmi, the implied narrator gave voice to the cultural caliber of those who are disposed to relate to Sephardic Jews in stereotypical terms. We hear Kedmi's thoughts concerning the secretary in his law office: "That aggrieved tone of voice. They can't forgive us for having rescued them from the caves of the Atlas Mountains and having introduced them to civilization" (p. 135). Thinking about his secretary, Kedmi concludes without any foundation that "her father must have beaten her. Those primitives run amuck before each Jewish holy day and maybe one of them is in jail already ... it was clever of them to plant a daughter in a lawyer's office for if you intend regularly to run afoul of the law you need dependable legal coverage" (pp. 37-38). It is, of course, highly doubtful that such a person lacking insight and sensitivity can provide "dependable legal coverage"; however, Kedmi speaks out of his need for self-importance as he fantasizes and distorts reality for the purpose of self-flattery. The English translation (p. 39) does not reflect another remark which appears in the Hebrew text: Kedmi speculates that his secretary's parents gave her the name Levana ("white") because "her parents thought that through the name they will overcome their genes" (Hebrew, p. 48). The secretary's "curly African head" (p. 41) disturbs Kedmi. He sees "her eyes going wild" (p. 43); in his eyes she is "this little darkie." He is worried: "Just imagine if every darkie around here should start opening his mouth and saying dark things. It's not enough that ninety percent of them are in court all the time. They want to give us lessons in etiquette too.... I'll show that little darkie yet" (p. 44).

Due to his disturbed personality, when Kedmi suspects that money was stolen from him he decides against calling the police lest they send a Sephardic-Jewish policeman: "I jumped for the telephone to dial the police but I know them; they'll just send me some illiterate Ali Baba" (p. 56, the original Hebrew, p. 64, reads, instead of Ali Baba, "some imbecile from Mesopotamia")--a Near-Eastern Jewish policeman. He considers calling his secretary in order to find out what happened to the check but then he remembers that "her family of cave men doesn't have a telephone" (p. 57). At his secretary's home he feels that "now the whole family has me surrounded; half a dozen short swarthy gangsters invite me to sit down ... all I need now's to have to sit down and eat eggplant, I turn to go opening a small door ... I am in a tiny bathroom facing an old witch sitting naked in yellow water lit by the lurid glare of the heat" (p. 58). Lacking any evidence, Kedmi suspects that a theft occurred. Due to his clumsiness and lack of sensitivity he does not apologize for intruding on the privacy of his secretary's family life and he continues to refer to her and her family in terms of stereotypes, as a superior person speaking of inferior people. His attitude toward the Sephardic Jews is purely stereotypical, the result of his mental deficiencies and of his own inferiority complex. His attitude toward them serves as a mirror reflecting his own limitations and his problems. However, his limitations, of which he is unaware, do not prevent him from concluding, "IQ. That's what it all boils down to. Their IQ evaporated in the Islamic sun. And that's something you can't give them along with their social security" (p. 58). In the light of his opinion of the Near Eastern Jews, Kedmi appears as a limited man, unrefined, suffering from an inferiority complex, and in belittling Near Eastern Jews he strives for some measure of self-confidence by viewing himself as belonging to a better class--the *Askenazim*.

The Sephardic-Ashkenazic issue appears also in other contexts within the novel (pp. 175, 185, 193, 197, 198, 190-191, 272-273). Of course one finds conflict not only between the Sephardic and the Ashkenazic sectors of the population--a conflict with potential to attract the reader--but also within the Sephardic community itself. Calderon, for example, differentiates between the "true, old-time *Sephardim*" and the "trouble-makers from North Africa. They really have a wild streak in them." Calderon is worried about the image of the "true, old-time *Sephardim*" lest someone might confuse the two groups (p. 213). Nevertheless, he betrays the secrets of his employers in order to win Zvi's favor.

The relationship between Calderon (a Sephardic Israeli) and Zvi (an Ashkenazic Israeli) may constitute an implied general statement. Zvi gives his body to Calderon in exchange for inside bank information as well as money; Zvi's lust for money causes him to submit to Calderon's lust. Both Zvi's lust for money and Calderon's for sex are stronger than their moral restraints.

A Late Divorce describes some changes in the social structure in Israel. An Ashkenazic Jew such as Kedmi discovers that he lacks the tools for his desired success, while attorney Mizrahi ("Eastern") prospers. Levana, Kedmi's secretary, is protective of her own self-respect, and her silence is a threat to Kedmi who is aware deep inside of his very real limitations. The stable lawyer Mizrahi is surrounded by such people as Yehuda, a teacher, Asa, a lecturer, Dina, a poetess, and Zvi, a parasitic speculator. The spiritual world of these people, however, does not solve their problems.

In *Five Seasons*, Yehoshua treats the Sephardic-Ashkenazic issue in a most settled manner. Molkho's wife, a German-born Israeli, is pessimistic. Her political criticism of Israel is cutting (pp. 33, 183); she prophesies catastrophes for the country (pp. 37, 183). Her father, a pediatrician upon whom people depended to cure their children, could not cure himself and he committed suicide (p. 72). His education did not assure him a love for life. While Molkho learned very clearly how to translate his love in a practical way to prolong his wife's life and to comfort her most compassionately, her father abandoned her by taking his own life. Molkho's love enhances life more than does the education of his German-born father-in-law.

Yehoshua was asked why he matched the Israeli-born Sephardic Jew, Molkho, with a *yeke* (German-born) wife. He responded (Fuks, 1987):

> The *yekim* are a special group in Israel. They came to Israel against their will, feeling that they were thrown out of a high culture. The *yekim* live here in a kind of insult because they were told insolently: You do not belong [in Germany - L.H.] ... they are critical of the Israeli reality; they have difficulties in adjusting to the customs, to the language ... they do their work faithfully ... but they are full of criticism and bitterness all the time.... On the other side, the type of Molkho, like the old Sephardic settlers, does not have any criticism; impotent Jews, they could sit another two hundred years without doing anything for Zionism.

The distinction is made between Molkho, who uncritically accepts Israel, and those bitterly critical of it. However, Molkho is identified also by some form of ideological passivity. Molkho views Israel as his homeland, and like his Sephardic forefathers he has no need for large words concerning a new and exemplary society or about Messianic-socialist-religious tidings. While Molkho's bitterly critical wife foresees destruction, Molkho himself points to the constructive side (p. 170):

> If you believed half you heard, the whole country had been falling apart for years, and yet everything was still there. In fact, wherever you went, there was a tractor clearing new ground.

With his representative attitude, Molkho, in contrast to his wife, can locate the optimistic, the positive, the hopeful dimension in the Israeli reality.

Molkho is not an intellectual, but he does possess wisdom. It is inaccurate to conclude from the novel that he is uneducated or unwise (Boshes, 1987). For him, life is not a series of career-oriented goals and achievements but rather emotional fulfillment with meaningful relations. In a moment of perspective Molkho defines the main characteristics of his wife: "She was an intellectual ... she was very honest ... I mean, very critical ... of herself too. An intellectual. Nothing was ever good enough for her. She never felt fulfilled or happy. And maybe she never even wanted to be" (p. 138). In contrast, the Sephardic emphasis is on happiness rather than achievement. Molkho recognizes that he himself is not an intellectual (pp. 138, 212), his mind is banal (p. 99), and he is aware of his own cultural and intellectual disadvantages (p. 121), but he does not have an inferiority complex. Furthermore, his common sense, practicality, and sensitivity give him an advantage over the more sophisticated people around him. He is more in control of his life than they are. He has more feeling: he loves his wife, loves music, loves his children. The "cold, intellectual glitter" (p. 138) does not threaten him--"It's a lucky thing we're not on the same flight tomorrow, he told himself," looking at the eyes of the adviser, "whose feverish glitter repelled him, the gleeful, intellectual glitter of her clever, twist-all mind" (p. 139). This explains his role vis-a-vis intellectual women in the novel--his wife and the legal adviser of the Ministry of the Interior, where he works as a certified public accountant.

Both his profession and his emotional balance influence Molkho to be perceptive. He is capable of love, compassion, and satisfaction; he is sensitive to music, and so music becomes analogous to his life (Gilbo'a, 1987). He is not frustrated nor is he ambitious for the sake of ambition. While it has been claimed that Molkho is passive and dies a slow death (Paz, 1987), more likely the implied narrator is alluding to some essential differences between East and West and is illustrating the Sephardic qualities of moderation and lack of extremity. In many ways Molkho stands in contrast to his wife: she sees only the negative aspects, while he acts with patience and tolerance. In this sense he also provides comfort to his ill wife and does his best in difficult circumstances. The reader, however, should not ignore the argument of the legal counsel (p. 138):

> "You killed her little by little ... I only realized it today...." For a second he felt his blood curdle; yet at

once, as if a soft quilt were thrown over him, he felt a warm, rich happiness in his veins. Slowly his eyes met hers. The thought was not new. "You are killing me," his wife used to say to him.... Wearily he smiled.... "You should know," he said brightly, "that I did my best to take care of her." "Yes, I do know," she answered with compassion, "I know everything. I want you to try to understand ... I mean unintentionally, I felt today as if you wanted to put me to death...."

This argument haunted Molkho several times during the course of the novel. It is possible that his exceptional devotion and care for his wife were, in effect, a way to overpower her. With his wife he reached "sexual desperation" (p. 192); she castrated him, in a sense. His infinite giving to her can be viewed as a way of getting even with her: she is more intellectual, but she is in need of him, of his stability and support, and so he is no longer disadvantaged in relation to her. The same thing occurred to him in connection with the legal counsel: after she fell and hurt her leg, he sat near her bed to tend to her, "trusting once more in his patience to compensate for the intellectual superiority of its occupant" (p. 121); the new situation with the adviser appeared to him as an opportunity--"Now she'll see what I'm made of, thought Molkho" (p. 105). In this context the reader remembers that Molkho had been somewhat afraid of his wife (p. 344) and that he has satisfaction in controlling someone of whom he is, in other respects, afraid. We also recall in this context that Molkho's father admired the clerks of the Jewish Agency (Hebrew, 1987, p, 288), an attitude which he transmitted to his son.

Being an intellectual does not resolve anything in the novel. Molkho's wife's black irony (p. 37), her tendency to assume a leading role in conversations (p. 54), the fact that she supervised young teachers (p. 20) and was so interested in newspapers ("she had always been too tired to go anywhere on Saturday and had passed the time irritably glancing at the weekend papers and uttering her Jeremiads" [p. 183]), did not lend any real content to her life. In the novel we hear much concerning what she disliked: nature ("Like most intellectuals, she had never cared for Nature, which had bored her," p. 154), or the political situation in Israel--but we hear nothing concerning what she liked. She was essentially negative, an unhappy, negative critic who did not create very much. She saw in her husband's attempt to relate to reality in a moderate, balanced way "one more sign of the dangerously Levantine, a political naivete that was leading the country to catastrophe" (p. 183). Molkho's wife projects her problems onto the political situation for she cannot deal with her own problems. She does not accept herself and ultimately it is for this reason that she is so critical of Israel. She objects to visiting Germany (pp. 116, 146), but her tragedy is that she did not know how to adapt to and love her new home.

Another intellectual couple, Uri and Ya'ara, is childless; Ya'ara again and again becomes pregnant but the result, each time, is an aborted pregnancy. Uri's never-ending search for meaning (Uri is the "eternal Kierkegaardian-Buberian truth-seeker," p. 210) leads only to a chain of abortions. Similarly, the nine months which the Russian immigrant, Nina, spent in Israel ended as an abortive attempt and she returns to her native land. Nina, who did not acclimate to Israeli life at all, seemed to Molkho "a girl who did not develop well" (Hebrew, 1987, p. 306; English translation, 1989, p. 324: "a little woman barely taller than a child"), but when she crosses the Berlin Wall, "her poorly cut clothes seemed perfectly in place here" (p. 333).   Molkho also rejects the legal counsel, who resembles his late wife in many ways, and thus avoids a continuation of the kind of relationship he had known with his wife. ·Calderon (1987) composes an imaginative letter from the legal counsel to Molkho, in which she objects to the preconceived mold that Molkho had constructed for her and also for his wife, for Nina, and for Ya'ara. She also deals with the question, what of his own Sephardic origin and of her Sephardic origin (the Balkans) was preserved? She feels that in arguing he actually put his wife to death; she was wicked.

Generally speaking, the female intellectual characters do not redeem themselves in the novel and do not attain a stable emotional relationship with Molkho.   Perhaps this is because of Molkho's qualities which extend quite beyond the intellectual: he is wise and practical, wisdom provides him with an all-encompassing tool with which to relate to life, while it appears that intellect alone, when not coupled with wisdom, can be destructive.

Molkho's relationships with the Ashkenazic women in the novel explain his love and attraction to an eleven-year-old Cochin girl. In her presence Molkho feels alive. She is "red, tempestuous and a zealot" (Hebrew, 1987, p. 166; English translation, p. 184: "green with envy"), full of life and color and feelings which contrast with the way Molkho remembers his wife: tired, irritated, pessimistic, and always predicting troubles (p. 83). One cannot ignore the girl's dark eyes and her ivory-color skin which remind the reader of her origin. Molkho was attracted to an intellectual woman and their marriage ended with her cancer. Perhaps Molkho's life would have been very different had he married a girl like this--when grown up. It is only after he gains confidence in himself and after he has grasped that intellectual women will not necessarily bring him fulfillment that he is capable of such complete attachment to what the Eastern girl represents.

According to Yehoshua, "Molkho still did not digest his past. He did not make it an integral part of his identity. His Sephardic-Jerusalemite identity still lies in a drawer within him" (Fuks, 1987, p. 27). Perhaps Molkho failed to relate to that part of his identity in a systematic and intellectual manner, but his Sephardic identity, this reader believes, is well inscribed in his personality and explains his principal characteristics.

The Sephardic-Ashkenazic issue appears in the novel also in other ways. The reader confronts various Sephardic Jews in various situations in the course of the novel (pp. 17, 22, 23, 27, 28, 92, 144, 156, 160, 161, 163, 169, 174, 300). In general, Sephardic-Ashkenazic relations are treated in the novel with considerable compassion. Molkho cares for his mother-in-law, a German-born Israeli who "was a cultured, educated woman who read books and went to concerts" (p. 13). "Though she had never thought particularly highly of him, he knew that she felt a subtle affection for him" (p. 23). Molkho's mother, who "had always been afraid of her daughter-in-law" (p. 15) and who later wishes her widowed son to remarry, speaks of his choosing a woman who is suited to him, one with a mentality to which he is accustomed (Hebrew, 1987, p. 61), who is closer to him blood-wise (p. 150); she does not, however, explicitly mention the factor of being Ashkenazic or Sephardic. Molkho admires Jews of German origin as represented by his wife and her family. His attraction to Berlin, however, is motivated by his latent desire to take his deceased wife, who had never adjusted to Israel, back to Berlin. Since this is impossible, he takes Nina back to Berlin instead. Molkho's seriocomic complaint that he could "become a Christian ... even a Moslem," but there's no way he could "become a German Jew" (p. 53), reveals some awareness of the gulf separating him from Jews of German background. When Molkho meets the family of the legal adviser of his office, her family takes a liking to him and appreciates him. He makes a point of his being an "Asian" (p. 75) Israeli-born Sephardic Jew: "I'm a fifth-generation Sephardi in this country ... and Europe is another world to us" (p. 72).

A Jew of Indian origin sees Molkho as "one of them"--one of the Near Eastern Jews, and so he hopes that Molkho will not give them trouble for no reason (Hebrew, 1987, p. 167; English, 1989, p. 185: "I told him ... that you were a reasonable man and would give folks like us a fair hearing"). Molkho has never experienced the feeling of deprivation due to his Sephardic origin; only once he feels bitterness for having to carry a heavy box: "they took a *Sephardi* porter," he thinks when he has to carry Nina's heavy stuff (Hebrew, 1987, p. 272; English, 1989, p. 292: "they must think I'm their native porter").   However, this appears to be more like a humorous grumbling than a serious complaint.   The reader also may think of the story by David Shahar, "The Two Porters," telling about two Sephardic porters, one of whom is dishonest and violent.

Ben-Ya'ish, a practical local leader of Near Eastern Jews, reminds us of Yaish, the title character in Hazaz' four-volume novel of that name; the choice of that name might suggest the complex of virtues which stands out in Hazaz' description of the Yemenite Jews. Furthermore, in Arabic the word ya'ish means "will live"; unlike Molkho's wife, the practical Ben-Ya'ish will find a way to survive and to sustain others.   It is ironic that the Indian Jew describes the original population of Zeru'a as comprised of Indians, North Africans, and Tunisian Jews and "some Israelis" (Hebrew, 1987, p. 149; this is not reflected in the 1989 English translation, p. 164); he accepts that Sephardic Jews are not considered to share in the latter term.

Molkho's very practical profession, accounting, is not incidental.   It illustrates the sense that Sephardic Jews are involved more in the applied fields and occupations than in artistic fields.   In the novel, being an accountant connotes a mode of living and of character: it suggests keeping balance, order and thrift.   Molkho, however, is very conscious of his own "balance" and is free neither of greed nor of small deceits.

For a long time, Yehoshua avoided the subject of the Ashkenazic-Sephardic issue.   Both Ashkenazic and Sephardic authors who wrote about it were often trapped by such pitfalls as sentimentalism, stereotypes, or an extremist or apologetic approach. Yehoshua wrote more about Sephardim than about Near Eastern Jews: Arditi, Veducha, Calderon, Naomi (partially Sephardic), Molkho. Levana and Mizrahi (in A Late Divorce), Near Eastern Jews, are marginal characters.   In Levana, Yehoshua provided a clear example of prejudice against Near Eastern Jews.   Yehoshua's Sephardic characters--Arditi, Calderon--have serious faults. Yehoshua is not apologetic and has no need to beautify Sephardim. Veducha is fascinating; Molkho is not faultless.   The relationships between Sephardic and Ashkenazic Jews are troubled: the marriage of Naomi and Yehuda, the relations between Calderon and Zvi or between Arditi on the one hand and Adam and Asya on the other, the relations between Kedmi and Levana--all these are problematic. "Natalie" gives her body to Asa for money; Zvi gives his body to Calderon for money too, even though it is not done so blatantly. Even the relations between Molkho and his wife are complicated in many ways. Musa, having the advantage of physical strength over Yehuda, murders him.

Yehoshua's most important contribution to a literary depiction of this issue is probably the character of Molkho. Through this character Yehoshua conveys that balance, moderate attitudes, and wisdom are more important as individual and national assets than intellectualism; pessimistic criticism can be an individual and national burden, while wise, realistic acceptance is a virtue. Israel's future depends on the type of the Sephardic Molkho who despises the "feverish ... gleeful, intellectual glitter of ... clever, twist-all mind" (p. 139). Molkho is the author's literary response to all those who fear a future in which Sephardic views could constitute the dominant element in Israel. In the story "Extended Horizon" by Hayim Hazaz, one of the characters, a student, says:

> Within a few years the Near Eastern Jews will constitute a majority in Israel.... In the end, we will become a Near Eastern nation.... All the qualities which took root in us during two thousand years of exile and which made us a European entity will disappear. The question is: Is it possible to leave the Jewish people, Jewish history and, moreover, the destiny of the country in the hands of the Near Eastern Jews? Will they know how to develop it, defend it, to give their lives for it? I am very doubtful....

Jehoshua Kenaz in his 1986 novel *Hitganvut yehidim* presents similar opinions expressed by various characters (e.g., pp. 555-559). Molkho is the answer to these worries. Not only is he not a cause for worry, but he is the one who can secure Israel's future.

In my opinion, Yehoshua conveys a latent message to Israeli society: the future of Israel depends upon a moderate, well-balanced character as exemplified in the Sephardic Molkho and upon the stability and devotion which he inspires so that life can go on even considering the obstacles and the crises. In my opinion, Tsemah's understanding (1987) of Molkho's character has no foundations in the novel. Molkho is not monstrous or repulsive.

The Ashkenazic-Sephardic issue in the novel becomes one of differences between individuals rather than between social groups. In emphasizing the moderate, restrained aspect of Molkho's personality, the author expresses an idea which has been voiced numerous times: the Sephardic Jews are not extremist in their approach to things, and their moderation and deliberation in judgment is a national asset in Israeli society.

SECULAR AND RELIGIOUS JEWS

In *Early in the Summer of 1970* the reader meets the army chaplain, "a khaki-clad prophet." The father became attached to this "man of God" (p. 40) who treated him tenderly while the two were together for the purpose of identifying the son's corpse. The rabbi gives the father hope that perhaps out of the father's suffering, "a new rising may come"; yet, "he is very much afraid of false hopes" (p. 68). The father's attitude toward the chaplain is trusting, perceptive, and respectful.

In *The Lover*, Arditi joined the community of ultra-traditionalist Jews not as a result of personality change but of sheer calculation. In association with that ultra-traditionalist element which never accepted the values of the State of Israel he was best able to desert the army and disappear. For this purpose he painted his grandmother's blue car (symbol of Israel) black (popular color of the clothing of such ultra-traditionalist Jews). Shwartz, Dafi's secondary-school principal, does not forget to curse the "anti-Zionists" (p. 270) whose car collided with his due to his own error. On a symbolic level this collision may be understood as the confrontation between Shwartz's Zionist values and the anti-Zionism of that sector of ultra-traditionalist Jews.

Students of *yeshivot*, talmudic academies, appear on the battlefield: "They came to cheer us up, to restore our faith, sent by their yeshiva to circulate among the troops, to give out prayer-books, to bind *tefillin* (phylacteries) on the young men" (p. 300). But the soldiers knew: "These men are so free ... they come and go at will. They have no obligations" (p. 301). Even in time of war there is a definite gulf separating secular from religious Jews: "I could see that they were a little scared of us, a little wary" (p. 304). Arditi claims that he did not join the ultra-traditionalist Jews in Jerusalem out of choice: "Did I have an alternative? Where else could I go? Where could I hide ...?" (p. 311). He quickly perceived "how efficient they were, how well organized, how disciplined," unlike the secular Israelis. He learned that "they lived a life apart in the land in their closed order" (p. 316). He enjoys the shelter they provided for him while avoiding giving them "a clear sign ... that I linked my fate to theirs" (p. 318).

Reading the novel *A Late Divorce*, one witnesses many signs of a weakening of the role and status of religion in Israeli life. According to Kedmi, religious Israelis are "taking over this country" and "before long we won't even be allowed to drive a car on Saturday. We'll have to get around on roller skates" (p. 316). During the grotesque divorce ceremony when Rabbi Subotnik tries to convince Naomi that marriage is holy in God's eyes, Naomi responds, "God, what are you talking about? Who is that?" and again, "I don't want to hear another word about it. Not another meaningless word. Please understand that God means less than nothing to me. I don't want to hear another word about it" (p. 279). Naomi, of course, is not alone in this. For example, Dr. Ne'eman ("loyal," an ironic use of the word) of the mental hospital says that the Seder is "only a ceremony" and he adds, "I don't believe in it either" (p. 288). He is disloyal and unfaithful to his religion (unlike Dr. Ne'eman who represents Moses in Agnon's famous short story, "A Whole Loaf." The term "ne'eman" is used of a loyal and faithful person).

Gadi informs Yehuda, his grandfather, that he had never been in a synagogue until Yehuda came to Israel; Kedmi, the boy's father, had never taken him to a synagogue (pp. 311-312). And, of course, Yehuda doesn't enlighten his grandson concerning religious values either. When Gadi finally enters a synagogue building it is a nursery school temporarily serving as a synagogue and they come across it quite by accident. And his grandfather who took him there is also remote from religion.

The descriptions of religious ceremonies in the novel indicate a lack of intent, faith, and content. The family meal in a restaurant, a meal paid for by Calderon, is indicative of a distance from tradition, and one notes, for example, that the meal was served by an Arab waiter (p. 333). But it is the Passover season that most clearly reveals the crisis of religion and tradition in Israel. During the Seder, Jews emphasize their redemption from exile, their sense of family togetherness, and the importance of transmitting their heritage from generation to generation. Traditionally, the mother is the "queen" of the Seder; in the novel, however, the mother, a patient in the mental hospital, is unable even to be with her family on that occasion. Asa goes to his parents-in-law's for the Seder and so he, too, is not with his own family; and the father, traditionally looked upon as the "king" of the Seder, is planning his return to the Diaspora as a matter of his own choosing. Kedmi has bread in his house, and the family is marked with hostility and separation. Instead of redemption there is Yehuda's plan to leave Israel to return to the Diaspora; instead of transmitting the Jewish heritage and honoring it, one notes only the desecration of that heritage. The five ceremonies of the Seder nights are, hence, not indicative of fulfilling the way of tradition but rather of the destruction of that tradition in the lives of Israelis. Kedmi wrapped the *matsa* (unleavened bread) in a newspaper and he gave his son wine to take with him to school for the Seder ceremony after he himself "tasted it and made a face" and he gave him "some old leaves" of lettuce (p. 4) to take to the same Seder. It should not come as a surprise that when Gadi was asked about the school-Seder and about what he did in it, he responded that he had Seder at school, that he recited the prayers and sang, but also that all this meant nothing to him (p. 9). A feeling of family disintegration pervades the Seder at Ya'el's house; there is bread in the house and no meaningful attitude toward the festival. Then at the grotesque Seder in the mental hospital, the zealot, Rabbi Subotnik, tells the mental patients, "... but also, you are chosen, do you know? Also you have sparks of holiness; also you belong to God's covenant ... all of you" (p. 293). Further examples abound. On the Seder night at Dina's parents, Yehuda asked Dina and Asa about their Seder and Asa snapped with a sharp sideways look that the Seder was "Sederlike" while Dina "didn't turn to look at him" (p. 324). Asa's answer is clearly cynical and expresses contempt not only for that particular Seder but probably for the entire tradition of the Passover Seder. The destruction of his family life marks Calderon's Passover--motivated by lust, he drives to Zvi on Passover. The world and values of the Seder are turned upside down.

Even Dina who had come from a religious family left her parents' traditional way of life; she is detached, however, from her new environment. It is possible that her sexual problems, her inability to open up to her husband and to engage in sexual relations with him, are indicative of her fear of and reservations concerning the secular environment to which she is attracted but which she is unable to absorb and accept.

Religion still maintains formal strength in Israeli life. Naomi and Yehuda cannot obtain a divorce without the rabbi and without submitting to Jewish legal tradition in matters of marriage and divorce. (Yehoshua does not deal with the Jewish legal questions concerning the validity or lack of validity of a bill of divorce given to a woman who is sufficiently mentally ill to be committed to a mental institution.)

In *Five Seasons*, Yehoshua describes two religious Israelis, Uri and Ya'ara. Both are searching for meaning in their lives and they live penniless (p. 220), remote from the materialistic way of life of many Israelis. Uri offered to let Molkho marry Ya'ara, who was unable to bear children to Uri, so that Uri could then marry another woman. Ya'ara appears as the sad response of a certain Israeli song, a nostalgic song which raises the question, where are those girls of the pre-State period with their pony-tails and pioneer-type dresses (*sarfan*)? Ya'ara, one of those devoted, idealistic, charming girls, grew up and is now searching for meaning in her life; she is economically destitute and has had numerous miscarriages. She is the answer to the question in the enchanting song. She is strange, slow, fearful, passive, without a real vocation, working as an uncertified nursery-school teacher's aide. Molkho wonders: "Was she still bleeding from her miscarriages? Would she be penetrable or blocked by debris? Was he meant to heal her or put her out of her misery? For he did want to heal her, he thought" (p. 232).

Her husband, Uri Adler, is an intellectual, a former follower of Joseph Shekhter (p. 210), who constantly inquires about the meaning of life and who, at the time of the story, is attempting to understand the world and life of Orthodox Jews. Uri is genuinely interested in the way authentic Jewish tradition relates to moral issues (p. 210, 212-213), and to this end he is interested in being among Orthodox Jews and acquiring their confidence. But while Uri is "looking for the Meaning," "for the purpose of it all," Molkho asks mockingly: "He told us that in the movement thirty years ago--but what has he found since then?" (p. 244).

The relationship between secular and religious Jews in Israel sometimes culminates in a hostility accompanied even by physical violence. Yehoshua does not take any extreme stand regarding this issue. The army chaplain in *Early in the Summer of 1970* is described through the eyes of the father as a caring and compassionate man; the ultra-traditionalist Jews in *The Lover* are described through the sympathetic eyes of Arditi, who required their shelter and who, as an outsider, became an uncommitted insider. In *A Late Divorce* we witness the weakening of the role and status of religion in Israeli life. The implied author relates to this phenomenon with pain; on the one hand the characters have a certain need for tradition and they comply with some of its ceremonial aspects, but tradition cannot contribute meaning to their lives because their actions are superficial and lack intent and belief. Uri and Ya'ara in *Five Seasons* did not resolve their search for purpose and meaning in life by being among Orthodox Jews. As in the case of Arditi in *The Lover*, the secular Uri and Ya'ara join religious Jewry at a time of crisis and are both inside participants and outside observers at the same time.

In his book *Bizkhut hannormaliyut* (pp. 27-73; 105-140), Yehoshua maintains that life in the Diaspora avoids the conflict between religion and secularism, between state and religion, because there the foreign state decides such matters. The strongest expression of the conflict between state and religion is found in *The Lover*, when Arditi avoided military service by joining the ranks of ultra-traditionalist Jews.

Rather than take a clear-cut stand, Yehoshua's novels depict the complexity of the issues involved in the relationship between religious and secular Jews in Israel. The issues are many and their resolution complicated. Yehoshua's contribution is evident in his relating to them in a moderate manner, depicting the characters on both sides as human beings with both virtues and faults, in his avoiding preconceived hostile attitudes, and in his presenting complexities of some problems and conflicts related to some of these issues rather than seeking a simple, one-sided solution.

EMIGRATION - "THE ILLNESS OF DIASPORA"

In his book *Bizkhut hannormaliyut* (pp. 27-73, 105-140), Yehoshua states that the Diaspora was not imposed upon the Jew but rather that the Jew desired it and still desires it. That desire, to his way of thinking, constitutes a kind of mental ailment.

The source of difficulties in resolving the relationship between state and religion, he claims, is the authoritative image of God, the father-image, while the image of the homeland as a soft mother is repressed. The attitude toward the father, the God, is one of awe; the attitude toward the mother, in contrast, is described in erotic concepts of love and infidelity. The meaning of Zionism is the cessation of the desire to live in the Diaspora and the demand to return to what Yehoshua considers to be a normal, healthful life. The reader notes that in *A Late Divorce*, when Yehuda betrayed the Zionist dream he died.

In the context of discussing his book *Bizkhut hannormaliyut*, Yehoshua explained (Carmel-Flumin, 1986):

> Living in Diaspora seems to be an abnormal situation, a distorted and dangerous one, and normality is to return to your country and to live in the full context of your national identity. The contents of this identity is a separate issue. This belongs to the struggles that every nation leads in relation to the contents of its identity which continuously undergoes change, one connected with

the history, the language and the character of the nation....

In an interview with Shwartz (1986), Yehoshua added:

> I am worried because of this illness which is called Diaspora; I am absolutely frightened in confronting the deep tie of the Arabs to the land and their large population in the area surrounding us.

In *Bizkhut hannormaliyut* (p. 71), Yehoshua thinks that Israel should expose the pathology of the Diaspora, the fact that its existence is schizophrenic. The condemnation of those Israelis who emigrated from Israel (*yordim*) will have a moral validity only when Israel condemns and rejects all of Jewish existence outside of Israel. Arditi in *The Lover*, Yehuda Kaminka in *A Late Divorce*, and Nina in *Five Seasons* may serve as literary examples for Yehoshua's position (ibid., pp. 31-34) that the Diaspora was not something imposed upon the Jews but that they, in fact, desire it. Yehoshua points to the paradox in that while Jews detest the Diaspora, they nevertheless struggle constantly to continue their existence in it rather than fulfill the dream of returning to their own land.

In *The Lover*, Arditi returned to Israel only in order to claim his legacy and then leave again. In the Diaspora he earns his living by various kinds of work, from teaching Hebrew to translating materials for Zionist publications of the Jewish Agency (p. 103). This, of course, is ironic. Gabriel's living among that group of ultra-traditionalist Jews which does not support the Zionist state is only a variation on his leaving the country and deserting the army. Yehoshua recognized that after the 1973 war there were Jews who felt that Zionism had failed and who expressed doubts as to the justification of the existence of the Zionist state; he created Arditi in order to demonstrate an anti-Zionist possibility (according to Yehoshua's own testimony, Baretsky, 1977).

The author relates the story of Israel here through an object, a 1947 Morris car, which symbolizes the State in the novel. The automobile is a British product; this may remind the reader of the Balfour Declaration, a declaration of support for Jewish Zionist aspirations of the British mandate. (The Declaration was approved in 1920 and was incorporated in the Mandate on Palestine conferred upon Great Britain in 1922.) The light-blue color of the automobile suggests the two light-blue strips of the Israeli flag. When the automobile was conscripted for military use its color was light-blue but the car was painted black, alluding to a coffin during the 1973 war, a time of crisis and death in Israel. It was "a very old model" (p. 88). Gabriel thinks that "the engine won't start, there's a screw missing" (p. 89). Metaphorically, the one "missing screw" can cause the failure of the entire engine; the experienced eye, however, perceives that not only a screw but the engine itself is "ruined and rusted" (p. 90) and needs to be restored. Gabriel tells Adam that he "only came to pick up the inheritance"; he "wouldn't have come back for the load of junk," the Morris, but rather for the "old Arab house" (p. 92). The car is a very old model "painted bright blue"; it is a "little car" (p. 88). Veducha kept the interior of the car in good shape but she required the help of an energetic grandson to take care of the engine; the grandson, however, sees the Morris as "junk" and as a source of money. Adam comments that twenty-five years ago he had a "car exactly like it ... but I don't feel any great nostalgia for it," and now only "some nut, some antique collector" (p. 90) would want it, even though "it's basically quite sound" (p. 92). Twenty-five years ago Adam's desires, values, and problems were also different. During that interval of time it is in his and Arditi's hands—the grandmother had left the 1947 model to Arditi, but he decided to leave and go elsewhere (Yiftah-El, 1977, *Shedemot*). At the end of the novel Adam feels that "the car is going to fall apart under me" (p. 350), and after he drops Na'im in Peki'in he is "standing beside a dead old car from '47 and there is nobody to save me" (p. 351)—he is no longer the miracle repairman and it is Hamid, the Arab leader of his employees, who must come to his rescue. The disintegration of the car is analogous to the problems which threaten to destroy Israel.

The repair of the car, its restoration and "resurrection" allude to the restoration of the State of Israel. During the war it resembled a coffin. Given into the hands of Arditi, nothing is going to help it, and it is only bound to disintegrate by the end of the novel. Hamid, the Arab, is the only hope for saving Adam by repairing the "dead old car." In this context of emigration the reader recalls that Gabriel could not afford to repair the car which his grandmother had preserved. In order to evade his obligations to the Israeli army he altered the color of the car and he waited for his grandmother's death in order to sell it and leave. But even Adam, who is able to repair and maintain it, is tired and needs the Arab's help in order to repair the "dead" car (p. 351), while he himself does not feel "any great nostalgia for it" (p. 90). The signals point to a clear danger to Israel's future.

Yehoshua maintains that a connection exists between his essays and the book *Bizkhut hannormaliyut*, and his novel *A Late Divorce*. This he expressed in an interview with Beser (1982):

... here is in this novel an ideological layer ... which is connected with questions that I have been dealing with over these last years; these questions are Diaspora and Israel and the homeland, the disturbed balance (as I wrote in my book, *Bizkhut hannormaliyut* ...) between the father and the mother in the consciousness of the Jewish people--the father, God, the mother, and the homeland--the disturbance of this balance is very ancient in our collective consciousness, in our collective myth; this matter is present in the novel and it exists in some ideological foundations of the novel.

The sixty-six-year-old Yehuda Kaminka is willing to surrender his share of their community-property apartment for the divorce so that he can go back to the United States, marry Connie, and live in physical and spiritual exile. Kaminka, who had previously immigrated from Russia to Israel, now chooses to return to the Diaspora. Initially sent by Israel, he decided to remain after his official position terminated, "The Apostle to the Exile who reexiled himself and now spends his days in heated underground shopping centers fingering the fabric of dresses, checking out the millinery aisles waiting for Connie" (p. 314). Yehuda, the Israeli who is not capable of living in peace with himself and his family in his own country, was sent to help Jews elsewhere. Yehuda himself, however, blames Israel for his decision to leave:

... during my first year abroad I missed the landscape terribly; afterwards I grew attached to others so breathtaking especially in autumn and in spring. We who saw this country being born thought we could always bend it to our will, always correct it if it went off course; yet here it was out of control full of strange mutations: different, odd permutations, new sources of unexpected energy. The clear lines have been hopelessly smudged. If only it could at least be a homeland. When will it settle down to be one? (p. 313)

Despite the fact that it was his own decision to leave Israel he nonetheless thinks, "And me with my bridges burned. Disinherited. Homeland, why weren't you a homeland?" (p. 345). And again, "Homeland, why can't you be a homeland?" (p. 348). Yehuda also blames his wife for his moving to Diaspora: "I've signed away my home ... so she's finally drawn me away. At last she has managed to uproot me. I am being punished by her for not being crazy too, for not having gone over the brink with her" (p. 325). Yehuda will not assume responsibility for his decision not to fulfill his responsibilities as an Israeli citizen. Precisely because he feels guilty he cannot admit that he made an independent decision and instead casts the blame upon the State or upon his wife. Eventually, he decides that he did not want to give away his "home"; he recognizes his inability to detach himself from his homeland as well as from his share of the property. This novel suggests that the Israeli emigrant wants the benefits of the divorce; he desires the bill of divorce which will enable him to begin a new life but he is unwilling or unable to take the divorce seriously.

Yehuda Kaminka is ill; his malady is the illness of the Diaspora. Even though he did not achieve any meaningful success in America, he nevertheless prefers remaining there to living in Israel. His attempt to detach himself from his past, from his homeland and family, culminates in his being murdered and so he could not enjoy the love, appreciation, and success he hoped to find in the United States. The murder-scene in which Yehuda faces the fence, the wall of the mental hospital with the pitchfork, symbolizes the dead-end situation of the emigrant who leaves but cannot detach himself from his Israeli homeland. Yehuda's physical death at the end appears to suggest the emotional death of those Israelis who attempt to detach themselves by pretending to find success, status, and perhaps love in Diaspora.

Other characters in the novel might actually share the same illness. For example, when Asa asked the prostitute who called herself Natalie, "Are you Israeli?", she responded, "For the time being" (p. 63). Might the Israeli dream of emigration be depicted here as a dream of prostituting one's skills in order to attain an unrealistic dream elsewhere? When Kedmi tells his son, Gadi, that Yehuda, the boy's grandfather, will go back to America after being in Israel "for a few days to take care of some business" (p. 3), the boy asks, "For good?", and Kedmi responds, "For the time being," the identical answer that Natalie, the prostitute, gave to Asa. It would appear then that the Jew is still a wandering Jew lacking any stable attitude as to where he wants to live and with a constant desire to live in the Diaspora. Kaminka says to his daughter-in-law, Dina, "There is so much to see in the world—me, I am always curious for more. I have told him [Asa – L.H.] that the two of you should come to stay with us for a while in America. I will find him some work there, some postgraduate position" (p. 107). We do not hear any word of protest from either Dina or Asa regarding such a proposal.

Both Arditi in *The Lover* and Yehuda in *A Late Divorce* remain problematic characters for whom leaving Israel does not help to rid themselves of their neurotic existence in the country. The connection with the Diaspora is tempting and emigration is viewed as a national danger.   The Diaspora appears as a neurotic solution for a neurotic existence in Israel, one which does not resolve the real problems of the characters but nevertheless endangers Israeli existence by way of its temptations.

In *Five Seasons*, Molkho accepts Israel and it never crosses his mind to leave. His wife, however, is bitter and pessimistic, unhappy and critical (pp. 28, 33, 37, 44, 138); her intellectual qualities contribute neither to her happiness nor to her acclimation.   Her cancer is symbolic of the problems of European Jews in Israel as the author perceives them: "the cancer of his wife symbolizes the illness of European Jews in Israel. Molkho is a native, in the most natural sense. He accepts Israel unconditionally" (Huppart, 1987, quoting Yehoshua).   The criticism of Israel by Molkho's wife ends with an illness which can be neither controlled nor cured; the diseased cells spread and eventually lead to her death.   A person who criticizes Israel so severely, it appears, either completely loses or decides to do what Nina did: she came to Israel from Russia, but never liked the country, and Molkho helped take her back to Berlin whence she managed to return to Russia.   It is most interesting to note that in this novel, the bitterness often ascribed to Sephardic Jews is given instead to these two characters (Nina and Molkho's wife), both Jews of European origin.   The Indian Jew from Zeru'a overcomes his illness, but Molkho's wife succumbed because of her lack of positive spirit.

Returning the Russian woman to Russia is a symbolic act: Molkho takes the immigrant who so disliked Israel back to her place of origin.   His own attraction to Berlin is explained not by his attitude toward the legal adviser who failed to seduce him but rather by his desire to send his deceased wife back to Berlin since she had never adjusted to Israel.   (In this context, note the description of Berlin in the article of Tsippora Kagan, Yehoshua's colleague at Haifa University, in *Igra*, 1984, edited by Zakh, a German-born Israeli colleague of Yehoshua.) Yehoshua views the Holocaust as the final and absolute proof of the failure of the Diaspora (*Bizkhut*, p. 19), and it is significant, in his eyes, that the Germans--with whom the Jews thought they shared a cultural and spiritual symbiosis--provided Jews with this proof, one which, in the novel, however, does not lessen the bitterness of Molkho's wife who is incapable of acclimating and enjoying life in her new country.

In a 1987 interview, Yehoshua anticipated that should Russia allow Jews to emigrate, they would either remain there or go to America.   This is "the eternal amusement of the Jews, their pseudo-masochistic games: when they can go to Israel, they don't; and when they cannot, they long for it" (Levi, p. 23). Nina, in *Five Seasons*, is the literary substantiation of this argument.

In each successive stage of Yehoshua's writing the emigration problem appears more important. In *Early in the Summer of 1970* when the son returns to Israel with his wife and son, both American citizens, we find no evidence of hesitation: the son wishes to apply his knowledge acquired in America for the benefit of Israel. In *The Lover* only Arditi emigrated from Israel, but he is a detached man, with a psychiatric history; he came to Israel to claim his legacy, to sell the house of his grandmother and go back. Yehuda in *A Late Divorce* was willing (at the beginning) even to give up his share of the house (his home, his attachment to his homeland) in order to be free to leave Israel as a divorced man. Even though Yehuda is literally insane, his emigration is even more alarming due both to his age and to the fact that he was once an idealistic pioneer and educator; he has strong roots in Israel, children and grandchildren, and his ties to the Hebrew language are exceedingly strong.

The religious background of Yehuda's daughter-in-law, Dina, and her creative work in Hebrew do not lead her to protest her father-in-law's suggestion that she and her husband stay in America for a while (p. 66). The prostitute "Natalie" is not permanently committed to Israel (p. 63)--her dream of emigration is not different from those of Yehuda and Arditi. They utilize the skills they acquired in Israel in order to make a living in Diaspora. But the problem of emigration appears even harsher in *Five Seasons*--not because of the Russian Jewish Nina who craves Russia so much and cries for it, but because of Molkho's wife, a representative of a large segment of the population: Israelis who live in Israel without ever adjusting to it, who constantly criticize it--as rooted as they are in Israeli life, their heart is elsewhere. The fact that Molkho's wife was an educator who also trained young teachers (p. 20) reminds us of another educator--Yehuda Kaminka--who actually left Israel.

Emigration appears as a harsh reality of Israeli life. In the works of Yehoshua the harshness grew gradually. In his latest novel, *Five Seasons*, Yehoshua has made a critical statement: one has to accept Israel in order to adjust to it and constructively contribute to it. Physical presence is not a sufficient commitment--the heart and body should be committed in order to be an active participant in solving its problems in place of creating them or criticizing their existence.

CONCLUDING REMARKS, AND THE CRITICS ON A. B. YEHOSHUA

Nurit Gerts (1976) contends that the fiction of the literary generation of the 1960s in Israel that includes Yehoshua, Oz, and Kahana-Karmon, shares a common thematic structure which is composed of four stages: 1) The characters yearn for nature, people, Godlike authority, for a time beyond the present and for a different space in which dramatic and exceptional events will occur; meanwhile, they live routine lives in a desolate reality.   2) In the plot, the characters attempt to connect with the world of their yearnings through exceptional dramatic events in distant places.   3) The attempt connects instead with destruction or death.   4) Ultimately the characters return to the initial stage of detachment and to their desolate daily reality and abandon their yearnings.

This thematic structure, according to Gerts, dominates poetic aspects such as style, structure, characters, and the narrator-type. Furthermore, Gerts contends that this thematic structure not only is applicable to the individual characters but parallels the social reality: 1) Society is under siege and experiences alienation; having failed to deepen its roots in nature, Israeli society is composed of lonely individuals who lack contact with one another, common ties with a meaningful past, and hope for a meaningful future.   2) This society attempts to fulfill a Zionist dream of social redemption, but the dream is distorted. The subjects of yearning are a hostile nature (one in which the Jew did not successfully integrate), and present enemies (who were also the enemies of past generations). These enemies pose threats of war and of destruction through war; hence the contact with them is through war.   3) The movement of redemption, fulfillment of the distorted dream, is war.

In a later publication (1983, pp. 79-82), Gerts discusses *Early in the Summer of 1970* and *The Lover*. There she contends that Yehoshua's characters are marked by absolute loneliness and detachment. A drastic disastrous event disrupts their loneliness. The change, it turns out, is merely imaginary and simply restores the original situation of detachment.

Gerts' model, even considering its rigidity and questionable aspects, is nevertheless applicable, to a significant but qualified extent, to the principal characters in the works we have examined, except *Five Seasons*. The father in *Early in the Summer of 1970* is isolated and lonely. His loneliness is disrupted when he is informed of the death of his son; once he has learned that his son is still alive he again becomes lonely and isolated. Adam, in *The Lover*, is lonely, isolated, and bored. War took the lover away and provided him with a task: to search for the lover. Once he has found him, he resumes his state of isolation. The Kaminkas, in *A Late Divorce*, appear lonely. Divorce brings a certain degree of intensity to their lives, but this leads to an even worse situation as Yehuda is killed. Gerts' model might not apply at all to *Five Seasons*, for in that novel, despite the death of Molkho's wife, there is a way out: with the passage of time, Molkho recovered and, through his self-awareness, found a key to the resolution of his situation following her death. Gerts' model is not as applicable to the social structure. The weight, meaning, and place of the nature, the enemies, the siege, and the war differ from one work to another to such a large extent that generalizations become hardly applicable.

There is no question that in these novels Israeli society is described in dark colors. One might view this in perspective by remembering that the characters are individuals, that the narrator intentionally chose to focus on particular sectors of Israeli society, that the tone of these works comes to warn of what may happen, and that only particular periods of the history of Israeli society are described in the novels. But even allowing for all these factors, the cumulative portrayal of Israeli society in Yehoshua's novels is harsh. A society characterized by such a degree of excitement and intensity, a society with such ambitions and aspirations, heritage, and struggles, pays the price for them.

Natan Zach (1983) attempted to address the question why contemporary Israeli writers such as Tammuz, Shabtai, Be'er, Oz, Kenaz, and Yehoshua deal to such an extent with madness, suicide, murder, alienation--in sum, with the dreadful aspects of life. The Holocaust, war, and rapid changes in Israel, he suggested, may explain the frustration, the helplessness, and the distress of the characters in contemporary Hebrew fiction. Zionism did not achieve the shaping of a new and healthy human being in Israel; instead, man as reflected in literature is quite ill. The strangeness, the distress and loneliness, the folly and death and alienation in contemporary Israeli prose might be explained also by the struggle between the generations, by the collapse of ideology and values, by the sobering reaction to hopes that were perhaps larger-than-life, by the lack of cultural identity on the part of the second and third generation of Israelis, and perhaps by the fact that literature, in this case, precedes reality and serves as a mirror reflecting the moods, the fears, and the yearnings of a new generation. According to Zach, many characters in the stories and novels of contemporary Israeli writers die because they are romantic characters who lack the ability to survive in an unromantic world. Their authors, he asserts, must instead allow their characters to live in a normal reality which is neither hell nor paradise, one free of fictitious, unattainable models and abstract and absolute ideals.

Zach's contention is insightful and enlightening. But it does not provide a complete answer to the question. The problem of the characters in Yehoshua's novels does not lie in their being romantic characters unable to survive in a non-romantic world. Their difficulty is absolute, not simply relative to a non-existent, naive, and romantic model, to some abstract ideal or paradise. His characters do not suffer simply because they have discovered that the Israeli state, that Zionism, socialism, love, etc., are subject to compromise (see Zach, p. 22), that they live in the shadow of some naive and romantic model, but because their lives themselves are unbearably troubled.

The disintegration of the Israeli family is a microcosm which mirrors the shattering of the Zionist dream. The family unit is composed of troubled individuals who suffer not only because of their own problems but also because of the other members who compose the family--spouse, parents, offspring. Along with emigration, the Ashkenazic-Sephardic and the religious-secular conflicts weaken Israel. While the Israeli has attained a certain measure of economic satisfaction, he is crushed by his emotional problems. The Arabs, in contrast, are awake, potent, and energetic. Consumed from inside, the Israeli society will not endure unless it becomes aware of its ailments and determines to cure them.

The basic contribution of these novels to Israeli society lies in the vivid portrayal of the internal destruction that is occurring, a destruction which Israeli society refuses to see as marks of national disaster. One may emphasize Yehoshua's successful portrayal of characters in a way which is indicative of perspective, balance, and sensitive perception free of stereotypes--Arabs, Sephardic Jews of the old Israeli settlement, religious Jews, emigrants, and others; one may emphasize Yehoshua's success in perceiving emigration from Israel as symptomatic of a larger problem which he calls "the illness of Diaspora"; or his success in illustrating the destruction which Israel will inflict on itself if it does not cure the illnesses involving family life, relations between Arabs and Jews, conflict between Ashkenazic and Sephardic Jews, between religious and secular Jews, emigrants and faithful citizens.

But Yehoshua's major contribution, we might suggest, is his creation of the character Molkho. The implied author of these literary works resembles Molkho in his patience, moderation, and sense of balance, in his ability to perceive many facets, in his lack of pretensions as he prefers wisdom to sharpness for the sake of sharpness, and in his being able to weigh things and his appreciation of the art of survival.   When Yu'ara tells Molkho that her husband Uri is searching for a purpose in life, Molkho says: "But isn't life itself a Purpose ... To get through as best you can before Death comes for you?" (p. 244). The fact that Molkho is imperfect does not prevent him from being a constructive, stable, reasonable citizen. He is a positive human element in the Israeli society. The Israeli society does not need to wait for perfect characters in order to assure its survival.

Survival in itself is a task: it is also the prerequisite for any betterment.

Israeli society accepts Yehoshua for his literary achievements. But it is also in need of a preacher who denounces it for its illnesses and who cares enough for it to diagnose these illnesses and to tie his destiny with its own. As someone concerned with curing the ill spots, Yehoshua would find as many ill parts or more in any other society. He is concerned, however, with the cure of Israeli society.   The question is, "Will you still murder and commit adultery ... and walk after other gods ... and come and stand before me in this house ... and say: 'We are delivered?'" (Jeremiah 7:9-10). Posing the question is the first step toward betterment. Recalling that "Thy destroyers and they that made thee waste shall go forth from thee" (Isaiah 49:17), is a summons to take the precautions necessary to assure the continuation and survival of a strong nation in a strong land.

NOTES

1.   The term "Sephardic" here includes Near Eastern Jews.

BIBLIOGRAPHY

Aharoni, Mikhal.   "Na'ar aravi bemishpaha Yehudit."   *Bemahane Gadna'*, no. 3 (449), Nov. 1978, 10-11.

140   EQUIVOCAL DREAMS

Alter, Robert, ed. *Modern Hebrew Literature.* Behrman House, New York, 1975, 353-356.
Balaban, Avraham. "Hamme'ahev--de'ah aheret." *Yediot aharonot,* April 15, 1977, 3.
Baretsky, Nurit. "Nahuts omets lev likhtov." *Ma'ariv,* Feb. 18, 1977, 6.
Bartana, Ortsion. "Sippur marshim--umefutsal." *Davar,* Masa, March 6, 1987.
Barzel, Alexander. *Mashm'aut vetsura.* Cherikover, Tel-Aviv, 1976, 76.
Barzel, Hillel. "Pritsot tabu". *Alei-Siah,* Dec. 1977, no. 4-5, 7-18.
_____. "Gerushim me'uharim." *Alei-Siah,* no. 19-20, 86-108.
Barzilai, Yitshak. *Lashon, sifrut ve'arakhim.* Hadoar, vol. 63, no. 33, Aug. 10, 1984, 535-537.
Baumgarten, Murray. "The Car Key." *The Jerusalem Post Magazine,* July 19, 1977, 13.
Beser, Yakov. "Hammoah hu hammiklat ha'aharon shel haherut." *Hotam,* June 11, 1982.
Betsalel, Yitshak. *Hakkol katuv besefer.* Hakkibbuts hammeuhad, Tel-Aviv, 1969, 151-158.
Blat, Avraham. "Bema'galei hazman." *Hatsofe,* Nov. 11, 1977, 4.
_____. "Haroman bekhoved hazman." *Hatsofe,* Nov. 12, 1982.
Boshes, Heda. "Sofer hatsuy me'od." *Ha'arets,* March 6, 1987.
Carmel-Flumin, Nili. An interview. "Min habbeged el ha'or." *Yediot aharonot,* Aug. 15, 1986.
_____. "Bignut happarshanut ha'alegorit." *Itton 77,* Sep. 1982.
Cole, Diane. "A Superb Portrayal of the Israeli Psyche." *The National Jewish Monthly,* Washington, D.C., Feb. 1979.
_____. "Israeli life: Turmoil on the Home Front." *Wall Street Journal,* Europe, Brussels, Feb. 23, 1984.
Feldman, Yael S. "Hatsiyonot al safsal hanne'eshamim." *Hadoar,* vol. 65, no. 14, Jan. 31, 1986.
_____. "Zionism on the Analyst's Couch in Contemporary Israeli Literature." *Tikkun,* vol. 2, no. 5, Nov. 12, 1987, 31-34, 91-96.
Fuchs, Esther. "The Sleepy Wife: A Feminist Consideration of A. B. Yehoshua's Fiction." *Hebrew Annual Review,* vol. 8, 1984, 71-81.
Fuks, Sarit. "Molkho Sephardi tahor." *Ma'ariv,* Jan. 3, 1987, 26-27.
Gants, Hayim. "Haherut lelaket zeradim." *Siman Kri'a,* no. 5, Feb. 1976, 291-294.
Gerts, Nurit. "Me'ora dramati uzmannim aherim." *Siman Kri'a,* no. 6, May 1976, 380-393.
_____. "Sifrut, hevra, historia." *Siman Kri'a,* no. 9, May 1979, 422-443.

_____. "Temurot bassifrut ha'ivrit." *Hassifrut*, no. 29, Dec. 1979, 69-75.

_____. *Hirbet Hiz'ah vehabboker shelemohorat*. Hakkibbuts hammeuhad, Tel-Aviv, 1983.

Gilbo'a, Menuha. "Arba onot ve'od ahat." *Ma'ariv*, Feb. 27, 1987.

Haefrati, Yosef. "Ktsat textim veharasim." *Siman Kri'a*, no. 1, Sep. 1972, 156-159.

Huppart, Shmuel. "Hammerkaz she'ibbed 'et koho hammelaked." *Zehut*, vol. 3, Summer 1983, 190-195.

_____. "An Interview with A. B. Yehoshua." *Hadoar*, vol. 66, no. 16, March 6, 1987, 15-18.

Kagan, Tsippora. "Sifrut al hakkir." *Igra*. Keter, no. 1, 1984, 59-74.

Kalderon, Nissim. "Kalkalot besifrut." *Siman Kri'a*, no. 1, Sep. 1972, 313-316.

_____. *Beheksher politi*. Sifre Siman Keri'a, Hakkibbuts hammeuhad, Tel-Aviv, 1980.

_____. "Hayoetset hammishpatit kotevet leMolkho." *Moaznayim*, vol. 61, no. 2, June 1987, 10-14.

Kaplan, M. S. "A Late Divorce." *International Herald Tribune*, Paris, March 16, 1984.

La'or, Dan. "Ben hammetim uven hahayim." *Ha'arets*, Feb. 27, 1987.

Levi, Gid'on. "Hahitpaysut." *Ha'arets*, Musaf, May 15, 1987, 21-24.

Lewis, Anthony. "Corruption Of Power." *New York Times*, April 19, 1979.

Lewis, Stuart. "A Late Divorce." *Kansas City Jewish Chronicle*, March 2, 1984.

Madison, Charles. "A Late Divorce." *Jewish News*, Detroit, Michigan, March 23, 1984.

Meron, Dan. *Pinkas patuah*. Sifriyat Poa'alim, Tel-Aviv, 1979.

Mintz, Alan. "New Israeli Writing." *Commentary*, N.Y., Jan. 1978, 64-67.

_____. "A Late Divorce." *Hadassah Magazine*, March 3, 1984.

Moked, Gavriel. "Sipporet bemivhan." *Ha'arets*, Sep. 17, 1982.

Navot, Amnon. "Dyokan mishpahti bir'y akhur." *Ma'ariv*, Aug. 16, 1982.

Ohad, Michael. "Me'ahev mehapes me'ahev." *Ha'arets*, Feb. 25, 1977.

Oren, Yosef. "Hazono shel A. B. Yehoshua." *Ha'arets*, May 4, 1977, 18, 19.

_____. "Pegishat hamma'arav im hammizrah." *Yediot aharonot*, July 9, 1982.

_____. "Ketsad mitpatterim meidiologia." *Moznaim*, vol. 61, no. 2, 1987, 59-62.

Parlis, Iza. "Hame'ahev--roman hadash shel A. B. Yehoshua." *Hadoar*, vol. 56, no. 36, Aug. 19, 1977, 596-597.

Paz, Miri. "Hakkol ba'arets mitporer veshum davar lo mitporer." *Davar*, March 20, 1987.

Perets, L. "Min hamme'atim hamme'anyenim vehaproblematiyim."
    Zu Haderkh, July 13, 1977, 12-13.
Peri, Menahem, and Kalderon, Nissim. "Likhtov proza." Siman Kri'a,
    no. 5, Feb. 1976, 276-288.
Pomerantz, Marsha. "A Country on the Couch." The Jerusalem Post,
    March 11, 1983.
Ramras-Rauch, Gila. "Motiv hashomer: tenudut utmurot." Bikkoret
    ufarshanut, no. 11-12, Jan. 1978, 151-165.
_____. "Mesirut nefesh 'o hona'h 'atsmit?" Hadoar, vol. 66, no.
    36, Sept 23, 1987, 42-45.
Ra'anan, Natan. "Al nefashot shemats'u mehabber." Proza, Nov.
    1982.
Rotem, Gid'on. "Akudim umutashim." Shedemot, no. 47, Summer
    1972, 57-61.
Rothschild, Sylvia. "The Lover." Jewish Advocate, Boston, Nov.
    1978.
_____. "Noted writer A. B. Yehoshua on Israel's Literary
    Crisis." Jewish Advocate, Boston, Feb. 9, 1984.
Sadan-Lovenshtein, Nili. A. B. Yehoshua—a Monograph. Sifriyat
    Poa'alim, TelAviv, 1981.
_____. "Hamme'ahev." Ma'ariv, March 25, 1977, 37-39.
_____. "Ambivalentiyut ben adam lisvivato." Itton 77, Sep.
    1982.
_____. "Hen vehesed verahamim." Al-Hammishmar, Nov. 5,
    1982.
Shaked, Gershon. "Haomnam rak bithillat kayits--1970?" Siman
    Kri'a, no. 1, Sep. 1972, 150-155.
_____. "Hatsel happarus al kulanu." Yediot aharonot, Feb. 25,
    1977, 1-6.
_____. "Me'ahore kol ze mistater shiga'on gadol." Moznaim,
    Sep. 1982, 12-16.
_____. Gal ahar gal bassifrut ha'ivrit. Keter, Jerusalem,
    1985, 39-64.
_____. Gal hadash bassipporet ha'ivrit. Sifriyat Poa'alim,
    Tel-Aviv, 1971.
Shalev, Mordekhai. "Missipur aktuali letext rituali." Ha'arets, March
    29, 1972, 18-19; April 4, 1972, 14-15.
Shalgi, Mordekhai. "Siyutei or kayits." Davar, July 7, 1972.
Shamir, Ziva. "Arba'a kenisot lapardes." Yediot aharonot, April 29,
    1977, 2-3.
_____. "Ben gola lig'ula." Ha'arets, Nov. 19, 1982.
_____. "Gerushim meuharim--tragikomedia shel ta'uyot."
    Hadoar, vol. 65, no. 1, Nov. 1, 1975, 16-20.
Shenhar, Aliza. "'Etsem mea'tsmenu uvasar mibbesarenu." Al
    hammishmar, April 22, 1977, 6-7.
Shlonski, Rahel. "Gerushim meyuttarim." Ma'ariv, Nov. 9, 1982.

Shwartz, Dror.   An interview.   "Hassofer ke'idi'olog."   *Hadoar*, vol.
   65, no. 60, June 20, 1986, 16-18.
Silver, Marc.   "A.B. Yekoshua's '*The Lover*' a Tour de Force."   *Jewish
   Times*, March 21, 1980.
Strouse, Evelyn.   "Anarchy in Translation."   *The Jerusalem Post
   Magazine*, Feb. 2, 1979, 23.
Tamar, David.   "Ta'uyot sofrim vahakhamim."   *Yediot aharonot*, Dec.
   23, 1977, 2.
Tsammeret, Tsvi.   "Ben 'hamme'ahev' ve'tor happla'ot."   *Shedemot*,
   no. 69, Fall 1979, 106-107.
Tsemah, Adi.   "Kol dor ohev et happoza."   *Maariv*, Oct. 14, 1987.
Urian, Yehudit.   "Lehamit be'ahava."   *Yediot aharonot*, June 2, 1987,
   20.
Yehoshua, A. B.   *Early in the Summer of 1970*.   Doubleday & Co., Inc.
   New York, 1977.
_____.   *Bithillat kayits—1970*.   Schocken, Jerusalem, 1972.
_____.   *The Lover*.   Translated by Philip Simpson.   Doubleday &
   Co., Inc.   Garden City, N.Y., 1978.
_____.   *Hasmme'ahev*.   Schocken, Jerusalem and Tel-Aviv, 1977.
_____.   *A Late Divorce*.   Translated by Hillel Halkin.
   Doubleday & Co., Inc.   Garden City, N.Y., 1984.
_____.   *Gerushim me'uharim*.   Sifre Siman Keri'a, Hakkibbuts
   hammeuhad, Tel-Aviv, 1982.
_____.   *Bizkhut hannormaliyut*.   Schocken, Jerusalem and Tel-
   Aviv, 1984.
_____.   *Five Seasons*.   Translated by Hillel Halkin.   Doubleday &
   Co., Inc.   Garden City, N.Y., 1989.
_____.   *Molkho*.   Sifre Siman Keri'a, Hakkibbuts hammeuhad.
   Keter, Jerusalem, 1987.
_____.   "La'amod mul hammetsi'ut velishpot otah."   *Al
   hammishmar*, April 30, 1971, 8.
_____.   "Any muda' lekhakh shetadmiti kesofer nifga'at 'ekev
   pe'iluti happolitit."   *Maariv*, May 13, 1977.
Yerushalmi, Joseph.   *A. B. Yehoshua—Bibliography 1955-1979*.
   Sifriyat Poa'alim, Tel-Aviv, 1980.
Yiftah-El, Ester.   "Mea'hev ve'ohev."   *Shedemot*, no. 64, Summer
   1977, 61-65.
_____.   "Al shne 'inyanim be'hamea'hev'."   *Alei-Siyah*, no. 4-5,
   Dec. 1977, 34-35.
Yudkin, Leon.   "Multiple Focus and Mystery."   *Modern Hebrew
   Literature*, Tel-Aviv, vol. 3, Autumn 1977, 38-40.
Zach, Natan.   *Kave avir*.   Keter, Jerusalem, 1983.
Zandbak, Shimon.   "Roman shel kolot bilvad?"   *Yediot aharonot*, July
   17, 1983.

DAVID VOGEL AND NATAN ALTERMAN:

A COMPARATIVE STUDY

This study focuses on two poems--one by David Vogel (1891-1944?), the other by Natan Alterman. The study of these poems serves as a point of departure for a discussion of certain poetic and thematic elements found in Vogel's poetry and in Alterman's collection, *Kokhavim bahuts* (*The Stars* Outside, 1938).

The opening poem in David Vogel's volume *Lifne ha-sha'ar ha'afel* (*In Front of the Dark Gate*, 1923), presents major thematic and poetic elements found in much of his poetry,[1] and serves as a motto to Vogel's poetry. In my analysis of the poem, I will refer to those elements that are so typical of much of Vogel's poetry.[2]

The first poem in Alterman's *Kokhavim bahuts* is also a motto to his volume and reflects some of the main poetic and thematic elements of the volume. A comparison of the two motto poems will bring out the differences between the poetic approach of Vogel with his free verse and Alterman with his strict, systematic prosodic devices.

Vogel's first poem is a short lyric poem, as is much of his verse:

לְאַט עוֹלִים סוּסִי
עַל מַעֲלֵה הָהָר,
לַיְלָה כְּבָר שׁוֹכֵן שָׁחוֹר
בָּנוּ וּבַכֹּל.

כְּבֵדָה תַחֲרֹק עֶגְלָתִי לִרְגָעִים
כַּעֲמוּסָה אַלְפֵי מֵתִים.

זֶמֶר חֲרִישִׁי אֶשְׁלַח
עַל פְּנֵי גַלֵּי הַלַּיְל,
שֶׁיַּעֲבֹר לַמֶּרְחָק.

סוּסִי מַאֲזִינִים וְעוֹלִים לְאָט.

My horses climb slowly
On the slope of the mountain,
Night dwells black
In us and in all.

My cart, heavy, squeaks at times
As if burdened by thousands of dead.

I cast a soft song
Upon the waves of the night,
To stretch out to the distance.

My horses listen and climb slowly.

This verse concentrates on the speaker's feelings in the described atmosphere. Typical of Vogel's poetry is that it is not bound to any historical or social events. It does not hold any social or national "message." Time and place are described merely as "night" and a "slope of a mountain"--the immediate components essential for shaping the poetic atmosphere which exist in any country, any year. It is due to the mountain and the silence of the night that the poet's soft song can carry to a distance. Mountain, horses, cart, distance, silence--these convey a feeling of a place far from the city. Indeed, many of Vogel's poems describe village sights and sounds far from the tumultuous urban scene.

The speaker appears as a wanderer making his way alone in darkness on a mountain slope. Wandering, going astray in the darkness on the roads of the world, is a frequent setting for Vogel's poetry. In such a setting darkness is often associated with death. Roads on the mountain slopes, darkness, the wandering of poor, lonely people--a symbolic situation that describes, in many of his poems, the immediate situation, and, poignantly too, the poet's point of view concerning the course of life. The feeling is of pervasive ennui, poverty of hope.[3] The poet says: "We are tired / Let's go to sleep /The edges of the days are tucked in the night, / Are tucked in the death" ("We Are Tired").

Loneliness and death dominate the atmosphere: "But here is night-- / Besides him no one. / Somewhere / An empty wagon escapes down the hill's slope / From the midst of our childhood-- / We all of us died--" ("But Here Is Night"). And in another poem: "We wander through life / Weeping / With empty palms/Held out shaking/ To every passer-by" ("Our Childhood"). Or: "Under a heap of strange shadows, / Beside a black silence / I shall lie / And my heart will ache /And ache" ("A Calm Evening Will Flow").

He sees that "a deep night," blacker than the blackness "of the beloved woman's eyes" has fallen silently on the world ("How Can I See You?"). People in Vogel's poetry "are sitting in darkness." They say, "Our shadows are bigger than we are." The speaker's loneliness in the darkness continues in other poems: "But all I held dear / Have gone into the wilderness/ And I can stretch out a hand / To no one. / I am happy to rest / In the black cradle of night ..." ("I Saw My Father Drowning").

Another time the speaker feels that "Tomorrow won't come. /Tonight will last long. / Children will wake up while it's still dark. /Not knowing for what" ("The Mountain Tops Are Covered in Snow"). In another poem he says: "Through black night / The journey will sweep / Taking me somewhere" ("Through BLack Night").

Again, he says: "In the darkening side-streets / Days will crumble, sunless" ("These Great, Silent Houses").

The poet's view in general is that "All of us, for many days and nights, / Will go secretly ... / Till we come / To the great, dark gate" ("Black Flags Are Fluttering").

Thus Vogel's opening poem expresses the atmosphere and feeling of loneliness, darkness, hard climbing on a mountain slope, and the squeaking of a wagon as if it were loaded with thousands of dead. The poet's imagery is often nonrealistic, full of associations of horror and the domination of death. Vogel avoids demonstratively rich figurative language. In the above poem, sight and sound together shape the feeling of death and straying, darkness and wandering, tiredness and isolation. There are no sharp, visual pictures in the poem. The moody, internal night is drawn by the mind of man, not by his eye.

The situation stressed in Vogel's poetry is typical of people's lives--at least of those lonely ones--wherever and whenever they are. Specific indications of time and place are unnecessary. In the first stanza the speaker states the situation bluntly to himself and to others: "Night dwells black/ In us and in all." If one insists on interpreting "in us" as meaning the speaker and the horses (and not as meaning "in us," the people), the end of the stanza enforces the darkness on everyone and everything. This way of generalizing, through the use of "us" and "we," all lonely people, is typical of Vogel's poetry.

The song serves the speaker of the poem as a means of communication which will redeem him from his loneliness and break his isolation by stretching out to the distance. His song (*zemer*), at the beginning of his poetry volume, expresses the hope that it will serve as a link between him and others. The lines "I cast a soft song /Upon the waves of the night, / To stretch out to the distance," echo the biblical verse, "Cast thy bread upon the water, for thou shalt find it after many days" (Eccl. 11:1). Here the words imply the speaker's hopes that his poetry will be sung far and wide. While Vogel's vocabulary is mainly biblical, direct allusions to the Bible in his poetry are few. The closure of the poem cannot hold hope for the immortality of his poetry because the only visible listeners are his horses, and they are too tired to give him their alert attention. Vogel's unconventional objects are used to describe a given situation, and at times the marginal nonrepresentative aspects and objects are chosen to express the atmosphere, as the slow, tired horses here do by being the listeners of the speaker's song.

Characteristically, the speaker does not claim any impressive virtues: Vogel does not use the chastising tones of social condemnation or the viewpoint of a "prophet-poet."

One notices in the Hebrew version of the line "To stretch out to the distance" (*Sheya'avor lammerhak*) a lack of subordinating and conjunctive links; this seems to be typical of his writing.

The typical closure of the poem--turning us back to the opening sentence with a feeling of cyclic motion--suits the feeling of a man who contemplates his return to dust and his viewing life as a deadlock. The last line is arresting in its cyclic repetition, but also in its second strategic place (first the opening line, then the closing line)--this time as a stanza by itself, the shortest one in the poem. This ending of the poem, which goes back to the beginning, gives a feeling of completion and continuation, implying the endless time of going astray.   The last line is striking because of the rhythmical structure of the poem: until the last line of the third stanza every two lines made a syntactical and rhythmical unit. With the break of this rhythm at the end of the third stanza, one takes a longer pause between the third and the fourth stanzas, with a resulting emphasis on the last two lines of the poem.

One notices a slowing of the rhythm in the second stanza in harmony with the physical heaviness of the cart. This deceleration is most noticeable in the fifth line, which is relatively long--there are long Hebrew words in this line as well--and by the fact that, in contrast, the stanza itself is short.

Each stanza consists of one short sentence which breaks up into short lines, a form which contributes to the unity of each stanza. The sentences are syntactically simple.[4]   Now, the tendency of Vogel's stanza to consist of one short sentence broken up into very short lines, and the lack of syntactical complexity that we find in this poem, are typical of Vogel's poetry in general.   Each line is a syntactical and rhythmical unit; Vogel rarely makes use of enjambement.

The sound of *l*, which appears here 18 times, contributes to the softness of the sound and the atmosphere or mood.   In the second stanza, *g*, *k*, and *q* contribute to the expression of effort, heaviness, and the squeaking of the cart.   The silence and softness are deeper in the third stanza due to the *l*, *sh*, and *z* (*Sheyavor, zemer harishi 'eshlah*); perhaps one can hear in this portion the sounds of *ka'amusa, susay ma'azinim*.   While examining rhymes, sounds, and rhythm, one must keep in mind that the poem is written in Ashkenazic pronunciation,[5] in free verse.   This form, too, is typical of Vogel's poetry.   With a few exceptions, he did not write in a Sephardic pronunciation, and the majority of his poems do not have systematic rhymes or stanza structure.   In most cases they do not have a metrical scheme.

In the course of analyzing Vogel's poem, I mentioned some typical components of it--and they relate to different aspects of his poetry--themes, sights, the basic way the speaker views the world, structure, vocabulary, syntax, and prosody.   I referred to Vogel's usage of the short lyric poem in which many times the closure of the poem takes us back to its beginning and gives us a cyclical motion. Vogel's lyric poetry does not contain social-national messages.   The speaker does not claim any large impressive dimensions, and his poetry is not a "prophecy."   His dimensions are human and his concerns are more individualistic, without pretensions of ideological or national messages.   When Vogel writes "we," he does not refer to a definite ideological, social, or national group with a common experience.   Instead, he refers to people who have common emotional experiences such as loneliness, tiredness, longing for childhood, etc., which bind them to one another.   The speaker appears in the poems as a tired wanderer who is going astray in the darkness; landscapes favor the rural over the urban view; death is found everywhere and dominates every situation.   Vogel's descriptions avoid the direct view. Situations and atmosphere indicate his view of life.   His nonrealistic, horror-filled imagery simply demonstrates his capacity to astonish readers with his imagination.   In Vogel's poetry the nonconventional, marginal object or aspect is preferred for describing feeling, atmosphere, or situation, so that the marginal becomes the

representative.   Vogel's stanzas consist of short sentences which
break to very short lines.   He rarely uses enjambement.   In most
cases his sentence structure avoids syntactical complexity.   Although
he writes in free verse, he devotes special attention to rhythm and
many of his lines are syntactical and rhythmical units.

Alterman, in *Kokhavim baḥuts* (*The Stars Outside*, 1938), uses
the same device: the opening poem of the volume portrays major
thematic elements of the poems that follow.[6]   Alterman's opening
poem is short:

א

*

עוֹד חוֹזֵר הַנִּגּוּן שֶׁזָּנַחְתָּ לַשָּׁוְא
וְהַדֶּרֶךְ עוֹדֶנָּה נִפְקַחַת לָאֹרֶךְ
וְעָנָן בְּשָׁמָיו וְאִילָן בִּגְשָׁמָיו
מְצַפִּים עוֹד לְךָ, עוֹבֵר־אֹרַח.

וְהָרוּחַ תָּקוּם וּבְסִיסַת נְדֻדוֹת
יַעַבְרוּ הַבְּרָקִים מֵעָלֶיךָ
וְכִבְשָׂה וְאַיֶּלֶת תִּהְיֶינָה עֵדוֹת
שֶׁלִּטַּפְתָּ אוֹתָן וְהוֹסַפְתָּ לֶכֶת – –

– – שָׁדַיִךְ רֵיקוֹת וְעִירֵךְ רְחוֹקָה
וְלֹא פַּעַם סָנַדְתָּ אַפַּיִם
לְחֻרְשָׁה יְרֻקָּה וְאִשָּׁה בִּצְחוֹקָהּ
וְצַמֶּרֶת נְשׂוּמַת עַפְעַפַּיִם.

I do not intend to offer a detailed interpretation of the poem, but
instead, will indicate some ways in which the poem serves as a motto
for the entire volume.

In Alterman's poem we find the "wanderer" (*over 'orah*) and the "tune" (*Nigun*)--two crucial elements in *The Stars Outside*. The "tune" is the poetry. The poet's efforts to desert the "tune" are in vain, because the "tune" comes back and imposes itself upon the wanderer-poet. What is permanent in the wanderer's life are the wandering and the "tune": his lack of ties to a definite social frame and his unbreakable tie to this poetry. "Road," "cloud," "tree," "sky," "rain," "wind," and "light," rather than home or wife are expecting him. And he caresses not the laughing woman but the lamb and the gazelle. To the woman, he only bows. Once he has caressed the lamb and the gazelle, he continues on his journey--poor, lonely, and far away from his city. There is no commitment in his life but to his "tune," i.e., to poetry and wandering. On his way he bows to a grove, to a laughing woman, and to the top of a tree, but he does not stop. The woman does not hold him back any more than the treetop or the green grove. They only elicit his admiration.

The poem is representative of Alterman's collection, *The Stars Outside*: in its imagery of the wanderer as the main character, his ties to his poetry, his attraction to the various sights and to their freshness, his attraction to softness, beauty, and innocence as exemplified in the lamb and the gazelle. But the poem is also representative of this poetry volume in its main theme, its vocabulary and figurative language, its meter, rhythm, and rhymes. One can mention here briefly the four-line stanzas, the anapestic meter, the intermittent rhyming, the breaking of the monotony in rhyme by systematic usage of penultimate and ultimate accents (*lashav geshamav; Orekh-Orah*, etc.); the attention to sound within the line--the internal rhymes (*vea'anan beshamav ve'ilan bigshamav; ve'isha bitshoka*); the delight of the insistent, splendid rhymes; the frequent usage of figurative language (*haderekh nifkahat la'orekh; betisat nadnedot ya'avru habberakim; tsameret geshumat afapayim*). Unlike Vogel, Alterman uses "classical" prosodic conventions.

In "The Foreign Poem," in *The Stars Outside*, Alterman deals with some aspects of his verse. He is conscious of the fact that his poetry follows conventional schemes of meter, rhyme, and stanza structure. His words are strong, therefore they do not cry in their poetic "cage"; his lines are recognized in the "strangeness of the metal, in the proud rhythm." The speaker is a poet who does with his words what an artist (e.g., a sculptor) does with his material. In the process of "building" his poem, the poet "tortures" his poem and demands that it "get broken and cry out!"--but the poem does not "break" the poetic conventions (i.e., his strict prosodic structure comes natural and ready, "organic") and the sensitive reader will communicate with it in spite of the "coolness of the clear rhyme" and the prosodic "games" and devices with which the speaker-poet dresses it.

One can mention here other aspects in which the motto poem is representative of the volume: the decorative usage of metaphoric language ("rainy eyelids of a treetop") remote from the concrete and the perceivable; the sentimental approach (the wayfarer caressing the lamb and the gazelle, bowing and worshipping a green grove); the "acrobatic" usage of light (the lights pass over the wayfarer in "a flight of see-saws"). Besides the imagistic aspects, one notices here the usage of symbolic objects and situations, and the shift from the concrete and immediate to the symbolic (e.g., the wayfarer poet who wanders on the roads of the world, the softness and beauty of the lamb and the gazelle). Also characteristic of The Stars Outside is the forming of a situation which does not "reflect" reality, e.g., the cloud and the tree are expecting him, but not the woman. One notices in this short poem the superabundance of sights--road, cloud, trees, wind, lights, grove, etc.--and this superabundance of landscapes is typical of The Stars Outside.

But unlike many other poems in the volume in this poem the abstract concepts and generalizations do not take over the concrete landscapes. In the meantime, we are aware that the concrete experience here is representative of the poet-wayfarer's way of life--his lack of social obligations and roots, his imposed devotion to his "tune," i.e., his poetry, his being empty-handed and in constant motion. This symbolic imagistic tendency is prevalent in The Stars Outside. Also typical of this volume is the poet's emotional distance form, e.g., the woman and the grove, while at times we find in other poems the deflating of the lofty. The positive attitude to the world in this particular poem is also common to the volume at large.

Vogel's poem serves as a motto to his volume, as does Alterman's poem to his volume. Besides the themes which declare their poet's worlds in each poem, the poetic devices used are typical of each writer's volume. Although in both poems one finds the conscious attitude of the speakers to the "tune" or "song" (i.e., poetry), and the main character in both is a wanderer, they differ greatly from one another in many of their poetic devices, and also in their approach to the described worlds: one finds the heavy feeling of death in Vogel's poem; in Alterman's poem there is the joy of life. Vogel's poem expresses a desire to communicate, while Alterman's expresses the desire of the poet to free himself from his "tune." But the poem imposes itself upon the poet and is a conscious choice of the wanderer to have a temporary, brief, unobligating tie with the fascinating sights of the world. Vogel's poem is perhaps a more egocentric one than Alterman's.

Shlonski and Alterman are disciples of the Russian modernist school, while Vogel's modern poetry is close in spirit to German Expressionism.[7]   Some critics express the opinion that Shlonsky treated Vogel's poetry contemptuously.   Vogel's attack on Shlonsky's poetry is devastating.[8]

These poets use different poetic devices and they have different themes and different approaches to the world--but each accomplishes the creation of a poetic work with unity, intensity, and complexity.   Vogel attains unity, intensity, and complexity in his free-verse poem, while Alterman expresses them with his strict attention to prosodic conventions.   Each poet in his own way is successful in making his "tune" or "song" a long-lasting communicative and expressive art.

NOTES

1.   The volume was published in Vienna in 1923.   In 1966 Vogel's collected poems were published under Dan Pagis' editorship. A revised and enlarged edition was published in 1971 by Hakkibbuts hammeuhad .   Pagis includes an introduction with Vogel's biography and the criticism of the poetry, then the poetry itself, indices, and source material.   Pagis' praiseworthy work is a very inspiring and helpful source for any discussion of Vogel's writing.   The third revised and enlarged edition was published by Hakkibbuts hammeuhad in 1975 under the title Kol hashirim.

2.   For translations of Vogel's poetry, see Pagis' index.   See also The Dark Gate, selected poems of David Vogel, translated by A. C. Jacobs (The Menard Press, London, 1976).   My Horses Climb and Other Poems were translated by Harold Schimmel with a "Note to a Translation of Vogel" in Orot: Journal of Hebrew Literature, August 1970, pp. 28-49.   My translation of the poem "My Horses Climb," printed here, differs from Schimmel's translation.

3.   The quotations that follow are from Schimmel's and Jacobs' translations.

4.   Some syntactical elements are discussed by Tsvi Luz in Shevile shira, Eqed, 1974, pp. 77-95.   (Luz's main concern is Vogel's motifs.)

5.   See Pagis, 3rd ed., pp. 52-55 and his article, "From Ashkenazic to Sephardic: A Crisis Reflected in Holograph of David Vogel" (in Hebrew), Hassifrut, vol. 3, no. 1, June 1971, pp. 157-164.

6.   This approach to this poem one finds explicitly in Dan Miron's article, "Nekuddat hammotsa," *Moznaim, Sidra hadasha,* vol. 31, no. 68, 1970.
7.   See Uzi Shavit's article, "Relations between Shlonsky and Vogel," in *Hassifrut,* vol. 4, no. 2, April 1973 (in Hebrew), pp. 251-257, about the relationship between Avraham Shlonsky and the Natan Alterman school.
8.   See Shavit's article (note 7) and also Vogel's lecture, "Lashon vesignon besifrutenu hatse'ira" in *Siman Kri'a,* no. 3-4, May 1974, pp. 388-391; also see there the introduction to the lecture by Moshe Hano'omi, pp. 387-388.

BIBLIOGRAPHY

Alterman, Natan. *Kokhavim bahuts.* Tel Aviv, 1938.
Luz, Tsvi. *Shevile shira.* Eqed, Tel Aviv, 1974.
Miron, Dan. "Nekuddat hammotsa." *Moznaim,* Sidra hadasha, vol. 31, no. 68, 1970, 5-12.
Pagis, Dan. "Measkenazit lisfaradit: livte ma'avar bikhtav yad shel Fogel." *Hassifrut,* vol. 3, no. 1, 1971, 157-164.
Shavit, Uzi. "Ben Shlonsky lefogel." *Hassifrut,* vol. 4, no. 2, 1973, 251-257.
Vogel, David. 3rd ed. *Kol hashirim.* Pagis, Dan, ed. Hakkibbuts hammeuhad, Tel Aviv, 1975.
_____. *Poems.* Translated by Harold Schimmel. *Orot, Journal of Hebrew Literature,* 9, 1970, 28-49.
_____. "Lashon vesignon besifrutenu hatse'ira." *Siman Kri'a,* no. 3-4, May 1974, 388-391.
_____. *The Dark Gate.* Translated by A. C. Jacobs. Menard, London, 1976.

"A POEM TO THE WISE LOVERS" BY NATAN ZACH

AN INTERPRETIVE RESOLUTION OF A POEM WHICH HAS POSSIBLE INCOMPATIBLE INTERPRETATIONS

The Israeli writers who are known as "The Palmach Generation" or "The 1948 writers" experienced together the historic events of the 1940s. They shared a cultural and literary background. Most of them were associated with the tradition of the Israeli labor movement and their poetry identified with its aspirations. They spoke as "we" in poems to indicate their identification with the desires and life of the Jewish population. Even when the poetic speaker expressed tension between himself and his environment he still believed in Jewish pioneering and in humanitarian values. Among the representatives of this group one may mention H. Guri (born in 1926), B. Galay (b. 1921), A. Hillel (b. 1926), and Natan Yonatan (b. 1923).

Natan Zach belongs to a different literary generation. In 1953 a group of young writers, including Zach (b. 1930), Y. Amihai (b. 1924), and D. Avidan (b. 1934), established the Jerusalem periodical, *Likrat.* This founding group was influenced by Western and Hebrew traditions. It strived for stylistic changes, emotional restraint, linguistic precision and concentration, the use of colloquial Hebrew, and "daring" metaphors. It also strived for a more subjective, individualistic approach and expressed skepticism toward official social ideals. It examined the values of Israeli society, and expressed a crisis of values in ironic, egocentric lyrics.

Zach's "A Poem to the Wise Lovers," translated and discussed here, should be read against this stylistic climate. "A Poem to the Wise Lovers" (*Kol hehalav vehadvash,* 1966, p. 92) allows for an interpretive resolution when two incompatible and disparate interpretations are possible:

שיר לאוהבים הנבונים

שִׁיר לָאוֹהֲבִים הַנְּבוֹנִים
אֲשֶׁר בִּתְבוּנָה יֶאֱהָבוּ.
יְמֵיהֶם בַּנְּעִימִים יַחְלְפוּ,
גַּם בְּרִדְתָּם שְׁאוֹל לֹא יַזְקִינוּ,
נֶצַח לֹא יִפָּרְדוּ, יַחַד יִחְיוּ
בְּבַיִת אֶחָד.

שִׁיר לָאוֹהֲבִים הַנְּבוֹנִים
עַל מִשְׁכָּבָם בְּאֵין מִלָּה.
בְּיָד אַחַת אֶת הַמְּנוֹרָה יְכַבּוּ,
יַחַד יַעַצְמוּ אֶת עֵינֵיהֶם,
זֶה אֶת זֶה יְבָרְכוּ,
וּבְעֵת הָאֶחָד קוֹרֵא –
אֶת הָאוֹר הַקָּטָן יַדְלִיק הוּא.
אֶת נְשִׁימַת יַלְדֵיהֶם שׁוֹמְעִים שָׁעוֹן
וְרוּחַ חֲצוֹת.

שִׁיר לָאוֹהֲבִים הַנְּבוֹנִים
אֲשֶׁר בָּנוּ לָהֶם בַּיִת וְאֶת דַּלְתּוֹ נָעֲלוּ.
הֵגִיפוּ הֵיטֵב אֶת הַתְּרִיסִים, בַּחוּץ קַר
וְרוּחַ וּמְצַפִּים בַּחוּץ לְמָטָר.
אוֹרֵחַ לֹא יָבוֹא בְּלַיְלָה אֲשֶׁר כָּזֶה
וְכִי יָבוֹא – אַל תִּפְתְּחוּ אֶת הַדֶּלֶת. מֵאָחָר
וְרַק קַר נוֹשֵׁב בָּעוֹלָם. וְגַם הַמְשׁוֹרֵר
מִמְּצוּקָה, לֹא מִשֶּׁפַע הוּא שָׁר. הִשָּׁאֲרוּ
חֲבוּקִים.

A poem to the wise lovers
Who love wisely.

Their days pass with delight,
Even when they go down to the grave they will not age, they
will never Separate, together they will live, in one home.

A poem to the wise lovers loving
On their bed speechless.
With one hand they turn off the lamp,
Together they shall shut their eyes,
They bless each other,
And when one of them reads
He turns on the little light.
The clock and the midnight wind
Hear the breath of their children.

A poem to the wise lovers
Who built for themselves a house and locked its door.
Shut the shutters well, outside it is cold
And wind and rain is expected outside.
A guest will not come in such a night
And if he does--do not open the door. It is late
And only cold is blowing in the world. And the poet too
Sings out of distress, not from plenty.
Remain embraced.

One can easily understand the poem's words, grammar, and syntax.
There remain, however, serious issues of explication, elucidation, and
interpretation that the reader must confront.

Determining the "contextual meaning" of word-groups in this
poem and what Beardsley (1958, p. 401) calls their "ranges of
connotation" is a difficult task.   The poem has deceptively simple,
basic vocabulary.   But what is the connotation of "wise lovers / Who
love wisely"?   Is it possible to be "wise lovers" and to "love wisely,"
or are wisdom and love normally incompatible?   The lovers are "On
their bed speechless."   Is this because they simply do not
communicate?   Is their nightly routine indicative of satisfaction,
calm and consideration, or of rigid routine?   Attempting to
understand the two characters and their motives "not explicitly
reported" (ibid.) in the poem, the reader wonders about the central
pair.   Is their consideration of each other motivated by love, or do
they simply co-exist comfortably because their arrangement is
habitual?   What is the extent of this "love" which is so "wise"?   The
answers to these questions and others cannot be easily found.

Interpreting (ibid., p. 403) "A Poem to the Wise Lovers" or
"stating the 'ideas' or propositions ... its 'message' or 'ideology'"--to

use Beardsley's language (1968, p. 232)--becomes difficult. We have tools to "validate" both optimistic and pessimistic interpretations of this poem; to show, that as Hirsch (1967, p. 171) suggests, each may "probably [be] true on the basis of what is known." We will have a more difficult time deciding which of the two interpretations "is the most plausible one available" (ibid.).

TWO INTERPRETATIONS OF "A POEM TO THE WISE LOVERS"

The major problem we face in interpreting the poem is characterizing the love of the poem's characters. Various statements suggest that the "wise lovers" lead an ideal life of love and harmony. Their days are full of joy, they do not age, they are inseparable. They do not need verbal communication ("On their bed speechless") because they have perfect understanding of each other. They care for each other, even helping with little chores; their timing is coordinated ("With one hand they turn off the lamp, / Together they shall shut their eyes"); they do not take each other for granted and they treat each other politely (they "bless each other"). They are considerate of each other: when one reads while the other sleeps, he reads only by a small light. They live together in their home with their children; at midnight they are all asleep so that only the clock and the wind can hear their children's breathing. After they lock the door, they sleep embracing each other in the house they built for themselves. Cold, rain, darkness, and distress do not intrude upon their well-protected home.

However, the poem lends itself to a different and contrasting interpretation, according to which this idyllic picture of familial and individual contentment is nonexistent. The poem could suggest a relationship emptied of emotional content and true love. We do not witness mutual communication ("On their bed speechless"), vivacity, or spontaneity. We witness routine (turning off the lamp and shutting their eyes) but no renewal; politeness (their blessing of each other and keeping the little light on), but no passion; wisdom, but little emotion (the irony of to "love wisely" and the irony regarding such "wisdom"). These could be married individuals who live next to each other but not with each other. They have community property and children in common, but it is doubtful that they have anything else in common. Routine replaces love, security replaces passion, and comfort replaces emotional depth in their lives. The door of the house is locked: their communion with the world is limited. They have shut themselves off from the world. Self-protectiveness and selfishness is present in their relationship and is expressed in their attitude toward the outside world. They do not extend the "warmth" of their locked house to the needy. The speaker's instructions to the lovers to shut their shutters well and not to open their door to anyone may reflect his irony, his anger, his frustrations, his bitter knowledge that they would never be tempted to open the door. The "outside" is symbolically portrayed as cold, windy, rainy. It is possible that the speaker of the poem and the poet in the poem who sings "out of distress" are identified with the man outside, standing in the stormy night. It is questionable whether the speaker, who understands the distress of the poet and of the lonely people out in the cold, would instruct the "wise lovers" to "lock their door" with a straight face.

These two possible interpretations, based on different emphases, are disparate and incompatible. Since they describe two irreconcilable meanings, we experience a sense of conflict in recognizing both of them. Each interpretation alters the controlling conception of the text's meaning and the emphasis that informs the other interpretation.

How should such a situation be tackled by the reader? Should the individual reader decide which interpretation is "better"--the one depicting joyful relations or the one depicting emptiness--according to his own values, experiences, and preferences?

Hirsch (1967, pp. 172-173) describes a situation in which there are two strongly compelling and mutually incompatible interpretations of the same work:

> Sometimes ... definite decision is impossible.... it may be simply that the two hypotheses are ... equally probable, and that no definite choice can be made. One may conclude that interpretation A is more probable than B, that it is less probable, or that neither of these conclusions is warranted.... two disparate interpretations cannot both be correct.... We can reach and agree upon the most probable conclusions in the light of what is known.

In discussing the issue of disparate interpretations, Hirsch (ibid., p. 197) views the reader as a judge who must consider all relevant evidence, both internal and external. The reader is capable of formulating a reliable interpretation on the basis of hypotheses resulting from such evidence. Insecurities and uncertainties are resolved by the logic of common sense when the interpreter strives to establish the most probable context and to adjudicate between the two interpretations.

Hirsch recognizes that "not all plausible interpretations are compatible" (ibid., p. 128). My own interpretation of "A Poem to the Wise Lovers" is incompatible with each of the two others.   In presenting a third reading, I am conscious that "Interpretive disagreements do exist, and they are not always partial or trivial disagreements" (ibid.).

THE THIRD INTERPRETATION OF THE POEM

This article suggests a third interpretation of "A Poem to the Wise Lovers," one that seeks to account for the entire text while guarding against excessive dependence on a single emphasis.   My interpretation represents Zach's poetic attitude to love ("relevant external evidence," ibid., p. 197)--its importance, its rarity, its mixture of the romantic and the bitter. The first two interpretations of the poem are mutually exclusive, not only by giving their own meanings to various statements in the poem but also by electing to exclude alternatives.   The third interpretation enumerates the components of the text, without intentionally skewing the evidence, and takes into account the poetic structure and the poet's own emphasis in "A Poem to the Wise Lovers." Each of the first two interpretations attempts to impose different emphases on the various components of the poem; they thereby restrict poetic meaning.

Hirsch (1967) contends that the poem's interpreter must determine probable structure by determining the relative emphasis of the poem's components. His rule is, "Whenever a reader confronts two interpretations which impose different emphases on similar meaning components, at least one of the interpretations must be wrong. They cannot be reconciled" (p. 230). Such reasoning applies to my interpretation of Zach's poem.   I hold the first two interpretations wrong, because they emphasize one possibility at the expense of the other. For example, the first interpretation would contend that the phrase "wise lovers / Who love wisely" indicates a harmony in which wisdom supports emotions. The second, ironic interpretation would contend that wise love includes self-preservation and calculation. The first interpretation would hold that locking the door to avoid an unwelcome intrusion proves a satisfying relation that needs no outsiders. The second interpretation would contend that the selfish, lonely individuals in the poem treat the outside world as they treat each other: they are self-centered and ungiving.

According to my interpretation, the poem embodies an ironical acceptance of life that can offer either the loneliness of the individual in "rain" and "cold," or preferably, the compromised relationship of a man and a woman in a life of consideration but little spontaneity. In this reading of "A Poem to the Wise Lovers," the relationship of the wise lovers is viewed as faulty; however, the empty alternative is worse. They have attained the best possible, the lesser of two evils, because the alternative is greater loneliness, distress, cold, rain, and wind, presented by the "guest" and the "poet." The world of the "wise lovers" is not full of harmony, passion, and vividness, but neither is it empty. The couple have attained balance, consideration, security, and earthly comfort; they have children and warmth. The couple's life contains some fulfillment, understanding, and a secure and stable expectation system. This is clear from the conduct of the "... wise lovers loving / On their bed speechless." Their locked door and shutters do not conform to humanitarian values; however, the lovers don't have any aspirations to improve the world. He who dreams of a loftier life, such as the "poet," ends up in distress, losing all that the wisdom of compromise could give him. It is possible that the speaker, like the poet in the poem, prefers the distressed world in which he articulately struggles to the secure but flawed life of those "inside" and the distress of those who are "outside."[1] But one who prefers this "distress" to the wise lovers' life should not ignore its blessings, which remain meaningful despite the poet's irony.

By taking into account both the "negative" and the "positive" aspects in the life of the couple, we did not attempt to trace the poet's "intent," but simply to understand the poem itself. It is possible that the intent was to mock the "positive" aspects. However, the poem itself is indicative of some form of maturity and reconciliation and reduction of expectations, which makes for an appreciation of the "positive" aspects in the couple's life.

A close reading of the poem will now follow in the light of Zach's early poetry. Zach's critical writings of 1959, 1966, and 1976 alert the reader to his poetic characteristics regardless of the validity of Zach's arguments (Golomb, 1969, 1976). Some poetic and thematic elements in this poem are typical of Zach's early poetry (1974, 1966). I shall refer to some of these typical elements here.[2]

My reading of this poem avoids sentimentalism by introducing the tension between irony and romanticism.[3] Irony, humor, and wit play a role in the description of the wise lovers when they are bitterly instructed to disregard the needy.

The poem abjures flowery language.[4] The world of the lovers is described in its natural dimensions in conversational tones which emphasize the human voice in a nondidactic manner. The poem is not written in the first person; however, the speaker seems to enter the reality of their lives when he advises the lovers to keep their doors shut. The speaker does not appear as a lofty, chastising prophet.[5] He does not preach that the house should be opened to the needy or that the lovers should strive for a more meaningful relationship.

The conversational style and tone of the poem are expressed in the rhythm, diction, vocabulary, and syntax.[6] We find in the poem prosaic objects of the modern world: a lamp, a small light, a clock, shutters. The poem does not strive for a "beautiful" style. Zach avoids figures of speech which are merely decorative and does not employ many metaphors. The personification in the poem in which the clock and the midnight wind hear the lovers' children breathe illustrates the calm life of the family. The emotional subject of Zach's poem comes to the surface through tension between the romantic and the ironic, conversational language, and through a "prosaic" atmosphere, all of which reduce the sentimental, the dramatic, the pathetic. On a deeper level, Zach sharpens the reader's sensitivities to the pains described. In this poetic world, one may be lonely when single like the "guest" and the poet, or lonely when married, like the "wise lovers."

"A Poem to the Wise Lovers," written in free verse, is typical of Zach's rejection of any preconceived structure. The number of lines in the stanza is determined by the ideas being expressed within the structural unit. The flowing, somewhat monotonous rhythm[7] in the first two stanzas of "A Poem to the Wise Lovers" reflects the stanzas' meaning; the slower rhythm in the last stanza makes us concentrate on the speaker's interference and its meaning. As in the beginning of the poem, no preconceived metrical scheme controls the last stanza. Instead, the loose structure of the line "And only cold is blowing in the world. And the poet too" implies that the poet, too, is a cold wind "blowing in the world."

The Hebrew original of "A Poem to the Wise Lovers" can demonstrate some of the characteristics of Zach's rhymes in his early poetry. In the last stanza we find *kar* (cold), *matar* (rain), and *meuhar*" (late) at the end of three of the lines, and *shar* (sings) inside another line. These rhymes sound faded, intentionally monotonous, and their unexpected place is effective. These rhymes affect the rhythm by creating tension between the poetic line and the sentence. "Cold," "rain," and "late" all refer to the world outside the house; "sings" is related to these terms as well, because the distressed, singing poet is identified with the cold, rainy, dark, lonely world outside. Such rhymes stress meaning and not decorative richness. There is no particular rhyme scheme.

Zach uses a setting which represents the technological world and does not use banal and conventional items which are connected to love, i.e., in this poem one does not find "roses" but a little light, a clock, and shutters.[8]

Throughout Zach's early poetry, words such as "wind" and "night" form repetitive patterns. Here, too, Zach employs repetition of words and phrases. For example, the phrase "A poem to the wise lovers" is repeated four times including the title. This repetition emphasizes the subject of the poem and its frame with musical effect. It also brings in its wake some reduction of the poem's vocabulary. Zach's richness of style is based not on verbal richness, but on syntax, enjambements, musicalization, and elliptical statements that demand the reader's participation to fill the gaps.

Zach's poems leave room for the reader's imagination. The reader has to supply the missing pieces, an effort which requires labor and generates hesitation and reevaluation. The resulting understanding is based on experiencing the total poem.

It is typical of Zach's early poetry that this poem is a short lyric whose speaker is not representative of any formal social or political group. His experience is individual, not national.[9] In Zach's later poetry the poetic speaker's identity and surroundings come to comprise an increasing part of the poetry.

When Zach's theme in his early poetry is grief and agony, he uses logic, perspective,[10] and emotional self-control to restrain hyperbole, self-indulgence, self-pity, and sentimentality. This effort implies that the poetic speaker views sentimentality as a poetic fault. The restraining devices simultaneously decrease the sentimental and stress it: the conscious effort to restrain sentimentality, to avoid inadequate transformation of pathos into poetry, indirectly implies that grief and agony are an integral part of the human condition. In reading "A Poem to the Wise Lovers," the reader who has in mind ideal love relations may pity the "lovers" who have routine, security, and comfort but not love (as depicted in the second interpretation). However, logic, perspective, and disillusionment (the third interpretation) point out the necessity of accepting a reduced life.

In her analysis of the irony in Zach's poetry, Shohet-Meiri (1972, pp. 61-107) claims that in most of Zach's poems the poetic form "collides" with the theme and as a result the poem becomes ironic. This contention is backed up by Shohet-Meiri's numerous examples. In Zach's pessimistic poem "Shum davar" (1974) the discrepancy between the gay, light, mischievous style and the gravity of loneliness is ironic. In many other poems biblical allusions are used as an ironical device, because we at first believe that the speaker uses them to portray sacred harmony, faith, hope, and trust. However, the practical or even cynical soberness of the speaker makes such a belief absurd. These allusions, through secularization, reveal as hopeless the life of man in a world in which God himself is lonely, in need of man's company, restless and hopeless.[11] In another example, "Sir Katan Leeres" (1966), the little child is ironically instructed not to fear, because man and his world are worthless and weak like clay.[12]

The irony in "A Poem to the Wise Lovers" is built up in the poem gradually. In the first stanza the reader is aware of the qualified "wisdom" of the "wise lovers." Irony arises from the implicit or explicit contradiction between "love" and "wisdom." The reader of the first stanza keeps in mind the ironic implications of the apparent naivete of the idealistic poetic speaker. As the reader progresses into the second stanza, irony arises from the word "speechless." The reader suspects that the "lovers" don't have much to share with each other; however, they do treat each other with consideration. It seems that in the third stanza the "lovers" should open their door for the very reasons that the speaker instructs them not to: someone out in the cold and wind and rain may need them and they should not be indifferent to him. The irony of the poem reminds us of Zach's "Shir katan laeres" (1966), a "lullaby" that has the "comforting" message that man and his acts are as fragile as clay and his world is composed of cold, loneliness, and darkness.

In the present poem, we witness the ironic passion of its speaker, who points out that our alternative to loneliness is simply another sort of loneliness. Our idealistic attitude toward potential loving relationships is shattered when it is confronted with disillusioning reality. Zach suggests the ideal, the dream, but through irony and cynicism he reminds us that such an ideal is only a dream. His fundamental pessimism and skepticism explain why dreamlike imagery does not occupy substantial room in Zach's poems. After disposing of illusions and romantic dreams, the reader of this poem must face the ironic reality and the price of compromise.

However, the negative aspects in the life of the "wise lovers" are not the only aspects. One should not disregard the couple's children, comfort, consideration, security, stability. Considering the alternative this imperfect life seems acceptable.

Using Hirsch and Beardsley as a theoretical framework, I have tried to illustrate an interpretive technique which helps the reader decipher confusing signals in Zach's "A Poem to the Wise Lovers." This resolution can also help decipher other poems of Zach.

NOTES

1.   Zach's poetry struggles with issues related to poetry, art, and artists. See, for example, *Mivhar*, 1974, pp. 66, 73, 85, 100; and 1966, pp. 5, 11, 36, 50, 68, 77, 86, 93.

2.   The poetic and thematic world of the early poetry of Zach is described in my book (1979, pp. 102-163), in which the reader may find examples of the poetic and thematic elements discussed here.

3.   For Zach as a bitter romantic poet, see Barukh's book (1979).

4.   Zach tends to use the vocabulary, diction, rhythm, and spontaneity of spoken Hebrew. See for examples 1974, pp. 23, 90; 1966, p. 41.

5.   The poems of Zach, 1974, pp. 20, 99; 1966, pp. 16, 22, can well demonstrate a poetic speaker who is not godlike or prophetic, but human, lustful, or rigid, or disposed to spit in someone's face.

6.   For examples of Zach's effort to achieve a casual conversational tone see 1974, pp. 44, 38; 1966, pp. 41, 8.

7.   Zach's analysis of specific examples of rhythm (1966, p. 57) and his academic focus on it at various points in his career leave no room for doubt about his poetics: rhythm is of primary importance, as is his consistent emphasis on organic forms.

8.   See his poems: 1974, p. 63, knee, lamp, table, and undershirt are used to describe loneliness; and 1966, p. 61, newspaper, a shirt, a closet, a taxi, a package with a gift and a clock.

9.   One may find some rapport with specific reality in poems such as 1966, p. 8, and 1974, p. 87, but one generally does not find specific references to specific national reality or affiliation.

10.   For use of a distanced perspective see Zach, 1966, p. 15. Distance is achieved by the use of parable; 1974, p. 34. Sentimentality is avoided by an ironical anticlimax in 1974, p. 20.

11.   See for example in Zach's poems (1974) "Levado," "Rega ehad," "Keshelohim amar bapa'am harishona," and (1966) "Loa kevod hammenatseyah," "Bahoshekh heamok," "Al tahshov li zot leavon," "Lifamin mitgageya."
12.   See Hakak (1979, pp. 108-112) for detailed examples from the comic-ironic poem "Enosh kehatsir yamav."

BIBLIOGRAPHY

Barukh, Miri. *Haromantikan hammar*. Alef, Tel-Aviv, 1979.
Beardsley, Monroe C. *Aesthetics: Problems in the Philosophy of Criticism*. Harcourt, Brace, & World, Inc., New York, 1958.

_____.   "Interpretation."   In *Dictionary of World Literature*, Shipley, J. T., ed. New Jersey, 1968, 232-233.
Golomb, Harai, and Tamir, Naomi.   "Simhat mo'adim: teaur veainterpretatsia shel shir me'et Alterman." *Hassifrut*, vol. 2, no. 1, 1969, 109-193.
_____.   "Yareyah beor Zach - levayat nituah haritmus beshir shakul." *Hassifrut*, no. 23, 1976, 7-22.
Hakak, Lev.   "Klale parshanut veherut hakkore - al shir ehad shel Natan Zach." *Al hammismar*, Jan. 30, 1976.
_____.   *Im arba'a meshorerim*. Eked, Tel-Aviv, 1979, 102-163.
Hirsch, E. D., Jr. *Validity in Interpretation*.   Yale University Press, New Haven and London, 1967.
_____.   *The Aims of Interpretation*. The University of Chicago Press, Chicago and London, 1976.
Jakobson, Roman, "Concluding Statement: Linguistics and Poetics." In *Style in Language*, Sebeok, T. A., ed., Cambridge, Mass., 1960, 350-377.
Peri, Menahem.   "Ma'galim nehtakhim." *Siman Kria'a*, no. 1, 1972, 269-281.
Raz, Avraham.   "Simhat aniyim vehabbikkoret al shirat Alterman."   In *Natan Alterman mamarim al yestirato*,   Am Oved, Tel-Aviv, 1970, 212-217.
Sachs, Arieh.   "Raiti," "Mishana leshana ze," "Kishalon."   In *The Modern Hebrew Poem Itself*, Burnshaw, Stanley, ed. Schocken (2nd ed. 1971), New York, 1966, 180-185.
Shohet-Meiri, Haviva.   *Al hatshok bassifrut hayisraelit*.   Sifriyat Poa'alim, Tel-Aviv, 1972.
Tsalka, Dan.   "Kavim litsirato shel Natan Zach."   Introduction to: *Natan Zach—mivhar shirim*. Mahbarot lesifrut, Tel-Aviv, 1962.

Zach, Natan. *Shirim shonim.* Expanded edition, Hakkibbuts hammeuhad, 1974.

_____. *Kol hehalav vehadvash.* Am Oved, Tel-Aviv, 1966.

_____. 1974. *Mivhar.* Hakkibbuts hammeuhad, Tel-Aviv, 1974.

_____. "Hirhurim al shirat Natan Alterman." *Akhshav,* no. 3-4, 1959, 109-122.

_____. *Zeman veritmus etsel Bergson uvashira hammodernit.* Alef, Tel-Aviv, 1966.

_____. "Leakliman hassignoni shel shnot hahamishim vehashishim besifrutenu." *Ha'arets,* July 29, 1976.

_____. *Against Parting.* Translated by Jon Silkin. Royal Press Ltd., London, 1967.

ESTRANGED NIGHTINGALES:

ON POETRY WRITTEN BY NEAR EASTERN JEWS
IN ISRAEL

While poetry written by Near Eastern Jews in Israel generally follows
the forms of Israeli poetry, their poetry does not simply emulate the
writing of Israeli poets of European origin; rather, it sometimes
introduces unique settings, themes, and metaphoric language drawn
from the specific background of poets of Near Eastern origin. It is,
therefore, important to recognize the unique contribution of this
poetry within the context of the larger corpus of Israeli poetry.
Eben-Zohar (1973, p. 431) sets a minimal requirement for determining
whether a literary work belongs to "Israeli literature" or not. He uses
"territorial criteria": if a literary work belongs to the place, to the
population, to the language and culture of Israel--then it is an Israeli
literary work. On the basis of Eben-Zohar's territorial criteria the
poetry of Near Eastern Jews in Israel certainly belongs to Israeli
literature: it belongs to Israel, to its population, to its language and
culture.

The beginning stages of modern Hebrew literature in Israel
occurred from about 1880 through the end of World War I. The end of
that war marked the beginning of an accelerated process (1920-1935)
which made Israel the center of Hebrew literature. With that shift of
the center of Hebrew literature to the land of Israel, Near Eastern
Jews began contributing to Hebrew literature on a more regular
basis. In his introductory essay on Hebrew literature, Sadan (1950,
pp. 53-55) describes the beginnings of the participation of Sephardic
Jews in Hebrew literature in Israel, first in prose and later in poetry,
and he indicates that, in time, Jews of all backgrounds will express
themselves in that literature. Indeed, the literary productivity of
Israeli authors of Near Eastern origin is a fact of the Israeli literary
scene today.

Near Eastern Jews in the land of Israel participated first in the
field of prose (Burla, Shami) and only later in the field of poetry.
Their contribution to the center of Hebrew literature in Israel

preceded the Palestinian period (1920-1947). Mordekhay Tabib (born in Rishon Letsion in 1910, of Yemenite origin) began his literary career as a poet; his first poems appeared in the supplement of *Davar* in 1938. It was only after the mass immigration of Near Eastern Jews to Israel in the 1950s, however, that Hebrew poetry began to be published on a regular basis. Since then they have contributed to Israeli poetry at a steadily increasing rate.

Some of these poets wrote first in other languages (Arabic, English, French), shifting to Hebrew when they immigrated to Israel. The fact that many of them already knew some Hebrew made it easier for them to shift to writing in Hebrew. Shlomo Zamir, Shalom Katav, and Aharon Zakay, for example, wrote and published in Arabic in Iraq, but they wrote in Hebrew after immigrating to Israel. Zakay and Zamir published their volumes of poetry a relatively short time after coming to Israel, Zakay in 1957[1] and Zamir in 1960 (in 1961 he was awarded the Shlonsky prize).[2]   Needless to say, poets of European origin experienced similar difficulties in shifting to Hebrew.   Rahel and E. Zusman, for example, had started writing in Russian; Sh. Shalom, in German; Anda Amir Pinkerfield, in Polish.

Israeli poets of Near Eastern background who were born in Israel, such as Mordekhay Tabib and Aharon Almog, and also those who arrived in Israel at an early age--such as the twins Hertsel and Balfur Hakak who came to Israel at the age of two--did not have to confront this problem of changing their written language.

In an autobiographical publication (1986, p. 38), Sh. Shalom (born in Galicia, 1905) told about the first poems he wrote in German at the age of eleven, while living in Vienna. His teacher directed him toward being an important German poet, but he experienced a crisis and swore that he would no longer write in German but would instead strive to be a Hebrew poet.   A more detailed account of the difficulty in changing from one language to another was provided by Samy Michael, an Israeli writer born in Iraq.

Michael describes (1983, pp. 8-11) how Jewish authors immigrating to Israel from Iraq dealt with their new situations. Some of them continued to write in Arabic for the readers that they left behind in Iraq, and they became frustrated and resentful because little of their writing was published and they became unknown. Another group--including Shamuel Moreh, Sason Somekh, and David Tsemah, ceased publishing creative work and turned instead to the field of research in Arabic language and literature.   Only a few

writers from Iraq chose to write in Hebrew. In his autobiographical
essay, Michael describes how, in spite of the fact that he moved to
Israel in 1949 at the age of twenty-two, he is still bewildered--his
Hebrew literary work in Israel is neither typically Iraqi nor typically
Israeli. Michael discusses some ways in which he was affected by the
fact of being an Israeli writer whose origin is an Arab country: in
Iraq he belonged to a minority group (Jews) which had to live in
silence. Any attempt to raise his voice and protest against what was
done to Jews there was tantamount to committing suicide. Once in
Israel, he was able to write about the Arab-Jewish relations in Iraq
without feelings of guilt or fear. Not having studied in Israeli
schools, his knowledge of Hebrew, of Jewish sources, and of Hebrew
literature was limited, and for a long time he used translation
mechanisms (from Arabic or English) in order to write in a language
which is not his mother-tongue. Michael describes feelings and
problems typical of his generation of Near Eastern writers, and even
though he wrote prose, the issues he raised apply equally to poetry.

Generally speaking, due to language problems, most of the first
generation of Israeli poets of Near Eastern origin lacked a
sophisticated knowledge of one layer or another of Hebrew literature
and so did not use allusions as an important device in their poetry.
The result, in the case of Shlomo Zamir, was an innovative and
fascinatingly original poetry, free of tradition; sometimes, however,
these poets missed rich opportunities to exploit the powers of allusion
that Hebrew offers. Allusions are used in Hebrew with powerful
effect, thanks to the sources alluded to--the Bible, the prayer book,
and well-known writers in the field of modern Hebrew literature.
Michael's generation does not make an extensive use of allusion.
However, the generation which was born and educated in Israel does
make sophisticated use of allusion as we shall note in the case of
Almog's "Shahin" and "Look at the Ground" which allude both to
biblical verses and to modern Hebrew poems.

In some cases, a poet's poetic language is influenced by his
background. "I am a hoarse rabbabba in a black bosom," writes Erez
Biton (1979, p. 7), his metaphor referring to the musical stringed
instrument used by the Bedouins, usually around the camp fire at
evening. Yosi Ozer writes, "the dates which you ate just today, here
are their pits in my pocket since yesterday" (1981, p. 18), a
translation of an Iraqi-Jewish proverb, meaning: What you just now
grasped--I have already known for a long time. In another poem
(ibid., p. 20) Ozer uses the Jewish-Arabic idiom in its original
language. This idiom states that the "figs are dense [compact,

compressed - L.H.] and the nuts are noisy"--referring to two types of people: one who hides cunningly and one who is boisterous and candid.   Biton uses Jewish-Moroccan language in certain poems as if to say that the language and the event are inseparable--and he translates the Jewish-Moroccan into Hebrew within the poem itself (1976, pp. 32-33).   The lips of the bride in Biton's "Moroccan Wedding" (1976, pp. 36-39) are described in this way: "Your lips are two dates / of the Buskary kind which is the sweetest kind."

The Israeli poets of Near Eastern origin write without fearing "the authorities" and they enjoy freedom of speech in Israel. Michael, for example, describes how the Jewish writers in Iraq were silent after the 1941 riots against the Jews in Iraq, because protesting would endanger their lives.   But in Israel, the Iraqi-born (1931) poet Shalom Katav published poems (1973, pp. 73-96) in which he vividly described those riots.   He also wrote poems (ibid., pp. 124-148) to the memory of the Ten Martyrs in 1969 in Iraq.

It is noteworthy that some poets of Near Eastern background who were born in Israel (such as Aharon Almog and Tuvia Sulami) give special expression to their unique background within Israeli life.   But just as some Israeli poets of European origin wrote about Near Eastern Jews (e.g., David Shimoni, Natan Alterman, Yisrael Efrat), some poets of Near Eastern origin born in Israel (e.g., Shulamit Kohen) or immigrants to Israel (e.g., Aharon Zakay) wrote poetry lacking any thematic or stylistic traces of their origin.

Today, poets such as Erez Biton, Shlomo Avayo, Aharon Almog, Roni Somek, Gavriela Elisha, Shelley Elkayam, Peres Banay, Hertsel Hakak, Balfur Hakak, Shalom Katav, Moshe Sartel, and other Israeli poets of Near Eastern origin contribute regularly to the Israeli literary scene.   While today the literary work of Near Eastern Jews appears regularly in literary supplements and periodicals, the existing English anthologies of Hebrew poetry do not yet reflect this recent change and such poetry is inadvertently excluded from most of these anthologies.   For example, an anthology published in 1965, *The Modern Hebrew Poem Itself* (Burnshaw, Carmi, and Spicehandler) does not include a single Hebrew poem by a poet of Near Eastern origin; and neither do anthologies published later (Finer-Mintz, 1968; Bernhard, 1980; Carmi, 1981).   And even when some expression was given to this poetry, its real place was not reflected: in the anthology of Schwartz and Rudolf (1980) only four pages were devoted to translations of poems by poets of Near Eastern origin (Shulamit Kohen and Erez Biton).

The poetry of Near Eastern Jews has been overlooked in anthologies of Hebrew poetry in translation because for a long period it was also overlooked in the Israeli literary scene and establishment. Bringing an area of modern Hebrew poetry which has been largely ignored to the attention of the literary and scholarly world is therefore a significant task. The changes in the Israeli literary scene during the last decade--which integrated the poetry of Near Eastern Jews into the established corpus of contemporary Israeli poetry--are not yet reflected in anthologies of Hebrew poetry in translation. Poetic presentations of atmosphere, ways of life, customs, characters, historical events, and folkloristic characters from the background specific to Israeli poets of Near Eastern origin have not found their way into any anthology of contemporary Israeli poetry in translation. When this is accomplished, readers will be introduced to some poetic elements unique to these poets, such as the use of original or translated idioms from the Jewish dialect of a given poet which serves as an organic element in the world he describes, or the use of figurative language and emotional tone intrinsic to the events and ways of life described in the poem.

Selecting poems from the many volumes published by Israeli poets of Near Eastern origin is a pioneering task. Little research and few anthologies exist which could assist in selecting representative works.[3]

In this article I will attempt a close reading of four poems written by two Israeli poets of Near Eastern background--two poems each by Aharon Almog and Erez Biton. I will then use these poems to characterize some aspects of the unique contribution of Israeli poets of Near Eastern origin to Modern Hebrew poetry. Almog and Biton are important poets on the Israeli scene generally and two of the most prominent poets of Near Eastern origin. Their poetry combines both sophisticated use of poetic devices, demanding the reader's constant active participation, and frequently-expressed attachment to unique aspects of the life of Near Eastern Jews. Though Almog was born in Israel, many of his poems subtly exploit his Yemenite background; Biton's vivid, emotional, and sensual style uses distinctive details of his Bedouin origin. The four poems selected represent and demonstrate some of the unique characteristics of this poetry--in their descriptions, images, ideas, and treatments of the confrontation between East and West.

TWO POEMS OF AHARON ALMOG

The poetry of Aharon Almog, a third-generation Israeli-born (1931) poet of Yemenite origin, closely reflects some of Israel's compelling national and social issues. The trivia of daily reality are judged with perspective in his poems, some of which resemble narrative fiction. The fact that he was educated in Israel and that he is familiar with both modern Hebrew literature and older Jewish sources enables Almog to make sophisticated use of allusions. His poetic world draws from the poems of Bialik and Zach, from the Bible and the Talmud. The various effects attained through his use of allusions make of the heritage of the Hebrew language an enriching source of allusions and not a stylish burden. At times the reader senses the presence of humor in Almog's serious poems, and the impact of the allusion becomes seriocomic. For example, in his poem "'En kolno'wa' shderot" (1979, pp. 9–10), seeing a couple embracing, he demands of any witness to this loving act: "put off thy shoes from off thy feet"--the same language that God used when telling Moses to take off his shoes "for the place whereon thou standest is holy ground" (Exodus 3:5). The allusion simultaneously depicts the bond of love as holy and secularizes the sacred sources. After instructing the one viewing the embracing couple to take off his shoes, Almog now employs a curse in colloquial Arabic which was absorbed into Hebrew slang in order to reproach the viewer and to insure that he obeys the instruction. The effects of the allusion and the mixture of lofty biblical language with an Arabic curse in a Hebrew poem are left to the individual reader; they are serious and humoristic at the same time.

It is noteworthy that Almog's poetry, in spite of his being a third-generation Israeli-born, renders a sensitivity to his own specific community and to its social issues. He addresses himself in his poetry to social aspects of the life of Near Eastern Jews in Israel, as in his poem "Shahin":

שַׁהִין

שַׁהִין. מִי הָיָה מַאֲמִין שֶׁיֵּשׁ מִין
שֵׁם עִם קֶסֶם מִזְרָחִי כָּזֶה
בַּת מֶלֶךְ
נְסִיכָה וְלֹא הֻגַּד לָהּ
גַּם הִיא עַצְמָהּ לֹא יָדְעָה
גַּם לֹא הוֹרֶיהָ
וְכָךְ בָּאָה לְכָאן מִמִּזְרָח עִם אֲבוֹתֶיהָ
תְּחִלָּה מֵעֲבָרָה אַחַר כָּךְ צְרִיף רָעוּעַ
וּלְבַסּוֹף בַּיִת עִם גִּנָּה קְטַנָּה
רָאִיתָ בַּחוּרִים וַיְהַלְלוּהָ
הִכִּירָה אֶחָד מְמֻלָּח שֶׁהָיָה לָהּ כְּמוֹ אָח
שָׁאַל: מַה שְּׁמֵךְ?
אָמְרָה: שַׁהִין
(חֲמוֹר, לֹא הֵבִין)
שָׂכַר דִּירָה דָּאַג שֶׁתִּהְיֶה אֲוִירָה שֻׁלְחָן סַפָּה סָלוֹן מְכוֹנִית טֶלֶפוֹן
שְׁטִיחִים מִרְפֶּסֶת בַּלַּיְלָה אָמַר לָהּ אִי
לַאב יוּ שַׁהִין, בַּיּוֹם שִׂחֵק עִמָּהּ
תּוֹפֶסֶת. הוּא נֶהֱנָה הִיא נֶהֱנְתָה, וְכָךְ
מֵתָה לְאַט לְאַט אַגָּדַת
שַׁהִין.
שַׁהִין
סַבְלָנוּת
אֲנִי וְאַתְּ לְאַט לְאַט
תִּרְאִי

SHAHIN

Shahin. Who would believe that there is a name with such
Oriental enchantment
A king's daughter
A princess--although she was never informed

Even she did not know
Nor did her parents
And so she came here from the East with her patrimony
First a transit camp, then a rickety shack
Finally a house with a little garden
The young men saw her and they praised her
She met someone cool who was like a brother to her
He asked: What's your name?
She said: Shahin
(What a jackass; he did not understand)
He rented an apartment, he took care of the ambience--a table
A sofa, living-room furniture, car, phone
Carpets, balcony. At night he said to her: "I
Luv Yoo Shahin." During the day he played tag
With her. He enjoyed it. She enjoyed it, and
Thus slowly slowly died the legend of
Shahin.
Shahin
Patience
You and I slowly slowly
You see[4]

"Shahin" is the first of three love poems which appear at the
end of Aharon Almog's *Hatsda'a leyisrael - hilton yerushalayim* (1977,
pp. 69-71). "Shahin" (p. 70) focuses upon love for an Israeli woman of
Near Eastern origin and on the erosion of that woman's life.

Some of the poem's language suggests a light attitude on the
part of the poetic speaker toward his subject. The intonation of the
poetic speaker is restrained, he avoids explicit "protest," and agony is
tinged with some resignation. Disillusionment with the new Israeli
life style explains in a seemingly casual manner the presence of
agony in the poem. The casual attitude and undertone of frustration
elicit strong sympathy for the suffering characters in the poem--
Shahin and the poetic speaker. The poet uses both colloquial Hebrew
and highly poetic language to his purpose. In some lines, the
colloquial Hebrew rises to a poetic style due to its juxtaposition with
the lofty words, the rhythm, and the biblical allusions.

The poet employs a period only three times in the poem, twice following the name Shahin, which alludes to someone royal (the Persian King—is Shah). The entire opening sentence of the poem consists of the single word "Shahin." This Near Eastern name has a metonymic quality, enchanting in its very sound. The Hebrew text draws our attention to the name also because of the rhymes: "Shahin" "ma'amin" (*believe*) "min" (*such*, also *sex*). The enjambement at the end of the first line encourages us to connect Shahin and sex; the second line, however, emphasizes the origin of Shahin and renders the contextual meaning of "min" as "such."

As the poetic speaker moves to describe Shahin herself, he alludes to Bialik's poem "May my lot be with you." Bialik described, in that poem, the thirty-six righteous men who were believed to exist secretly in the world. Bialik's poem describes them as "rich—although you were never informed / Spiritual noblemen—and you did not know." The allusion presents Shahin as one of the thirty-six righteous people. Almog alters the language of the above-quoted second line of Bialik, substituting for Bialik's high and dramatic style a more colloquial Hebrew, more appropriate to the new time and place and the mundane reality. Shahin, by the power of the allusion, is perceived as a woman of rare virtues.

Shahin's parents and Shahin herself are innocent and unaware of her uniqueness. She herself did not know that she was a princess (in nature, in the eyes of the speaker), "Nor did her parents / And so she came here from the East with her patrimony." In the world of Shahin's family, her virtues are normal human qualities.

Employing both biblical and colloquial Hebrew, the poet describes briefly both Shahin's suffering and her gradual economic progress in Israel.

A well-known Israeli song (Mohar-Vilenski) portrays two men, one who lives in a rickety shack and one who lives in a palace. Like the first man in the song, Shahin started on the lowest economic level, living in a rickety shack (the transit camp of Israel in the 1950s). Only when she attained "Finally a house with a little garden" did young men discover her, they "saw her" and "praised her" —an allusion to the biblical Song of Solomon (6:9): "My dove, my undefiled, is but one; ... The daughters *saw her*, and called her happy: Yea, the queens and the concubines, and they *praised her*." The allusion to the Song of Solomon evokes all the unique qualities of the beloved woman of the Song of Solomon. The poem alludes also to another biblical source, the woman of valour (Proverbs 31: 10-31): "Her children rise up, and call her blessed; her husband also, and he praiseth her" (ibid., 31:28). The allusions to both the beloved woman of Song of Solomon and the woman of valour elevate Shahin to a lofty rank. In the Hebrew text of the poem, grammatical rhymes result from the structure of the suffixes ("horeha"--her parents, "avoteha"--her ancestors, here translated as "patrimony"). Sophisticated rhymes connect the modern Hebrew song and the biblical allusions: "ra'uwa" (rickety), "ra'uha" (saw her), "vayehalleluha" (and they praised her). Like the rhymes of this poem which fuse biblical allusions and modern Hebrew song, Shahin combines in herself both the great characteristics of the biblical woman and the contemporary Near Eastern woman who immigrated to Israel.

When Shahin lives as an Israeli petit bourgeois the legendary Shahin is no more.

The "cool" guy who met Shahin was practical, not sophisticated. Unlike the poetic speaker, it did not occur to him to compare Shahin to the beloved woman of the Song of Solomon, to the woman of valour, or to the thirty-six righteous people. She was "just a woman" to him and he did not understand her special virtues ("what a jackass"), but he had an effective way of tempting Shahin. He gave her all the status symbols of an aspiring Israeli couple--a rented apartment, living-room furniture, a car, a telephone, carpets, balcony.   The list is long and specific and definite--unlike the expansive and poetic terms with which the poetic speaker described Shahin, "a king's daughter," "a princess" in her nature. The "royal" terminology is supplanted by a mundane and materialistic reality. Shahin's husband is busy with his wife day and night. At night he applies his learning from American movies as he tells his wife in English, "I / Luv Yoo." The sound of "I" ending the line describing what he said to her at night is also a sexual allusion in light of the enjambement (only in the following line does it become clear that "I" is a transliterated English word and not merely a sound of excitement).

Shahin's married life signals the death of the legend. The speaker uses colloquial Hebrew to describe the sense of routine life of Shahin, and simple rhymes to underscore its repetitive nature: "Hikira" (she met)--"amra" (she said)--"avira" (ambience); "memulah" (cool)--"ah" (a brother); "Shahin"--"hevin" (he understood); "salon" (living-room furniture)--"telephone"; "mirpeset" (a balcony)-- "tofeset" (tag); "nehenta" (she enjoyed)--"meta" (died); "le'at" (slowly)--"agadat" (the legend of). Some of these rhymes serve to strengthen meanings: The "cool" guy (memulah) acts as Shahin's "brother" (ah) in order to acquire her innocent trust; the living-room furniture ("salon") and "the telephone" create ambince (avira) in the apartment (dira).   During the day Shahin's husband played tag (*tofeset*) with her on the balcony (*mirpeset*)--recalling an Israeli song describing a girl who had missed her opportunity because she rejected the boy who loved her and with whom she played tag on the balcony. The allusion to that song (about Yosi and Miryam) points to the immaturity of Shahin's husband and foreshadows Shahin's sad end. The ironically detailed description of Shahin's married life voices the scorn of the speaker. Shahin did not fulfill herself in a way suited to her unique qualities. The royal is exchanged for the trivial, the lofty and untouchable for the mundane and easy-to-reach.

The poem is not explicitly one of social protest, but it makes it clear that Shahin's life in the new land moves toward the bland and the trivial because of her innocence. The longest line in the poem, describing all the tempting acquisitions of the man whom Shahin met, is contrasted with the short lines in which she was described as "a king's daughter" and "a princess." The little possessions replace the royal and the lofty and bring death to the legend. The shortest lines convey inner wealth, while the longest, naming all the acquisitions, voices emptiness.

In the last four lines of the poem the speaker attempts to give hope to Shahin. They form an incomplete sentence. The speaker does not accept the death of the romantic legend. We were already told that Shahin's legend died "slowly slowly." The speaker now promises Shahin that "slowly slowly" he and she--but he does not complete the statement. Do those concluding lines voice his realization that it is too late for both of them, or his disbelief that anything will change in their life? What in fact occurred "slowly slowly" was the death of the legend and after that death nothing will revive. The Hebrew rhymes strengthen the meaning: "le'at-le'at" (*slowly slowly*)-"agadat" (*the legend of*)-"any ve'at" (*I and you*)--the slow death of the legend was also the death of the possibility that the speaker and Shahin will be united.

Pain and explicit social protest are well restrained in the poem. The factual narrative tone avoids emotionally charged language. Settled irony effectively replaces the need for explicit social protest. Humor ("... At night he said to her I / Luv Yoo Shahin") serves to achieve a low-key intonation. In the Hebrew text, rhythm expresses meaning and meaning contributes to establishing the rhythm. A slow rhythm pervades the first part of the poem; the marriage activity and business is then described in a rapid rhythm created by the syntactic structure describing the intensified activity, the list of possessions, and the many rhymes accompanying the colloquial Hebrew. At the conclusion the rhythm slows down again--paralleling the slow death of the legend and reflecting the resistant position of the speaker who can offer no comfort or message to Shahin and who is passive and thoughtful, unlike the "wise guy" who had married her.

The entire poem consists of one stanza. The length of the lines is determined by the meaning, the rhythm, and the linguistic tensions. The rhymes are casual. They are not decorative and give little indication of striving for a richness of sound. They also contribute to the meaning. Rhythm, not meter, is significant in this poem. The emphasis is not on astonishing metaphors but on organic form. The colloquial Hebrew and the biblical allusions are integral to the message.

A strong social message is hidden in the poetic lines even as they seem to convey a lightness of attitude. Shahin and her parents, like many other Near Eastern Jews, were transplanted to Israel; the real subject of the poem is the cost of that transplanting.

Another poem of Almog that contains a social message is "Look at the Ground" (1977, p. 63):

אָכְלוּ אֶת הַכְּבֵדִים שָׁתוּ אֶת כָּל
הַוִּיסְקִי וְהַבִּירוֹת (בְּבֵית שְׁאָן יְלָדִים רְעֵבִים)
אֶת הַפּוֹלְקָס שָׂמוּ בַּכִּיסִים לַכְּלָבִים (חָשְׁבוּ שֶׁאֲנִי
לֹא רוֹאָה) הוֹרִידוּ אֶת הַקְּרָמִים מֵהָעוּגוֹת.

הַחֲגִיגָה נִסְתַּיְמָה. יֵשׁ הוֹצָאוֹת. אֶצְלֵנוּ מֶלְצָרִים
מֵבִיאִים. שְׁנַיִם הִתְעַלְּפוּ כְּפִי שֶׁאַתְּ רוֹאָה.
אֶחָד זַ'ק שָׂם דַּק נַעֲלֵי לַק מְרַק
שַׁמְפִּנְיוֹן. אַהֲבָה זֶה לְחוּד. כָּל הַכָּבוֹד. בִּשְׁבִילֵךְ

עַד חֲצִי הַמַּלְכוּת. סַנְגוֹ אַחֲרוֹן סוֹלוֹ.
זֶה לֹא אָסוֹן גְּבֶרֶת חָסוֹן הַפָּקִיד
טָעָה. אֵין אָדָם

שֶׁאֵין לוֹ שָׁעָה. חֲבָל רַק עַל
דְּסִיקוֹת הַלֵּב. רְאִי אֲדָמָה וְאֶת הַהוֹדָעָה
מַס הַכְנָסָה בְּטֵלָה וּמְבֻטֶּלֶת.

LOOK AT THE GROUND

They ate the livers drank all the
Whisky and the beers (In Bet-She'an there are hungry children)
They put the drumsticks in their pockets for the dogs (They
thought that I
Didn't see) they took the frosting off the cakes.

The party is over. There are expenses. We only use imported
Waiters. Two of them fainted as you can see.
One is Jacques--a thin mustache polished shoes champignon
Soup. Love! That's something else. With all due respect. For
you

Up to half the kingdom. A Last Tango, solo.
It's no disaster, Ms. Hason. The official
Erred. Every man

Has his day. It's not worth
Heart palpitations. Look at the ground and regard the notice
From the IRS as null and void.

The title of this poem alludes to a well-known Israeli poem by
Sha'ul Tshernihovski, "Behold, O Earth." Tshernihovski's title in
Hebrew is "Re'i, 'adama," and Almog's title is "Re'i 'adama"--the
same words without the comma. I have translated these words in two
different ways--"Behold, O Earth" for Tshernihovski's poem and
"Look at the Ground" for Almog's poem. (The translations reflect the
fine differences of the meaning.) Tshernihovski's poem, written in
1939, was published in 1940 in a poetry volume of the same title (p.
3). Tshernihovski addressed the earth of Israel in the name of the
Jews in Israel. Between 1936 and 1939 riots kept breaking out in the
land and Jews were murdered. The Jews in Israel, according to the
poetic speaker, were spendthrifts--instead of burying in the earth
such grains as wheat, spelt, barley, or oats, they planted the choicest
of their sons, who had sacrificed their lives for the defense of the
Yishuv. Tshernihovski found the desired bond between the people and
the land of Israel. The poem, which laments the death of Israeli
pioneers, also celebrates a national victory based on that love of the
land which justifies such a sacrifice: "Behold, O Earth, what
spendthrifts we are indeed! /... take you the best of our sons ...
/ Blest be their offering of death ..." (Silberschlag, 1968, pp.
177-178.)[5]

The speaker in Tshernihovski's poem addresses the land of Israel
in his monologue; in Almog's poem the speaker, an influential public

servant, talks to a woman at the end of a party, and in his monologue, he tells her to look at the ground (so that she will lie down, sleep with him) in consideration of the favor she has asked of him.

The allusion to Tshernihovski's poem directs the reader to a comparison of the pre-State generation of Tshernihovski's poem and the post-State generation of Almog's poem.   The idealism and sacrifice   of   the   pre-State   generation   darken   the   corrupt, materialistic and self-centered post-State generation.   The "nouveau riche" speaker represents a whole social class which exploits the state for its own lust.   The guests in Almog's poem "ate the livers drank all the / Whisky and the beers...."   Eating someone's liver, in Hebrew,   means   harassing,   exploiting,   someone.   The   relations between the host and the guests are not loving ones.   The first line continues and ends with an enjambement ("drank all the"), raising the expectation that the guests "drank all the blood"--and indeed the drinking of the whisky and the beers appears in the eyes of the speaker (metaphorically) like the drinking of his blood by his (metaphorically) "carnivorous" guests.   The implied author reminds the reader that while the guests ate delicacies and drank delightful drinks, children in the town of Bet-She'an remained hungry.   The impolite, abusive guests "put the drumsticks in their pockets for the dogs," thinking that the host did not see them, and "took the frosting off the cakes."   The atmosphere is one of "let us eat and drink for tomorrow we shall die" (Isaiah 22:13)--let us enjoy the present, trusting as little as possible to the future.

Now, at the end of the party, the host is left with the bills--but he is also left with one woman who remained after the party.   The shallow, vulgar host tries to impress her.   He boasts that the waiters are "imported"--a (typically) snobbish local attitude which prefers imported to local "merchandise."   The waiters were not accustomed to the level of stress to which they were exposed in Israel--"two of them fainted" and had not recovered yet as the woman "can see" for herself.   The shallow, silly speaker most clearly exposes his character in his boasting about the waiter, Jacques.

The use of three foreign words in one sentence (*Jacques*, *lacquer* for polished, *champignon* for mushrooms) is intended to impress the woman.   The implied poetic speaker is sarcastic.   The strong impact of the successive frequent rhymes expresses the shallow boasting attitude of the speaker; it accelerates the rhythm and lightens the style: "'Ehad Jacques safam dak na'ale' lak merak /champignon"--"One is Jacques--a thin mustache polished shoes champignon / Soup."   The rhymes place an emphasis upon the sound just   as   the   speaker   places   an   emphasis   on   external phenomena--mustache, polished shoes, foreign waiters, and a foreign recipe for soup.

At the end of the second stanza the reader comes to grasp more clearly the situation between the speaker and the woman. It seems that the woman, who stayed behind to be the last guest at the party, approaches the speaker in a "loving" way, and the speaker's response to her is: "Love! That's something else" --love is not bills and food, the speaker is open to it, "With all due respect." When the speaker says "With all due respect. For you," the reader may think that the respect is for the woman, but the enjambement prompts us to see that what the speaker has in mind for the woman is only "Up to half the kingdom" (Esther 5:3), a Hebrew idiom signifying a person's willingness to do his utmost for someone else, whatever it takes--and more. The speaker pretends to be magnanimous. The association with the movie "Last Tango in Paris" and with the sex between the American man and the young French woman in that film is legitimate. He agrees to dance "last tango, solo" with the woman and to determine in a very settled language the terms of their give and take: he will free her of her problems with the IRS after she sleeps with him. He immediately tells her that "the official / Erred." The poem may also allude to a poem of David Avidan who, in "Ad kan veloa yoter,"[6] writes that Ahusuerus meant that he will take only one half of the kingdom of the ladies (the upper part), so that he will not be accused of being the father of many children. The allusion directs the reader to think not in terms of the speaker's generosity but rather in sexual terms. The speaker in Almog's poem also offers half of the kingdom ... and the IRS clerk's notice to the woman (or her sender) should be regarded "as null and void." He is sorry for her frightened heart-palpitations when she received the notice. The word *defikot* in Hebrew, however, not only means "beats" or palpitations but, in slang, also refers to intercourse. The woman should "go down" and in consideration he will take care of her income tax file: "Look at the ground and regard the notice / From the IRS as null and void." This is his great day. The name of the woman is Hason--which means "brave," "strong"--a Hebrew name in use mostly among Near Eastern Jews. As "strong" as she is, she submits to someone who uses his authority to save her money without treating the matter on its merits. Both Hason, the weak party in this matter, and the speaker are corrupted--her monetary lust and his sexual lust motivate them respectively. While we do not know the woman's response, her conduct appears to accept the deal.

The comparison between the pre-State and the post-State generations is not at all flattering to the latter: corruption replaced idealism; depriving the State of its money replaced the sacrifice of life for the land; food and sex come before the national interest in determining behavior; extravagance prevails over modesty. Instead of investing that which is most precious--the lives of the best sons-- for the sake of the national future, the focus is now upon immediate pleasure.   Materialistic   life   overrides   all   other   values. Tshernihovski's poem ends with hope that the national future will justify the sacrifice (Silberschlag, 1968, pp. 177-178):

> And you shall cover all these. May the plant arise at
>   length!
> To its homeland's people sacred, in hundredfold splendour
>   and strength!
> Blest be their offering of death, by whose glory our lives
>   are freed ...
> Behold, O Earth, What spendthrifts we are indeed!

These hopes in Tshernihovski's poem compare with the ironic fulfillment of the dream as conceived in Almog's poem.

Almog defines his poem as a sonnet. It has fourteen lines and it mentions "love." The first two stanzas (octave, octet) are composed of four lines (quatrain) each, the last two stanzas (sestet), of three lines (tercet, triplet) each. No systematic rhyming or meter scheme is present in the poem. The rhymes, however, connect the stanzas both by their musical sound and by their semantic meaning. The following grammatical rhymes are based upon suffixes: "kevedim" (livers), "yeladim" (children), "re'evim" (hungry), "kisim" (pockets), "kremim" (frosts), "kelavim" (dogs), "meltsarim" (waiters), "meyuba'im" (imported). The first six of these words appear in the first stanza, the last two in the second stanza; together they focus mainly on the guests and their conduct.

The following are also grammatical rhymes based on suffixes: "birot" (beers), "hotsa'ot" (expenses), "defikot" (beats, "palpitations"). With this also rhymes "kol hakkavod" (with all due respect). In this group Almog relates the conduct of the host and the guests who are basically the same. Other rhymes relate to the "bargain" between the woman and the speaker: "ro'ah" (see), "sha'ah" (hour, "day"), "ta'ah" (erred), "hoda'ah" (a notice). Other rhymes are "ason" (disaster) and Hason (strong, brave): "solo" and "she'en lo" (who does not have). The poem conforms to some traditional structural elements of the sonnet while not complying with others; its noncompliance with some of the schematic elements does not indicate a lack of organizational elements but instead replaces them with an individual creativity.

TWO POEMS OF EREZ BITON

Erez Biton, born in 1942 to Moroccan-born parents who had moved to Algeria, immigrated to Israel in 1948. In his poetry, he introduces the Hebrew reader to new landscapes, events, and characters unique to his Jewish-Moroccan community. The use, within the Hebrew poem, of the native language of his community, striking metaphors, the richness of sensuality and colorfulness, the unique artifacts, the various characters from the folklore and specific background of the Jewish-Moroccan community, and details of its day-by-day life are some of the features which distinguish Biton's poetry. Unlike authors who attempted to portray the world of Near Eastern Jews as they perceived it as outsiders, Biton grew up in this world and describes it with an insider's perspective, portraying its beauty with neither nostalgia nor idealization. He is capable of discovering and focusing on the exceptional and attractive within the mundane. Biton depicts the enchanting within the concreteness of daily life. His pride and joy in his origin are presented not in a provocatively challenging manner, but rather in an inviting manner. The values of the Near Eastern Jews are not stated explicitly but are grasped by the reader, without the use of either polemic or a didactic attitude.

Biton's poem "Basic Background Comments" (1976, p. 28) provides some fundamental information about the poetic speaker's background. This poem may demonstrate the challenge to some of these poets of writing about their experience without being offensive to their own pride. The naive and helpless speaker's mother-world is described with compassion and enchantment, especially considering that for a long time the dominant attitude toward the heritage of Near Eastern Jews in Israel was an intimidating one.

While the language of the poem's title is formal and informative, the poem itself is pictorial and expresses strong emotions which are restrained by various devices. This is the opening poem in a section of a volume which deals with the life of Moroccan Jews; "Basic Background Comments" are indeed necessary in order truly to understand fully that section.

דִּבְרֵי רֶקַע רִאשׁוֹנִיִּים

אִמִּי אִמִּי
מִכְּפַר הַשִּׂיחִים הַיְרֵקִּים בְּיָרֹק אַחֵר.
מִקַּן הַצִּפֳּרִים הַמַּחֲלִיבוֹת חָלָב מָתוֹק מִכָּל מָתוֹק,
מֵעֶרֶשׂ זְמִירֵי אֶלֶף לַיְלָה וְעוֹד לַיְלָה.

אִמִּי אִמִּי
שֶׁהִרְחִיקָה רָעוֹת
בְּאֶצְבָּעוֹת צְרֵדוֹת
בִּהֲלָקָאוֹת חָזֶה
וּבְשֵׁם כָּל הָאִמָּהוֹת.

אָבִי אָבִי
אֲשֶׁר עָסַק בְּעוֹלָמוֹת
אֲשֶׁר קִדֵּשׁ שַׁבָּתוֹת בְּעִרְאָק נָקִי
אֲשֶׁר הָיָה בָּקִי מֵאַיִן כָּמוֹהוּ
בְּהִלְכוֹת בֵּית כְּנֶסֶת.

אֲנִי אֲנִי
שֶׁהִרְחַקְתִּי עַצְמִי
הַרְחֵק אֶל תּוֹךְ לִבִּי
שֶׁכְּשֶׁהַכֹּל הָיוּ יְשֵׁנִים
הָיִיתִי מְשַׁנֵּן
הַרְחֵק אֶל תּוֹךְ לִבִּי
מַסּוֹת קְטַנּוֹת שֶׁל בַּךְ
בִּיהוּדִית
מָרוֹקָאִית.

BASIC BACKGROUND COMMENTS

Mother mother
From the village of bushes that are green but a different green.
From the nest of birds that give milk, sweeter than sweet,
From the cradle of the nightingales of The Arabian Nights.

Mother mother
Who removed evil
With her middle finger,
By beating her breast,
And in the name of all mothers.

Father father
Who occupied himself with other worlds
Who blessed the Sabbath with pure arak
Who was more knowledgeable than all
In the synagogue lore.

And I, I
Who removed myself
Far into my heart,
Who would memorize
When all were asleep
Far into my heart
Minor masses of Bach
In the Jewish
Moroccan dialect.

The first two stanzas focus on the mother of the poetic speaker, the third one on the father, and the last stanza on the poetic speaker himself. The last stanza places the world of the poetic speaker at some distance from the world of his parents which he lovingly described in the previous stanzas.

The first stanza depicts the distinguished roots and background of the mother, which are distanced from the present reality. The "bushes that are green but a different green"--the (metonymic) bushes are unique like her. The intonation depicts the implied sorrow and the nostalgia of the mother who was taken from a certain reality and placed in a different one. The mother came from a fabulous legendary world, "From the nest of birds that give milk, sweeter than sweet, / From the cradle of the nightingales of The Arabian Nights." It is not the mother's village that has this kind of nest and cradle, but she herself came from this nest and cradle. She left her enchanted nest and cradle, her real roots, and came to live in a different landscape representative of a different way of life. The terminology and descriptions which refer to past and present are not specific and concrete but rather suggestive and leave considerable room to the reader's imagination.

The second stanza describes the simple beliefs of the mother, her initiative, her naive way of fighting evil, and her care for all other mothers. She "removed evil / With her middle finger, / By beating her breast, / And in the name of all mothers."

The poetic speaker depicts both the enchanting, altruistic, and gracefully innocent world of the mother and her helplessness and limitations. The son's pain for his mother, his nostalgic sympathy for her lost world, his sensitivity to her roots, and his perspective, frustration, and disillusionment lead to irony. The middle finger and the beating on the breast alone will not remove evil and will not provide the protection and safety desired by mothers.

The expected reader of the poem, like the poetic speaker, is more modern in his beliefs in comparison to the mother, but the reader is guided by the poetic speaker to be compassionate and not contemptuous of the mother.

The poetic speaker's father preserved Jewish tradition. He "occupied himself with other worlds"--according to legend God will provide 310 worlds for the righteous in the World-to-Come. The father was attuned to future mystical hopes. For blessing the Sabbath he used not wine but a stronger drink, "pure" arak, untouched by the hand of a non-Jew. The father's own world was one of faith and tradition both at home and in the synagogue. The use of arak and the strong interest in the mystical are treated with irony--the father was impractical and perhaps evasive of reality: preferring arak to wine, he liked to be tipsy. Yet the speaker treats him with compassion.

The way the speaker perceives his parents reflects upon his own character. In the last stanza, the speaker describes his close yet distanced relationship with his parents' world. This, the longest stanza in the poem, incorporates all the previous parts of the poem. In the speaker's introverted world East and West meet but the fusion brings pain. The speaker states that he removed himself but he does not indicate from what. It is probable that he removed himself from his parents' world in order to go "Far into my heart." The tortuous search for resolution is within himself, taking place "When all were asleep," and it demands a new melody: the "Minor masses of Bach /In the Jewish / Moroccan dialect"--a new, different melody which he creates within himself in his attempt to bring together East and West into harmony within his own life.

The Hebrew text of the poem distinguishes the formal, informative language of the title, "Basic Background Comments," from the poem's pictorial language. Punctuation, style, syntax, internal and grammatical rhymes, and the use of verbs are all employed in order to achieve changes in rhythm which express the difference between the worlds of the two generations: the rhythm in the fourth stanza is quicker than the one describing the motion of the traditional life of the parents.   Rhymes based on common grammatical suffixes support the rhythm: "hassihim" (bushes), "yerukkim" (green), "sipporim" (birds); "ra'ot" (evil), "esba'ot sredot" (middle fingers), "halka'ot" (beating), "immahot" (mothers); "olamot" (worlds), "sabbatot" (Sabbath days), "hilkot" (lore); and the rhyming of "naki" (pure) and "baki" (knowledgeable).

The traditional world of the parents is wholesome, innocent, and enchanting, while the son's world is one of searching alone in the dark.   The confrontation is between the past and present, between the parents' deeds within their Near Eastern Jewish setting and tradition and the son's search; it is a confrontation between home and the parents' Near Eastern background, and the son who seeks to find his way between East and West alone.   It is also a conflict between the enchanted, fabulous, and somehow mystic world of the parents and the disillusionment of the son, and between the parents, aware of their family needs and the needs of their community, and their introversive and individualistic son.   It is the contrast between the sensual world of the parents (sight--the green, taste--the sweet milk, hearing--nightingales; the smell is incidental to the arak, the touching to beating the breast) and the dark, physically inactive (few verbs describe the speaker's world), restlessly searching life of the son.   The son lost the wholesome world of his parents and did not develop another one.   The meeting between East and West inflicted loneliness, searching introversion, suffering.   What would Bach say about the poetic speaker's music?   What would the speaker's father say about it?   Can the sound of Bach's minor masses replace the sound of the nightingales and the blessings of the Sabbath?

The tension between East and West (Near Eastern Jews and European Jews) is communicated by an overtone describing the pain of the meeting between the two cultures.   The world of the parents exists vividly in the son's memory.   His own world includes, through those memories, the tradition, the objects, landscape, and faith which made his parents' world so beautiful in spite of its apparent deficiencies in the eyes of the speaker and of the reader.   The meeting between East and West stimulated creativity ("Minor masses of Bach / In the Jewish /Moroccan dialect")--but did not bring happiness.

The struggle between the heritage of the past and the changed present preoccupies the poetic speaker in another poem--"Reforming Odors" (1979, p. 13):

תִּקּוּן הָרֵיחוֹת

מָה אַתֶּם רוֹצִים מִמֶּנִּי
טַעַם עָרָאק וְרֵיחַ זַעְפְרָן צוֹרֵב,
אֲנִי כְּבָר לֹא אוֹתוֹ הַיֶּלֶד
אָבוּד בֵּין רַגְלַיִם שֶׁמְּשַׂחֵק סָנוּקֶר
בְּקָפֶה מָרְקוֹ
בְּלוֹד.
עַכְשָׁו חֲבֵרִים
אֲנִי לוֹמֵד לֶאֱכֹל גְּלִידָה מִבְּדֹלַח
מָאוֹטוֹ שֶׁמַּשְׁמִיעַ קוֹלוֹת שֶׁל צָפֳּרִים
בָּעֶרֶב,
אֲנִי לוֹמֵד לִפְתֹּחַ דְּלָתוֹת
בְּתֵבוֹת נְגִינָה עַתִּיקוֹת,

עַכְשָׁו
נָשִׁים בְּטַעַם תּוּת־שָׂדֶה
מְלַמְּדוֹת אוֹתִי לְהָרִיחַ כְּרִיכוֹת שֶׁל שֶׁקְסְפִּיר־
מִן הַמֵּאָה הַשְּׁבַע עֶשְׂרֵה
מְלַמְּדוֹת אוֹתִי לְשַׂחֵק בְּחָתוּל סִיָּמִי
בְּתוֹךְ סָלוֹן יָרֹק

חֲבֵרִים.

REFORMING ODORS

What do you want from me you
Taste of arak, you smell of pungent saffron,
I'm no longer the same kid
Wandering between the legs of the adults, playing snooker

In Marko's Coffee Shop
In Lod
Friends
I'm learning to eat ice cream now, from crystal,
From a truck that whistles like a bird
In the evening,
I'm learning to open the lids
Of antique music boxes.

Now
Women tasting like strawberries
Teach me to smell the Shakespeare bindings
From the seventeenth century
They teach me to play with a Siamese cat
In a green salon.

Friends.

East and West confront each other in this poem. The poetic
speaker, a Near Eastern Jewish Israeli, carries with him the taste of
the arak, the smell of pungent saffron, memories from the town of
Lod (populated mostly by Near Eastern Jews) and Marko's Coffee
Shop, where the speaker as a child played snooker. At the time that
the poetic speaker is writing the poem, he is occupied with learning
of the West as his Israeli guides understand it: ice cream eaten from
crystal goblets, a truck that whistles like a bird, antique music boxes,
women tasting like strawberries, old bindings of books, a Siamese cat
in a green salon.

The key to the poem is the intonation of the poetic speaker. On
the surface, it may seem that he is boasting, telling his friends about
his new learning which bestows on him a new social status. However,
a closer reading of the poem reveals his mockery and contempt for
the emptiness to which he has been exposed and which is surrounded
by expensive objects. Once he approached the world to which he is
attracted, he learned that it is a world which emphasizes earthly
rather than spiritual possessions; it is a world of acquisitions and not
one of human relationships; it is a world in which a book is judged by
its cover, and ice cream is judged by its dish.

In the poem's opening line, the speaker addresses himself, in a spoken Hebrew, to someone who imposes himself on him.   In the second line we find out that he is indeed talking to the taste of arak and the smell of saffron which he has personified (they "want").   He tries to rid himself of the distinctive taste of arak and the smell of saffron which represent the Near Eastern world of his childhood.   His contact with this world is not intellectual or conceptual; it is rather sensual, a part of his physical being.   A favorite Hebrew proverb states that there is no accounting for tastes--literally, no debate should take place regarding matters of taste and smell.   Prompted by his new affiliations he seeks to deny his ties with his childhood world--"I'm no longer the same kid"--but he will soon admit that he has not found a better alternative to it.   In his childhood he was "Wandering between the legs of the adults, playing snooker / In Marko's Coffee Shop / In Lod."   The coffee-shop atmosphere, its odors and tastes and its games, reflects a people-oriented life of sociable interaction between the players and onlookers.   Later in the poem there will be an implied confrontation with the objects-oriented world of the West. The setting changes from coffee shop to living room, "salon."   Now the poetic speaker begins to describe his new learning ("I'm learning ... I'm learning ... Teach me ... They teach me"), which, when examined, indicates a learning of a world empty of meaning but nicely covered up.   Contrasting with the taste of the arak, he now has the taste of ice cream and of women tasting like strawberries; contrasting with the smell of the pungent saffron, he has the smell of old book bindings; instead of Marko's Coffee Shop he now has a salon; instead of playing snooker he now plays with a Siamese cat.   His contact is now through objects and technological devices.   Instead of tasting arak, he tastes strawberries through the lipstick of women; instead of listening to the chirping of birds he hears a truck that whistles like a bird; instead of smelling "pungent saffron" he smells the covers of books; instead of playing snooker in a coffee shop he plays with a Siamese cat in a salon.   His new learning emphasizes the relations between people and objects, appearance rather than content, the mechanical and artificial rather than the natural. Women do not discuss Shakespeare's work with him but rather the binding of Shakespeare's books.   Cover, decor, and possessions all replace relationships.   The art of music serves the ice cream business and the music boxes.

No direct ideological statement is made in the poem, no declaration as to the distress of the speaker who is torn between his Jewish Eastern roots and the way of life to which he has been introduced (Western in essence) and to which he was attracted before he became closely acquainted with its emptiness.   The boasting way in which he addressed the "friends" regarding his new learning turned out to be ironic, mocking and contemptuous of his new affiliations. The West did not teach him to open doors to new wisdom but rather the doors of antique boxes. The West did not offer the reforming of the odors which he craved. The ironic poetic closure sends us back to the opening of the poem: once he discovered the West, his ties to the genuine, definite, strong odors of his childhood prevail because they came from a way of life which is people-oriented and does not focus on a superficial contact with objects.

This free-verse poem is written in a narrative-like speaking style without metaphors. It leaves the reader with the task of unveiling the irony and of gathering the message of the poem which is not expressed explicitly. East and West are confronted not through generalizations but through daily objects and activities. Even the reader who will conceive the East in the poem as a troubled world (Tuker, 1983, p. 68), one of arak and idleness in coffee shops, will perceive that the exposure to the new way of life was enticing but not enhancing. The speaker who had abandoned his Near Eastern way of life to find a better, Western life-style, found emptiness instead.

Erez Biton has poetically expressed some aspects of the life of Near Eastern Jews in Israel. In both poems the poetic speaker recognizes his own specific roots and heritage, clearly described as those of a Near Eastern Jew; in both poems the speaker strives to accept a different life style, closer to that of European Jews in Israel. In the poem "Basic Background Comments," this attempt ends up in creative pain when he adapts the music of Bach to his Jewish-Moroccan background; in the second poem, this attempt ends with recognizing the vanity of the glamour which had attracted him. The speaker recognizes his strong attachment to his roots which, in spite of their deficiencies for him, represent a better world than that to which he has been exposed.

THE POETRY OF NEAR EASTERN ISRAELI POETS AND THE WORLD OF THEIR ROOTS

The poets writing in Israel who are of Near Eastern background have brought to life, in the written word, much of their world, their tradition and culture--and also their dilemmas of adjustment in Israel. Biton and Almog are not exceptional in writing about characters from their own background. I. E. Shlomo Zamir, for example, wrote about the Jews who were hanged in Iraq; Roni Ozer wrote about a Jewish-Iraqi singer, Layla Murad.

Biton's two poems analyzed here present the painful difficulties in adjustment, past and present. He also wrote, however (1976, pp. 32-33), about wedding celebrations of Moroccan Jews. He wrote an elegy on a central lyric character in the folktales of the Jews of Algeria (ibid., pp. 34-35) who murdered his beloved because she deserted him, and he wrote about a Jew who was the king's singer in Morocco. He described a Jewish Moroccan wedding (ibid., pp. 36-39), with the "'ud" (lute), small barrels of arak, and clusters of dates. Specific events in the history of Moroccan Jewry and typical aspects of the life of Moroccan Jews are described as viewed by an insider. Biton has contributed to Hebrew poetry a description of a different way of life that is rich in its sounds, tastes, and sights. Selecting attractive concrete fragments of reality from the life of Moroccan Jews, he conveys the values of this Jewry without needing nostalgia or polemics.

Almog's "Shahin" establishes the Eastern enchantment of the name Shahin as a prelude to describing Shahin's coming from the East with her patrimony, to the wretched life of the Near Eastern Jews in Israel in the 1950s--"transit camp," "rickety shack." The poignant contrast makes the reader aware of the difficulties the Near Eastern Jewish immigrants faced in becoming absorbed into the old-new homeland.

In some of these poems the younger generation observes the suffering of the older generation. The parents in Biton's "Basic Background Comments" are helpless and unable to take rational steps to protect themselves. In Almog's "Shahin," her parents are not equipped to achieve a better life either for their daughter or for themselves. Similarly, Shlomo Avayo and Shalom Katav wrote about the suffering of the parents' generation.

Many Israeli poets of Near Eastern origin express in their poems a love of Israel, for example Shalom Katav, Rahel Parhi, Ratson Hallevi, and Amnon Shamosh. But some also express social protest, pain, frustration, estrangement, and tension between the various Jewish communities in Israel, and astonishment at the social gaps in that country. The fact that freedom of speech (including the written word) is so highly respected and protected in Israel enables these authors to express themselves without fear. Poems of Ratson Hallevi, Tuvia Sulami, Aharon Almog, the twin brothers Hertsel and Balfur Hakak, Tsvi Hakak, Yosi Ozer, Yacov Shaya, David Rabi, Shlomo Avayo, Erez Biton, Shalom Katav, and others voice disillusionment with the Israeli social reality. Shlomo Avayo (1976, pp. 23-24), for example, writes about the discrepancy between the Israeli Black Panthers' facade of strength and their concealing their tenderness and emotion; he writes (1973, p. 17) about the gap between and separate worlds of the maid's children and the lady's children. Shalom Katav described the prejudice against the Near Eastern Jews when they first immigrated to Israel, their harsh living conditions when they first came, and the lack of understanding they confronted on the part of Jews of European background (1973, passim).

Ratson Hallevi and Amnon Shamosh used some of the poetic forms of medieval Hebrew poetry. In the first part of his volume *Diwan Sefaradi* (1981) Shamosh writes poems in the same familiar categories of medieval Hebrew poetry--poems which voice love, boasting, or complaints. He uses a line divided into first (opening) part of the line (*delet*) and second (closing) part of the line (*soger*).

The themes and figurative language in the poetry of Israeli poets of Near Eastern origin contribute to the uniqueness of their poetic world. Paying special attention to this poetic world will be an aesthetically enriching experience.

NOTES

1.   Aharon Zakay, *'El hofo shel ra'ayon.*   Kiryat-sefer, Jerusalem, 1957.
2.   Shlomo Zamir, *Hakkol mibba'ad la'anaf.* Sifriyat Poa'alim, Tel-Aviv, 1960.
3.   Interesting and fundamental work related to the field has been done by by Avraham Shtal and Yafa Binyamini. For some of their works, see the bibliography of my book *Yerudim vena'alim*, Kiryat-sefer. Jerusalem, 1981. See also some of my publications in this field: *Four poets*, Eked, Tel-Aviv, 1979, pp. 165-192; *Yerudim vena'alim*, *Perakim besifrut yehude hammizrah.*   Kiryat-sefer, Jerusalem, 1985; "The Contemporary Literary and Research Activity of Iraqi Jews in Iraq and Israel" (co-author Shemuel Moreh), in *Mehkarim betoldot yehude Iraq uvetarbutam*, Merkaz moreshet yehude bavel, Or Yehuda, 1981, pp. 83-132; "The Contribution of Iraqi Jews to Hebrew Literature in Israel," *Forum*, Winter 1981, pp. 143-153; "The Image of Sephardic Jews in the Modern Hebrew Short Story," in *The Sephardic and Oriental Jewish Heritage Studies*, ed. Issachar Ben-Ami, Magnes, Jerusalem, pp. 297-310; "La'atsevet--sefer kritut hayad kotevet," in *Yad leheman*, ed. Tsvi Mala'akhi,

Makhon Haberman, 1983, pp. 197-209; "Shiratam shel yehude
hammizrah beyisrael," *The Proceedings of the Eighth World Congress
of Jewish Studies*, Division C, World Union of Jewish Studies, 1982,
pp. 283-288 (also published in *Yediot aharonot*, Sep. 4, 1981)
"Yetsiratam hassifrutit shel yots'e Iraq beyisrael," in *Mahatsit
ha'uma*, Bar-Ilan University, 1986, pp. 251-278.

4. All four poems discussed in this chapter were translated
from the Hebrew with the generous help of my colleague Professor
Herbert Davidson, University of California, Los Angeles. Another
translation of this poem may be found in the anthology of Schwartz
and Rudolf, 1980, p. 61.

5. See another translation of this poem by Kuselewitz, 1978.

6. "Ad kan veloa yoter," "mittokh esrim ushnayim shirim
shonim," in *Shire David Avidan*. A. Levin-Epstein Modan, p. 29.

Bibliography

Almog, Aharon. *Hatsda'a leyisrael—hilton yerusalayim*. Sifriyat
Poa'alim, Tel-Aviv, 1977.

Avayo, Shlomo. *Esev al hassaf*. M. Newman, Tel-Aviv, 1973.

———. *Bammar'ot hatsov'ot*. Hakkibbuts hammeuhad, Tel-Aviv,
1976.

Bernhard, Frank, trans. and ed. *Modern Hebrew Poetry*. University
of Iowa Press, 1980.

Biton, Erez. *Minha maroqka'it*. Eked, Tel-Aviv, 1976.

———. *Sefer hanna'na*. Eked, Tel-Aviv, 1979.

Burnshaw, Stanley, Carmi, T., and Ezra Spicehandler, eds., *The
Modern Hebrew Poem Itself*. Schocken, New York, 1965.

Carmi, T., trans. and ed. *Hebrew Verse*. Penguin Books, New York,
1981.

Eben-Zohar, Itamar. "Hassfirut ha'ivrit hayyisraelit: model histori."
Hassifrut, vol. 4, no. 3, 1973, 427-440.

Finer-Mintz, Ruth. *Modern Hebrew Poetry*. University of California
Press, Berkeley and Los Angeles, 1968.

Katav, Shalom. *'Al gedot hannaharayim*. Eked, Tel-Aviv, 1973.

Kuselewitz, David, trans. *Shaul Tchernichovky*. Tel-Aviv, 1978.

Michael, Samy. "Lihyot sofer mimmotsa iraqi." *Moznaim*, vol. 56,
no. 3-4, 1983, 8-11.

Ozer, Yosi. *Silan tahor*. Sifriyat Poa'alim, Tel-Aviv, 1981.

Sadan, Dov. *Al sifrutenu*. Reuven Mas, 1950.

Schwartz, Howard, and Rudolf, Anthony. *Voices Within the Ark*.
Avon, New York, 1980.

Shalom, Sh. *"Nihsba'ti bammezuza shello osif 'od likhtov germanit."* *Moznaim*, vol. 59, no. 9, 1986, 38.

Silberschlag, Eisig. *Saul Tschernichowsky; Poet of Revolt.* London, East and West Library; Ithaca, N.Y., Cornell University Press, 1968.

Tshernihovski, Sha'ul. *Re'i, 'adama.* Schocken, 1940.

Tuker, Naftali.   "Hamminha vehana'na: 'al shirat Erez Biton." *Moznaim*, vol. 56, no. 3-4, 1983, 66-68.

Zakay, Aharon. *'El hofo shel ra'ayon.* Kiryat-sefer, Jerusalem, 1957.

Zamir, Shlomo. *Hakkol mibba'ad la'anaf.* Sifriyat Poa'lim, Tel-Aviv, 1960.